Published for
**OXFORD INTERNATIONAL
AQA EXAMINATIONS**

International GCSE
BIOLOGY
Revision Guide

Jo Locke
Jessica Walmsley
Editor: Primrose Kitten
Elizabeth McCullough

Contents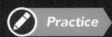

 Shade in each level of the circle as you feel more confident and ready for your exam.

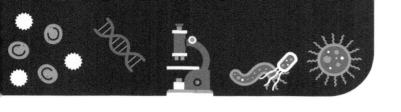

Answers

All of the **answers** are on the website at
www.oxfordsecondary.com/oxfordaqa-revision

How to use this book

This book uses a three-step approach to revision: **Knowledge**, **Retrieval**, and **Practice**. It is important that you do all three; they work together to make your revision effective.

1 Knowledge

Knowledge comes first. Each chapter starts with a **Knowledge Organiser**. These are clear, easy-to-understand, concise summaries of the content that you need to know for your exam. The information is organised to show how one idea flows into the next so you can learn how all the science is tied together, rather than lots of disconnected facts.

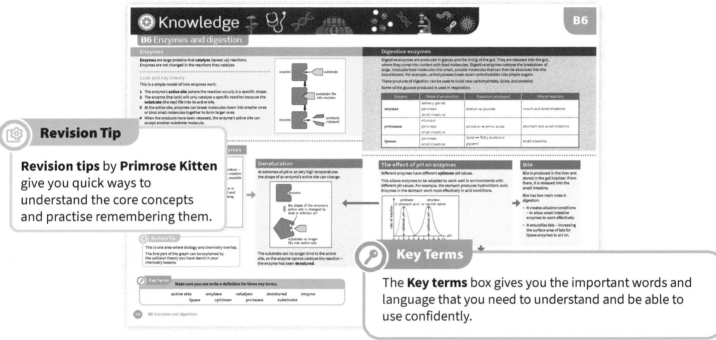

Revision Tip

Revision tips by **Primrose Kitten** give you quick ways to understand the core concepts and practise remembering them.

Key Terms

The **Key terms** box gives you the important words and language that you need to understand and be able to use confidently.

2 Retrieval

The **Retrieval questions** help you learn and quickly recall the information you've acquired. These are short questions and answers about the content in the Knowledge Organiser. Cover up the answers with some paper; write down as many answers as you can from memory. Check back to the Knowledge Organiser for any you got wrong, then cover the answers and attempt *all* the questions again until you can answer all the questions correctly.

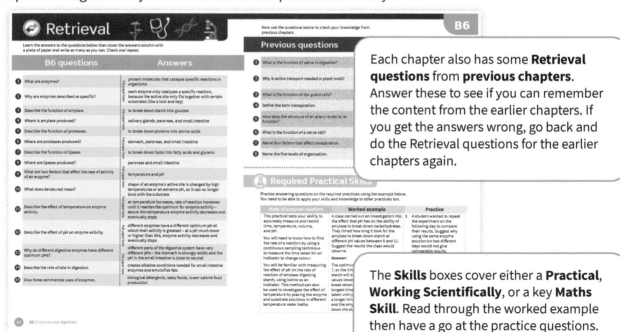

Each chapter also has some **Retrieval questions** from **previous chapters**. Answer these to see if you can remember the content from the earlier chapters. If you get the answers wrong, go back and do the Retrieval questions for the earlier chapters again.

The **Skills** boxes cover either a **Practical**, **Working Scientifically**, or a key **Maths Skill**. Read through the worked example then have a go at the practice questions.

Make sure you revisit the retrieval questions on different days to help them stick in your memory. You need to write down the answers each time, or say them out loud, otherwise it won't work.

3 Practice

Once you think you know the Knowledge Organiser and Retrieval answers really well you can move on to the final stage: **Practice**.

Each chapter has lots of **exam-style questions**, including some questions from previous chapters, to help you apply all the knowledge you have learnt and can retrieve.

Each question has a difficulty icon that shows the level of challenge.

 These questions build your confidence.

 These questions consolidate your knowledge.

These questions stretch your understanding.

Make sure you attempt all of the questions no matter what grade you are aiming for.

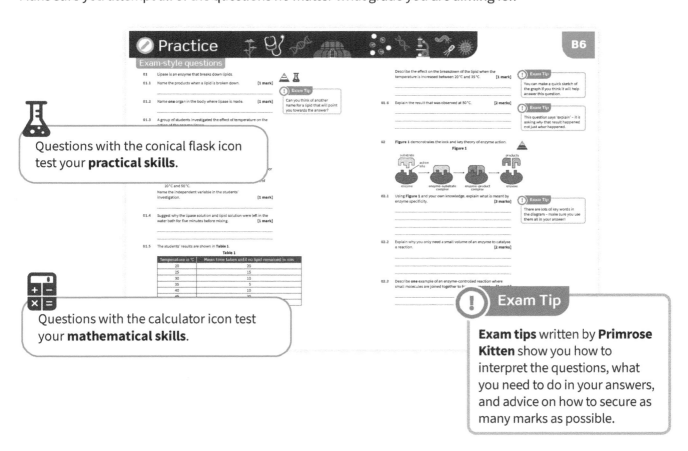

Questions with the conical flask icon test your **practical skills**.

Questions with the calculator icon test your **mathematical skills**.

Exam Tip

Exam tips written by **Primrose Kitten** show you how to interpret the questions, what you need to do in your answers, and advice on how to secure as many marks as possible.

B1 Cell biology

Eukaryotic cells

Animal and plant cells are **eukaryotic** cells. They have genetic material (**DNA**) that forms **chromosomes** and is contained in a **nucleus**.

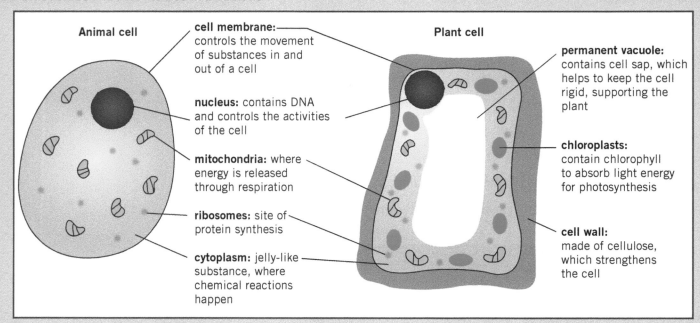

Animal cell

cell membrane: controls the movement of substances in and out of a cell

nucleus: contains DNA and controls the activities of the cell

mitochondria: where energy is released through respiration

ribosomes: site of protein synthesis

cytoplasm: jelly-like substance, where chemical reactions happen

Plant cell

permanent vacuole: contains cell sap, which helps to keep the cell rigid, supporting the plant

chloroplasts: contain chlorophyll to absorb light energy for photosynthesis

cell wall: made of cellulose, which strengthens the cell

Prokaryotic cells

Bacteria are single-celled organisms. They are made of a prokaryotic cell. **Prokaryotic** cells:

- have no nucleus – they have a single loop of DNA
- have small rings of DNA called **plasmids**
- are smaller than eukaryotic cells.

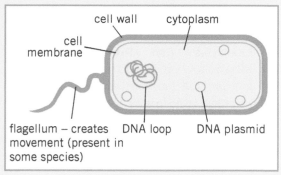

cell wall   cytoplasm

cell membrane

flagellum – creates movement (present in some species)   DNA loop   DNA plasmid

Comparing sub-cellular structures

Structure	Animal cell	Plant cell	Prokaryotic cell
cell membrane	✓	✓	✓
cytoplasm	✓	✓	✓
nucleus	✓	✓	—
cell wall	—	✓	✓
chloroplasts	—	✓	—
permanent vacuole	—	✓	—
DNA free in cytoplasm	—	—	✓
plasmids	—	—	✓

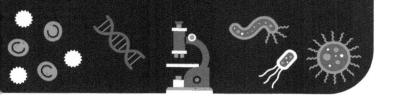

Specialised cells

Cells in animals and plants differentiate to form different types of cells. Most animal cells differentiate at an early stage of development, whereas a plant's cells differentiate throughout its lifetime.

Specialised cell	Function	Adaptations
sperm cell	fertilises an ovum (egg)	• tail to swim to the ovum and fertilise it • lots of **mitochondria** to release energy from respiration, enabling the sperm to swim to the ovum
red blood cell	transports oxygen around the body	• no nucleus so more room to carry oxygen • contains a red pigment called haemoglobin that binds to oxygen molecules • flat bi-concave disc shape to increase surface area to volume ratio
muscle cell	contracts and relaxes to allow movement	• contains protein fibres, which can contract to make the cells shorter • contains lots of mitochondria to release energy from respiration, allowing the muscles to contract
nerve cell	carries electrical impulses around the body	• branched endings, called dendrites, to make connections with other neurones or effectors • myelin sheath insulates the axon to increase the transmission speed of the electrical impulses
root hair cell	absorbs mineral ions and water from the soil	• long projection speeds up the absorption of water and mineral ions by increasing the surface area of the cell • lots of mitochondria to release energy for the active transport of mineral ions from the soil
palisade cell	enables photosynthesis in the leaf	• lots of chloroplasts containing chlorophyll to absorb light energy • located at the top surface of the leaf where it can absorb the most light energy

🔑 **Key Terms**

Make sure you can write a definition for these key terms.

cell membrane   cell wall   chloroplast   chromosome   cytoplasm   DNA

eukaryotic   mitochondria   nucleus   permanent vacuole

plasmid   prokaryotic   ribosome

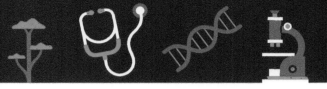

Learn the answers to the questions below, then cover the answers column with a piece of paper and write as many as you can. Check and repeat.

	B1 questions	Answers
1	What are two types of eukaryotic cell?	animal and plant
2	What type of cell are bacteria?	prokaryotic
3	Where is DNA found in animal and plant cells?	in the nucleus
4	What is the function of the cell membrane?	controls movement of substances in and out of the cell
5	What is the function of mitochondria?	site of respiration to transfer energy for the cell
6	What is the function of chloroplasts?	contain chlorophyll to absorb light energy for photosynthesis
7	What is the function of ribosomes?	enable production of proteins (protein synthesis)
8	What is the function of the cell wall?	strengthens and supports the cell
9	What is the structure of the main genetic material in a prokaryotic cell?	single loop of DNA
10	What are plasmids?	small rings of DNA containing extra genes (in addition to the DNA in chromosomes)
11	What is the function of a red blood cell?	carries oxygen around the body
12	Give three adaptations of a red blood cell.	no nucleus, contains a red pigment called haemoglobin, and has a bi-concave disc shape
13	What is the function of a nerve cell?	carries electrical impulses around the body
14	Give two adaptations of a nerve cell.	branched endings, myelin sheath insulates the axon
15	What is the function of a sperm cell?	fertilises an ovum (egg)
16	Give two adaptations of a sperm cell.	tail, contains lots of mitochondria
17	What is the function of a palisade cell?	carries out photosynthesis in a leaf
18	Give two adaptations of a palisade cell.	lots of chloroplasts, located at the top surface of the leaf
19	What is the function of a root hair cell?	absorbs minerals and water from the soil
20	Give two adaptations of a root hair cell.	long projection, lots of mitochondria

Put paper here

Maths Skills

Practise your maths skills using the worked example and practice questions below.

Resolution	Worked example	Practice
The resolution of a device is the smallest change that the device can measure. Selecting equipment with the appropriate resolution is important in scientific investigations. If the resolution of a digital watch is one second, one second is the smallest amount of time it can measure. Some stop clocks have smaller resolutions, for example a resolution of 0.01 seconds. This means that they can measure times of 0.01, 1.29, or 9.62 seconds, whereas a digital watch could not.	What is the resolution of the following equipment? The resolution of this thermometer is 1 °C, because this is the smallest change that it can detect. 40 °C 35 °C 30 °C 36.8 ℃ The resolution of this digital thermometer is 0.1 °C, because it can measure readings such as 1.1 °C, 8.9 °C, and 36.7 °C.	What are the resolutions of the following pieces of equipment? 1 2 302.16 g 3

Working Scientifically

Practise your working scientifically skills using the worked example and practice questions below.

Variables	Worked example	Practice
There are three types of variable in an investigation: • Independent variable: the variable that is changed in an investigation. • Dependent variable: the variable that changes as a result of changes to the independent variable. • Control variable: a variable that is kept constant in an investigation to ensure results are valid.	In an osmosis investigation, a student placed beetroot pieces in sugar solutions with different concentrations. They measured the mass of the beetroot pieces before and after leaving the beetroot in the solutions. They then calculated percentage change in mass. **a** Identify the independent and dependent variables. independent variable = concentration of the sugar solution dependent variable = mass of beetroot **b** Suggest three control variables for this investigation. temperature, time the beetroot is in solution, surface area of beetroot pieces	A student investigated how the wind speed affects the rate of transpiration in a plant. Identify the independent and dependent variables for this investigation, and three variables that should be controlled to collect valid data. **Revision Tip** Make sure you don't use the word 'amount' to describe variables. You need to be more specific. For example, instead of saying 'amount of beetroot' you should say 'mass of beetroot'.

 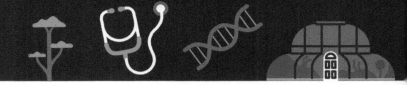

Exam-style questions

01   **Figure 1** shows a plant cell.

Figure 1

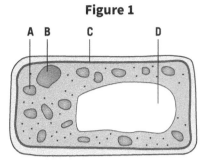

01.1   Identify parts **A–C**.   **[3 marks]**

A   _____

B   _____

C   _____

01.2   Explain the function of part **D**.   **[3 marks]**

_____

_____

_____

_____

> **Exam Tip**
>
> Labelling cells is a really common exam question. Take the time to become familiar with plant cells, animal cells, and prokaryotic cells.

01.3   Which feature in **Figure 1** allows you to conclude that this is a eukaryotic cell?

Tick **one** box.   **[1 mark]**

cell wall   ☐

nucleus   ☐

cytoplasm   ☐

cell membrane   ☐

01.4   The cell shown in **Figure 1** was taken from a plant.

Suggest and explain where in the plant this cell would be found.

                                                                       [2 marks]

_____

_____

_____

> **Exam Tip**
>
> Plants have a range of different specialised cells, but they will all share some common features.

02 **Figure 2** shows a cheek cell viewed under a light microscope magnified at ×1350.

Figure 2

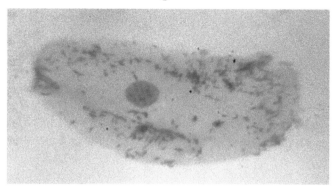

02.1 A student collected a sample of cells by taking a saliva swab from the inside of their cheek.

Explain **one** safety measure that the student should take during this procedure. **[2 marks]**

_____

_____

_____

> **! Exam Tip**
>
> For this question 'explain' is the command word so you need to say _why_ you have done something, not just what you have done.

02.2 The dye methylene blue was added to the cell sample on the slide. Suggest why this was added. **[1 mark]**

_____

_____

02.3 Explain two ways the student could tell they were looking at a eukaryotic animal cell and not a plant cell. **[4 marks]**

_____

_____

_____

_____

_____

> **! Exam Tip**
>
> Questions that ask you to 'suggest' something don't expect you to know the actual answer. They want you to use what you already know to make a sensible suggestion.

03 Red blood cells are an example of a specialised cell.

03.1 Describe the function of red blood cells. **[1 mark]**

03.2 Explain **two** ways a red blood cell is adapted to its function. **[4 marks]**

03.3 Red blood cells are eukaryotic cells. Explain why an image of a red blood cell could lead to it being incorrectly classified. as a prokaryotic cell. **[2 marks]**

04 **Figure 3** shows a single-celled organism called *Euglena*.

Euglena are found in ponds and lakes.

They survive by making their own food through photosynthesis.

In low light conditions they can engulf other microorganisms, such as bacteria and algae.

Figure 3

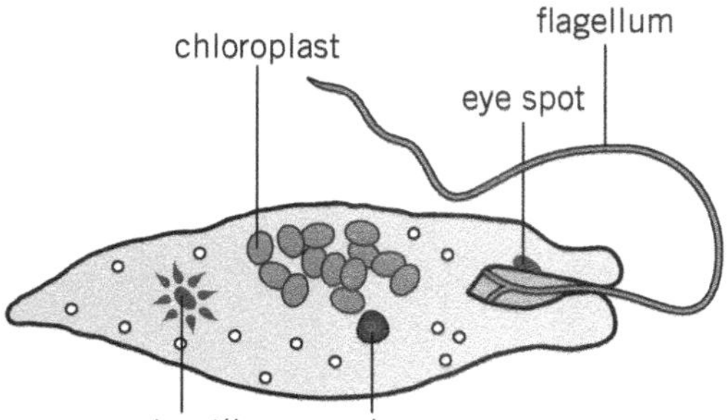

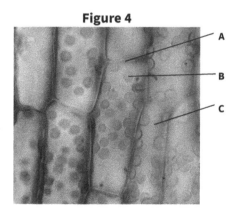

> **Exam Tip**
>
> You may not have come across *Euglena* before. Don't let this worry you! The exam has to include a lot of content you haven't seen before, so questions like this are designed to prepare you for that.
>
> Use the knowledge you have gained in class and practise applying it to this new situation. The more you try doing this, the better prepared you'll be for the unfamiliar contexts you will come across in the exams!

04.1 Identify which part of the *Euglena* traps light for photosynthesis. **[1 mark]**

04.2 The eye spot on the *Euglena* detects light.

Suggest how the flagellum and eye spot work together to maximise photosynthesis. **[3 marks]**

05 **Figure 4** shows some plant cells as viewed under a light microscope.

05.1 Identify the cell membrane in **Figure 4**. **[1 mark]**

05.2 Ribosomes are present in plant cells but cannot be seen using a light microscope. Describe the function of ribosomes. **[1 mark]**

Figure 4

05.3 Name **one** other subcellular structure that is present in plant cells but cannot be seen in **Figure 4**. **[1 mark]**

05.4 Describe the function of this structure. **[1 mark]**

06 Bacteria are an example of prokaryotes.

06.1 Identify which of the following is the most accurate size for a prokaryote.

Choose **one** answer. **[1 mark]**

100 nm   1 μm   10 μm   0.1 mm

06.2 Both plant cells and prokaryotic cells have cell walls. Describe **one** difference between the cell wall of a plant cell and the cell wall of a bacterial cell. **[1 mark]**

06.3 Describe the differences between the way genetic material is stored in a prokaryotic cell and in a eukaryotic cell. **[4 marks]**

06.4 Suggest which feature needs to be present on a bacterial cell if it needs to move in water. **[1 mark]**

07 Cone cells are a type of cell found at the back of the human eye.

They detect light and send information to the brain, which it then decodes, allowing us to perceive colour.

Figure 5 shows the main adaptations of a cone cell.

Figure 5

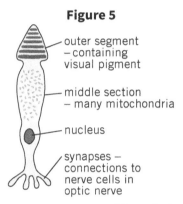

- outer segment – containing visual pigment
- middle section – many mitochondria
- nucleus
- synapses – connections to nerve cells in optic nerve

07.1 Use the information in **Figure 5** and your own knowledge to suggest and explain how the cone cell is adapted to its function. **[4 marks]**

07.2 There are approximately 6 million cone cells in the human retina. Three different types of cone cell exist:

- one to detect red light
- one to detect green light
- one to detect blue light

Assuming there is a roughly equal number of each cone cell type in a human retina, calculate the number of 'red' cone cells present in the retina.

Give your answer in standard form. **[3 marks]**

08 Muscle cells are an example of a specialised cell.

08.1 Define the term specialised cell. **[1 mark]**

08.2 The biceps contain muscle cells. Describe the function of a muscle cell. **[1 mark]**

08.3 In addition to providing movement to the skeleton, muscle tissue has other functions in the body. Describe **one** other example of where muscles are found in the body. **[2 marks]**

08.4 Explain why muscle cells have lots of mitochondria. **[2 marks]**

08.5 Explain **one** other feature of a muscle cell. **[2 marks]**

09 A student observed some onion cells under a microscope.

09.1 Give **two** features that help the student to know that they are looking at a sample of plant cells in **Figure 6**. **[2 marks]**

Figure 6

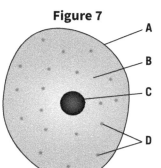

① Exam Tip

When measuring very small things, it is better to measure a group of them and then divide the measurement, for example, measure the width of ten onion cells then divide that measurement by ten.

09.2 The scale ruler in the diagram represents 1000 μm. Calculate the average width of an onion cell. **[2 marks]**

09.3 These cells were observed under ×100 magnification. Which of the following structures may have been visible under a higher magnification using a light microscope? Choose **one** answer. **[1 mark]**

vacuole   ribosomes   chloroplasts   plasmids

10 **Figure 7** shows an animal cell.

Figure 7

10.1 Which letter represents the cell membrane? **[1 mark]**

10.2 Describe the function of the cell membrane. **[1 mark]**

10.3 **Figure 7** shows a human skin cell. Explain how the cell would differ if it was a human nerve cell. **[4 marks]**

10.4 An animal cell is measured to have a mean diameter of 20 μm. Estimate the length of the cell membrane material in this cell. **[2 marks]**

10.5 The mean length of the molecules within the cell membrane has been estimated to be 4 nm. If we assume that the cell membrane is one molecule thick, calculate the total number of molecules contained in the cell's membrane. **[3 marks]**

11 In general eukaryotic cells are one order of magnitude larger than prokaryotic cells.

11.1 One type of virus is 100 nm in height. One type of algal cell is two orders of magnitude larger than the virus. Estimate the length of the eukaryotic cell. Give your answer in micrometres. **[1 mark]**

11.2 Compare the features found in eukaryotic and prokaryotic cells. **[6 marks]**

11.3 Cyanobacteria are a phylum of bacteria that are able to photosynthesise. Estimate the size of a cyanobacterial cell. Justify your answer. **[2 marks]**

11.4 Algae are aquatic organisms that belong to the kingdom Protista. **Figure 8** shows an algal cell.

Figure 8

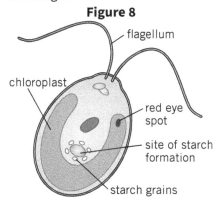

Use **Figure 8** to suggest why some algae have been classified as plants. **[3 marks]**

12 **Figure 9** shows a bacterial cell

Figure 9

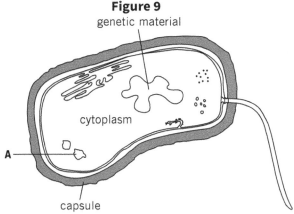

12.1 Give **one** reason from the diagram why it is not a eukaryotic cell. **[1 mark]**

12.2 Identify the cell component labelled **A**. **[1 mark]**

12.3 State **two** similarities between the bacterial cell and a plant cell. **[2 marks]**

13 **Figure 10** shows an epithelial cell from the small intestine.

Figure 10

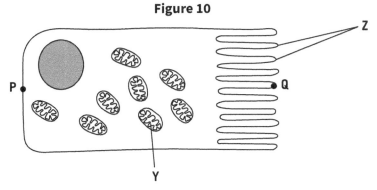

13.1 Identify the structure labelled P. **[1 mark]**

13.2 State the function of the mitochondria. **[1 mark]**

13.3 Suggest how this cell is adapted for its function. **[2 marks]**

 # Knowledge

B2 Cell transport

Comparing diffusion, osmosis, and active transport

	Diffusion	Osmosis	Active transport
Definition	The spreading out of particles, resulting in a net movement from an area of higher **concentration** to an area of lower concentration.	The **diffusion** of water from a **dilute** solution to a concentrated solution through a **partially permeable membrane**.	The movement of particles from a more dilute solution to a more concentrated solution using energy from respiration.
Movement of particles	Particles move down the concentration **gradient** – from an area of *high* concentration to an area of *low* concentration.	Water moves from an area of *lower* solute concentration to an area of *higher* solute concentration.	Particles move against the concentration gradient – from an area of *low* concentration to an area of *high* concentration.
Energy required?	no – **passive process**	no – passive process	yes – energy released by respiration

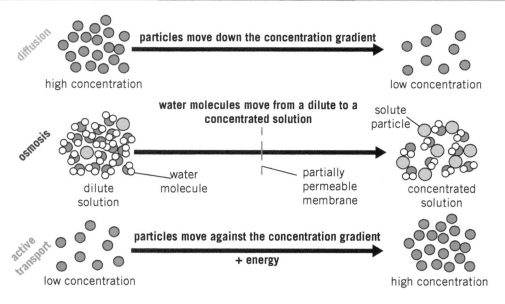

Examples	**Humans**	**Plants**	**Humans**
	Nutrients in the small intestine diffuse into the **capillaries** through the **villi**.	Water moves by **osmosis** from a dilute solution in the soil to a concentrated solution in the **root hair cell**.	**Active transport** allows sugar molecules to be absorbed from the small intestine when the sugar concentration is higher in the blood than in the small intestine.
	Oxygen diffuses from the air in the **alveoli** into the blood in the capillaries. Carbon dioxide diffuses from the blood in the capillaries into the air in the alveoli.		
	Plants		**Plants**
	Carbon dioxide used for photosynthesis diffuses into leaves through the **stomata**.		Active transport is used to absorb mineral ions into the root hair cells from more dilute solutions in the soil.
	Oxygen produced during photosynthesis diffuses out of the leaves through the stomata.		

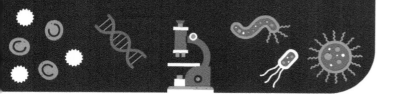

Factors that affect the rate of diffusion

 ① Difference in concentration

The steeper the concentration gradient, the faster the rate of diffusion.

② Temperature

The higher the temperature, the faster the rate of diffusion.

 ③ Surface area of the membrane

The larger the membrane surface area, the faster the rate of diffusion.

Hypotonic and isotonic

The concentration gradient can cause water to move into or out of a cell by osmosis:

- If the solution outside the cell has a lower concentration than the cell it is **hypotonic** – water moves into the cell.
- If the solution outside the cell has a higher concentration than the cell it is **hypertonic** – water moves out of the cell.
- If the solution outside the cell is equal to the concentration inside the cell, it is **isotonic**.

Adaptations for exchanging substances

Single-celled organisms have a large surface area to volume ratio. This means enough molecules can be transported across their cell membranes to meet their needs.

Multicellular organisms have a small surface area to volume ratio. This means they need specialised organ systems and cells to allow enough molecules to be transported into and out of their cells.

Efficient exchange surfaces have a large surface area that is thin. In animals, exchange surfaces have a good blood supply.

Villi in the small intestine

for absorbing nutrients

network of capillaries

large surface area due to folding

good blood supply

thin wall (only one cell thick)

Alveoli in the lungs

for gas exchange

network of capillaries provides a good blood supply

The rate of diffusion is increased because the membrane of the alveoli
- has a large surface area
- is moist
- is only one cell thick (short diffusion pathway).

Leaf

for gas exchange (for both photosynthesis and respiration)

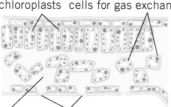

chloroplasts

big surface area on these cells for gas exchange

air spaces

stomata allow gases to diffuse into and out of the leaf

Root hair cells

for uptake of water and minerals

lots of mitochondria to take in mineral ions by active transport

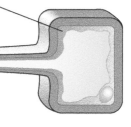

large surface area helps efficient absorption of water and mineral ions

 **Key Terms**

Make sure you can write a definition for these key terms.

active transport   alveoli   capillaries   concentration   diffusion
dilute   gradient   hypertonic   hypotonic   isotonic   osmosis
partially permeable membrane   passive process   root hair cell   stomata   villi

 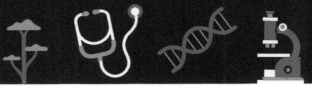

Learn the answers to the questions below then cover the answers column with a piece of paper and write as many as you can. Check and repeat.

B2 questions | Answers

1. What is diffusion?

net movement of particles from an area of high concentration to an area of low concentration along a concentration gradient – this is a passive process (does not require energy from respiration)

2. Name three factors that affect the rate of diffusion.

concentration gradient, temperature, membrane surface area

3. How are villi adapted for exchanging substances?

- long and thin – increases surface area
- one-cell-thick membrane – short diffusion pathway
- good blood supply – maintains a steep concentration gradient

4. How are the lungs adapted for efficient gas exchange?

- alveoli – large surface area
- moist membranes – increase rate of diffusion
- one-cell-thick membranes – short diffusion pathway
- good blood supply – maintains a steep concentration gradient

5. How are root hair cells adapted for exchanging materials?

- large surface area – for water absorption
- lots of mitochondria – to transfer energy for mineral uptake by active transport

6. What is osmosis?

diffusion of water from a dilute solution to a concentrated solution through a partially permeable membrane

7. Give one example of osmosis in a plant.

water moves from the soil into the root hair cell

8. What is active transport?

movement of particles against a concentration gradient – from a dilute solution to a more concentrated solution – using energy from respiration

9. Why is active transport needed in plant roots?

concentration of mineral ions in the soil is lower than inside the root hair cells – the mineral ions must move against the concentration gradient to enter the root hair cells

10. What is the purpose of active transport in the small intestine?

sugars can be absorbed when the concentration of sugar in the small intestine is lower than the concentration of sugar in the blood

Put paper here

Now use the questions below to check your knowledge from previous chapters.

Previous questions | Answers

1	What is the function of a cell wall?		strengthens and supports the cell
2	What is the function of a red blood cell?		carries oxygen around the body
3	What type of cell are bacteria?		prokaryotic
4	What is the function of ribosomes?	Put paper here	enable production of proteins (protein synthesis)
5	Give two adaptations of a nerve cell.		branched endings, myelin sheath insulates the axon
6	What is the function of a sperm cell?	Put paper here	fertilises an ovum (egg)
7	Give two adaptations of a sperm cell.		tail, contains lots of mitochondria
8	What is the function of the cell membrane?	Put paper here	controls the movement of substances into and out of a cell

Required Practical Skills

Practise answering questions on the required practicals using the example below. You need to be able to apply your skills and knowledge to other practicals too.

Osmosis in cells	Worked example	Practice
Different concentrations of sugar and salt solutions both affect the movement of water by osmosis, causing cells to lose or gain water and changing the mass of a tissue sample.	A sample of carrot was placed into a $0.75\,mol/dm^3$ sugar solution for 30 minutes. The mass of the carrot was recorded before and after this.	**1** Give one reason why it is important to dry the samples of carrot before they are weighed.
For this practical you need to be able to accurately measure length, mass, and volume to measure osmosis in cells.	Initial mass = 6.02 g Final mass = 3.91 g **1** Determine the percentage change in mass of the sample. $$3.91 - 6.02 = -2.11\,g$$ $$\left(\frac{-2.11}{6.02}\right) \times 100 = -35\%$$ (a minus sign is used because the sample has lost mass)	**2** When repeating this experiment using different concentrations of sugar solution, a student found that one sample did not change mass. Suggest what this tells you about the concentration of the solution. Assume no error in the experiment.
You will need to be comfortable applying this knowledge to a range of samples, not just to the typical example of potato tissue, because osmosis happens in all cells.	**2** Explain why this experiment should be repeated, and give one other variable that should be controlled. The experiment should be repeated to give a more reliable result, and to allow calculation of a mean loss in mass for the sample. The dimensions of the carrot sample need to be controlled between repeats.	**3** Two students set up this experiment. Student A said that each sample of carrot must have the same starting mass. Student B argued that each sample must have the same length and width. Explain which student is correct.

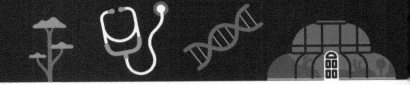

01   A group of students investigated how the mass of a potato sample changed over time, when placed into sugar solutions of different concentrations.

They set up their equipment as shown in **Figure 1**.

Figure 1

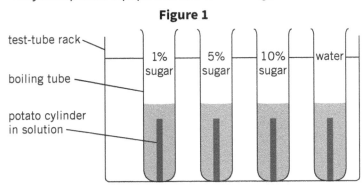

01.1   Name the independent variable in their investigation.   **[1 mark]**

_____

01.2   Identify **two** variables that the students controlled.   **[2 marks]**

1 _____

2 _____

> **! Exam Tip**
>
> Control variable are the ones we keep the same.

01.3   The students' results are shown in **Table 1**.

Table 1

Percentage sugar solution	0%	1%	5%	10%
Starting mass in grams	3.2	3.3	3.1	3.4
Final mass in grams	3.7	3.5	2.9	2.6
Change in mass in grams	+0.5	_____	−0.2	−0.8
Percentage change in mass	+15.6	_____	−6.5	−23.5

> **! Exam Tip**
>
> If you're not sure what to do, try using the values given for the 5% and 10% solutions as trials, and see if you can get the answer.

Complete the results table by calculating the change in mass and the percentage change in mass for the 1% sugar solution. **[2 marks]**

_____

_____

_____

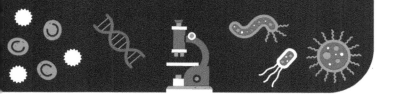
01.4 Plot the students' results of sugar concentration against percentage change in mass on the axes in **Figure 2**.

Draw a suitable line of best fit. **[3 marks]**

Figure 2

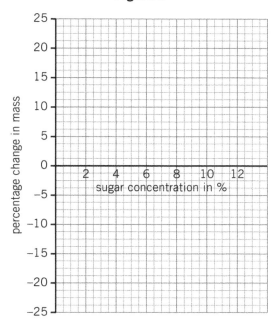

01.5 Determine the concentration of sugar present in the potato. **[1 mark]**

_____

01.6 Describe what the students should do to check that their results are reproducible. **[2 marks]**

_____

_____

_____

02 Multicellular organisms often have complex structures, such as lungs, for exchanging gases.

Explain why single-celled organisms, like _Euglena_, do not need lungs. **[3 marks]**

_____

_____

_____

03 **Figure 3** shows a plant cell before (**A**) and after (**B**) it was placed in a saltwater solution.

Figure 3

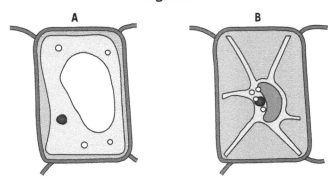

03.1 Name the type of solution that caused the differences observed in diagram **B**. **[1 mark]**

03.2 Explain the differences in the appearance of the plant cell after it was placed in the saltwater solution. **[6 marks]**

03.3 Explain why the cells in **Figure 3** are only found in this state in a laboratory. **[1 mark]**

> ⓘ **Exam Tip**
>
> The command word here is *explain*, so you need to say WHY the changes have happened.

04 **Figure 4** shows a number of different ways substances can move into and out of a cell. The dots represent the molecules of each substance.

Figure 4

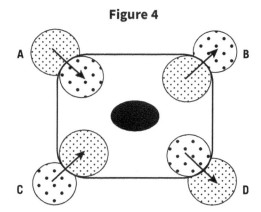

04.1 Name the cell structure that controls the movement of materials into and out of the cell. **[1 mark]**

04.2 Identify which arrow represents the active uptake of glucose by epithelial cells in the small intestine. Give a reason for your answer. **[2 marks]**

04.3 Explain why epithelial cells in the small intestine contain so many mitochondria. **[3 marks]**

> ⓘ **Exam Tip**
>
> Start this question by labelling the high and low concentrations.

05 Gas exchange in fish takes place in the gills (**Figure 5**). Fish breathe by taking in oxygen from their environment through opening their mouths underwater. This allows water, containing oxygen, to pass over their gills, causing the oxygen to pass from the water into the fish's bloodstream.

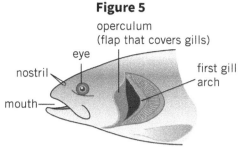

Figure 5

05.1 Describe what is meant by gas exchange. **[1 mark]**

05.2 Use **Figure 5** to suggest **two** ways in which fish gills are adapted for efficient gas exchange. **[2 marks]**

05.3 Students investigated the effect of temperature on the breathing rate of fish. They put same-sized fish in tanks of water at five different temperatures. They then measured the breathing rate of the fish by counting the number of times the fish opened their mouths in one minute.

The fish were placed in the water tanks for five minutes before the investigation began.

Suggest why the students included this step in their investigation. **[1 mark]**

05.4 The students repeated the test five times at each temperature then calculated the mean. Their results are shown in **Table 2**.

Table 2

Temperature of water in °C	Mean number of breaths taken per minute
5	20
10	38
15	45
20	57
25	70

Describe the trend shown in the results. **[1 mark]**

05.5 Identify which conclusion the students could draw from their results. Choose **one**. **[1 mark]**

The oxygen content of water remains the same regardless of temperature.

The oxygen content of water increases as temperature increases.

The oxygen content of water decreases as temperature increases.

06 *Crocodylus porosus* is a species of freshwater crocodile that normally lives in lakes and rivers. This species of crocodile is also able to survive in salt water because they have special salt glands in their tongues that remove excess salt from their bodies.

06.1 Explain why *Crocodylus porosus* have to use active transport to remove excess salt from their body when living in a saltwater environment. **[2 marks]**

06.2 Explain why the cells in the salt glands have large numbers of mitochondria. **[3 marks]**

06.3 Suggest **one** advantage to *Crocodylus porosus* of being able to inhabit both saltwater and freshwater habitats. **[1 mark]**

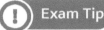

Exam Tip

Long Latin names can be confusing. I used to get my students to cross out the long confusing name and replace it with something friendly – just don't use the friendly name in your exam answer!

07 A scientist planned to carry out an investigation to determine which variety of apple was the sweetest. The scientist had access to the following equipment:

- range of different apples
- potato borer
- scalpel
- balance
- distilled water
- test tubes
- test-tube rack
- measuring cylinder
- sucrose solutions at six different concentrations

Plan an investigation the scientist could follow to determine the sugar concentration of each variety of apple. **[6 marks]**

Exam Tip

Planning an experiment is an important skill to practise.

Make sure you clearly plan out what you're going to do and think about safety.

08 Cell **A** is a spherical animal cell with a radius of 5 µm. Cell **B** is also spherical. It has a radius of 20 µm.

08.1 Identify which statement about these two cells is true. Choose **one**. **[1 mark]**

Cell **A** has a smaller volume than cell **B**.

Cell **B** has a smaller surface area than cell **A**.

Cell **A** has a smaller surface area to volume ratio than cell **B**.

Cell **B** has a larger surface area to volume ratio than cell **A**.

08.2 Cell **A** has a surface area to volume ratio of 0.6:1. It takes 5 ms for an amino acid to diffuse out of cell **A** into the bloodstream. Assuming that the rate of diffusion is proportional to the surface area to volume ratio of a cell, calculate the time taken for an identical amino acid to diffuse out of cell **B**. **[5 marks]**

Exam Tip

There are lots of areas where maths can be mixed with biology.

You may not have done this in class but don't let it worry you, just use your maths skills.

09   Plant roots absorb water from the soil by osmosis.

09.1   Define the term osmosis.   **[1 mark]**

09.2   Once inside the root, water continues to move from cell to cell as it moves towards the xylem vessel. **Figure 6** shows three cells within the root. Each cell contains a different concentration of salt.

Exam Tip

Think about which cell has the highest concentration of **water**, not just the salt shown in the diagram.

Figure 6

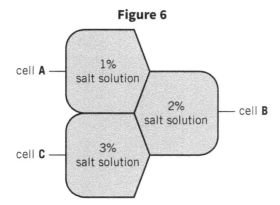

cell **A** — 1% salt solution

2% salt solution — cell **B**

cell **C** — 3% salt solution

Water can move from cell to cell in any direction. Identify which cell will gain water most quickly. Give a reason for your answer.

[2 marks]

09.3   Give one other factor that would affect the rate of water movement.

[1 mark]

10   The alveoli in the lungs are adapted for gas exchange. One adaptation is a large surface area to volume ratio.

10.1   Explain how a large surface area to volume ratio maximises gas exchange.   **[2 marks]**

10.2   Explain **one** other way the lungs are adapted for gas exchange.   **[2 marks]**

10.3   Alveoli can be modelled as spheres. The diameter of an alveolus is 300 μm.

The surface area of a sphere is calculated using the formula:
surface area = $4\pi r^2$

The volume of a sphere is calculated using the formula:
volume = $\dfrac{4}{3}\pi r^3$

Calculate the surface area to volume ratio of an alveolus.   **[4 marks]**

Exam Tip

This is a core maths skill in the biology specification, but is one that you don't get to practice often.

11 In many restaurants, vegetables are prepared in advance for the evening's meals. To prevent them turning brown, chefs often leave the prepared vegetables in slightly salted water. A chef wanted to know the ideal concentration of salt water to store potatoes. The chef used the following method:

1 Cut the potato into pieces of equal volume.

2 Measure the mass of each potato piece.

3 Place each potato piece into a different concentration of salt solution.

4 Leave for two hours.

5 Remove each potato piece and blot dry.

6 Measure the new mass of each potato piece.

The chef's results are shown in **Table 3**.

Table 3

Concentration of saltwater solution in M	0.0	0.5	1.0	1.5	2.0
Starting mass in g	2.8	3.0	3.1	2.9	2.9
Mass after 2 hours in g	3.1	3.0	3.0	2.7	2.4

11.1 Identify the solution in which the potato gained the most mass. **[1 mark]**

11.2 Explain why this potato gained mass. **[2 marks]**

11.3 Suggest which concentration of salt solution the chef should store the potato in. Explain your answer. **[2 marks]**

12 Substances such as water and ions need to move in and out of cells.

12.1 Draw **one** line between the process and the correct method of transport. **[2 marks]**

Process		Transport method
The movement of oxygen from the lungs into the bloodstream.		active transport
The movement of mineral ions from the soil into a plant root system.		osmosis
The movement of water into a plant cell.		diffusion

12.2 Complete the sentence using the correct words in bold. **[2 marks]**

Cells that carry out active transport contain **many / few** mitochondria so that there will be sufficient **chemicals / energy**.

12.3 Explain why active transport is required to move glucose from the small intestine into the bloodstream. **[3 marks]**

13   After eating, the body needs to absorb as much glucose from the digested food as possible. Glucose is absorbed into the bloodstream via the villi cells in the small intestine. **Figure 7** shows the cell membrane of a villus cell in the small intestine.

Figure 7

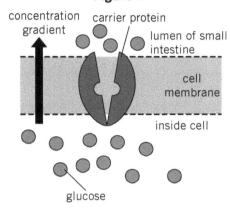

A carrier protein is used to transport glucose into the cell. The carrier protein binds to the glucose molecule and then rotates in the cell membrane to release the glucose into the cell. Using your own knowledge and information provided in **Figure 7**, explain how and why glucose is moved into the bloodstream by active transport and diffusion.   **[6 marks]**

14   Plant and animal cells share a number of common features.

14.1   Give the function of the cell membrane.   **[1 mark]**

14.2   Name **two** other structures found in both plant and animal cells.
                                                                   [2 marks]

14.3   Chloroplasts are a sub-cellular structure found only in plant cells. A student uses a light microscope to observe cells from an onion bulb. Explain why the student is unable to view any chloroplasts.   **[3 marks]**

14.4   Plant cells also contain vacuoles. Explain how the vacuole helps plants to remain upright.   **[4 marks]**

B3 Organisation in animals

There are five levels of organisation in living organisms:

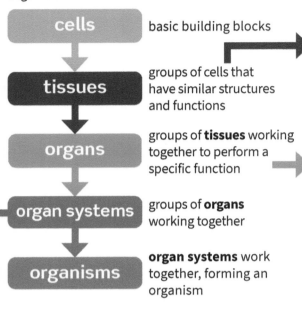

cells — basic building blocks

tissues — groups of cells that have similar structures and functions

organs — groups of **tissues** working together to perform a specific function

organ systems — groups of **organs** working together

organisms — **organ systems** work together, forming an organism

Examples of animal tissues

- muscular tissue – contracts to bring about movement
- glandular tissue – produces substances such as enzymes and hormones
- epithelial tissue – covers some parts of the body

Stomach

The stomach is an organ involved in the digestion of food.

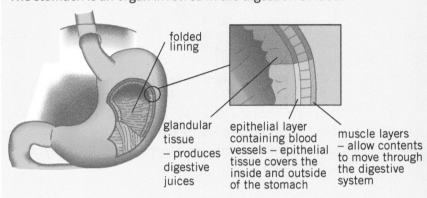

folded lining

glandular tissue – produces digestive juices

epithelial layer containing blood vessels – epithelial tissue covers the inside and outside of the stomach

muscle layers – allow contents to move through the digestive system

The digestive system

The digestive system breaks down food and absorbs nutrients.

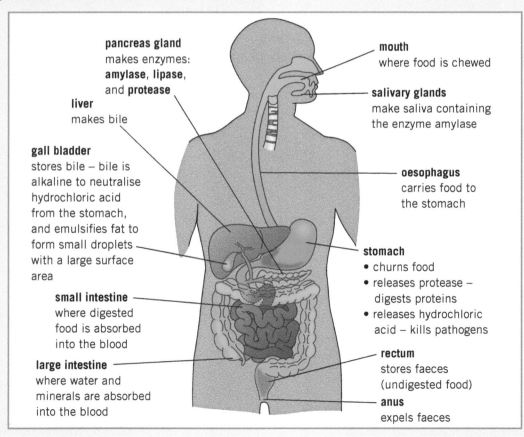

pancreas gland makes enzymes: **amylase, lipase,** and **protease**

liver makes bile

gall bladder stores bile – bile is alkaline to neutralise hydrochloric acid from the stomach, and emulsifies fat to form small droplets with a large surface area

small intestine where digested food is absorbed into the blood

large intestine where water and minerals are absorbed into the blood

mouth where food is chewed

salivary glands make saliva containing the enzyme amylase

oesophagus carries food to the stomach

stomach
- churns food
- releases protease – digests proteins
- releases hydrochloric acid – kills pathogens

rectum stores faeces (undigested food)

anus expels faeces

The respiratory system

The respiratory system takes air into and out of the body. When breathing in, air moves:

1. into the body through the mouth and nose
2. down the **trachea**
3. into the **bronchi**
4. through the **bronchioles**
5. into the **alveoli** (air sacs).

Oxygen then diffuses into the blood in the network of **capillaries** over the surface of the alveoli.

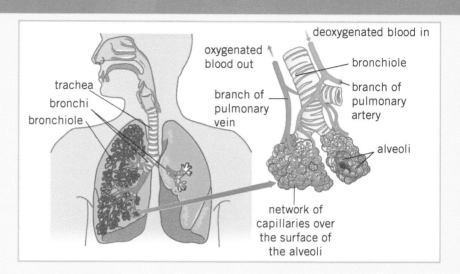

Ventilation of the lungs

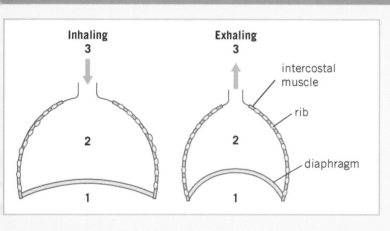

Inhaling

1. The **intercostal muscles** contract, pulling the **ribcage** upwards and the **diaphragm** muscles contract, causing the diaphragm to flatten. The volume of the **thorax** increases.
2. Increased volume means lower pressure in the thorax.
3. Atmospheric air is at a higher pressure than the chest, so air is drawn into the **lungs**.

Exhaling

1. The intercostal muscles and diaphragm muscles relax, allowing the ribcage to fall and the diaphragm to move up. The volume of the thorax decreases.
2. Decreased volume means increased pressure in the thorax.
3. Pressure in the chest is higher than outside, so air is forced out of the lungs.

Mechanical **ventilators** can be used to help patients to breathe:	• negative pressure **ventilators** – cause air to be 'drawn' into the lungs, by changing the air pressure surrounding the chest • positive pressure ventilators – force air into the lungs

 **Key Terms**

Make sure you can write a definition for these key terms.

alveoli	bronchi	bronchioles	capillaries	diaphragm
intercostal muscles	lungs	organ	organ system	ribcage
thorax	tissue	trachea	ventilator	

Retrieval

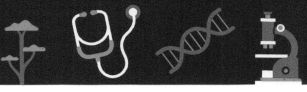

Learn the answers to the questions below, then cover the answers column with a piece of paper and write as many as you can. Check and repeat.

	B3 questions	Answers
1	Name the five levels of organisation.	cells → tissues → organs → organ systems → organisms
2	What is a tissue?	group of cells with similar structures and functions
3	What is an organ?	group of tissues working together to perform a specific function
4	What is the function of the liver in digestion?	produces bile, which neutralises hydrochloric acid from the stomach and emulsifies fat to form small droplets with a large surface area
5	What are the functions of saliva in digestion?	lubrication to help swallowing – contains amylase to break down starch
6	What is an organ system?	a group of organs working together to perform a similar function
7	Give three examples of animal tissues.	muscular, glandular, and epithelial tissue
8	Give two functions of glandular tissue.	producing enzymes and hormones
9	Name two structures in the digestive system that produce digestive juices.	pancreas and salivary gland
10	Name the muscles found between the ribs.	intercostal muscles
11	How is an alveolus adapted for gas exchange?	has a large surface area, thin walls, and rich blood supply
12	Describe the structural changes that take place during inhalation.	intercostal muscles and diaphragm muscles contract, pulling the ribcage upwards and causing the diaphragm to flatten
13	Describe the structural changes that take place during exhalation.	intercostal muscles relax and diaphragm muscles relax, so the ribcage falls and diaphragm moves up
14	Name the two main types of ventilators.	negative pressure ventilator and positive pressure ventilator
15	List the structures air passes through when breathing in.	mouth/nose → trachea → bronchi → bronchioles → alveoli

Put paper here

Now use the questions below to check your knowledge from previous chapters.

B3

Previous questions | Answers

1	What are two types of eukaryotic cell?	animal and plant
2	Where is DNA found in plant and animal cells?	in the nucleus
3	What is the function of chloroplasts?	contain chlorophyll to absorb light energy for photosynthesis
4	What is the function of mitochondria?	site of respiration to release energy for the cell
5	What is active transport?	movement of particles against a concentration gradient – from a dilute solution to a more concentrated solution – using energy from respiration

Put paper here *Put paper here*

Maths Skills

Practise your maths skills using the worked example and practice questions below.

Surface area to volume ratio	Worked example	Practice
Knowledge of surface area to volume ratio is important in biology, for example, it explains the body size adaptations of organisms and is important for the rate at which transportation processes such as respiration occur.	What is the surface area to volume ratio of the cube below?	Work out the surface area (cm^2), volume (cm^3), and surface area to volume ratio for cubes with the following dimensions.
To calculate it, you first need to calculate the surface area and volume of the object.	1 cm	**1** 2 cm × 2 cm × 2 cm
For the surface area of a cube, find the area of one face and multiply by six.	1 cm	**2** 5 cm × 5 cm × 5 cm
To find the volume of a cube, use: length × width × height	To calculate surface area (cm^2):	**3** 12 cm × 12 cm × 12 cm
	Area of one side of the cube = $1 \times 1 = 1 \, cm^2$	
	The cube has six sides, so:	
	surface area = $1 \times 6 = 6 \, cm^2$	
	To calculate volume (cm^3):	
	$1 \times 1 \times 1 = 1 \, cm^3$	
To calculate the surface area to volume ratio:	Surface area to volume ratio:	
surface area to volume ratio $= \dfrac{\text{surface area}}{\text{volume}}$	$\dfrac{6}{1} = 6{:}1$ ratio	

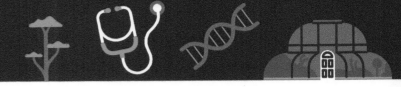

Practice

Exam-style questions

01 The events that occur during one breath – one inhalation and one exhalation – are known as one respiratory cycle.

Figure 1 shows change in the volume of the lungs in one respiratory cycle. The data were taken when the person was resting.

Figure 1

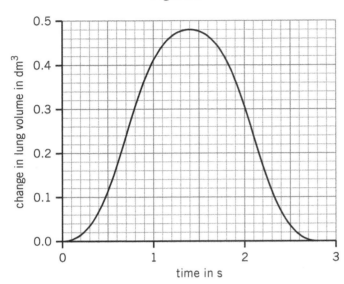

01.1 Use **Figure 1** to determine the volume of air taken in when the person inhales. **[1 mark]**

_____ dm³

> **Exam Tip**
>
> Draw lines on the graph to help you work it out!

01.2 The person's total lung volume after inhalation was 6.00 dm³. Calculate their total lung volume after exhalation. **[2 marks]**

_____ dm³

01.3 Calculate how many respiratory cycles will take place in one minute. Give your answer to **two** significant figures. **[3 marks]**

_____ per minute

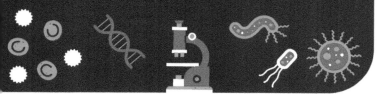

01.4 Explain how the structures in the chest cavity cause the changes in lung volume shown between 0s and 1s. **[4 marks]**

_____

_____

_____

_____

_____

01.5 A doctor measured another person's resting respiratory cycle. This person had 25 respiratory cycles per minute.

Suggest and explain **one** possible cause of this difference. **[2 marks]**

_____

_____

_____

02 **Figure 2** shows the main structures in the respiratory system.

Figure 2

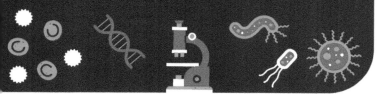

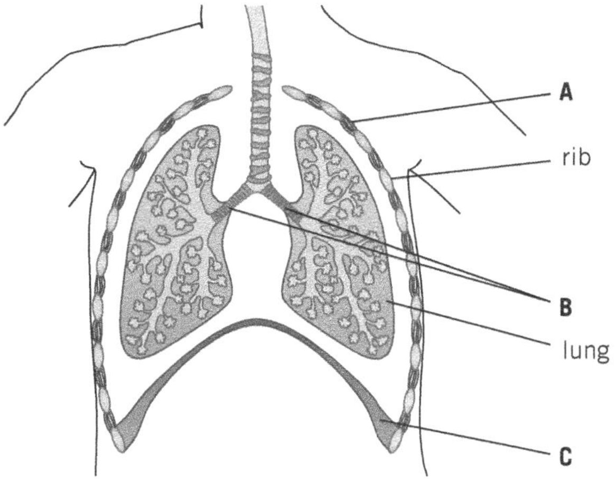

02.1 Identify structure **B**. **[1 mark]**

_____

02.2 Identify the trachea on the diagram by adding the letter **T**. **[1 mark]**

02.3 Describe what happens to structure **A** during inhalation. **[1 mark]**

_____

02.4 Explain the role structure **C** plays during inhalation. **[4 marks]**

_____

_____

_____

_____

03 Gluten is a form of protein found in some grains, for example, wheat.

03.1 Coeliac disease is a disease of the digestive system. It damages the lining of the small intestine when foods that contain gluten are eaten, resulting in a patient having a reduced number of villi. This causes a number of symptoms such as abdominal bloating and pain. A healthy person has on average 25 to 30 villi per μm^2. Calculate the density of the villi in the small intestine of a coeliac patient who has 50 000 villi in 7200 μm^2 of small intestine. **[2 marks]**

03.2 **Figure 3** compares a section of the small intestine of a person with coeliac disease with a person who does not have coeliac disease.

Exam Tip

For this question coeliac disease is used as an example. You may not have covered this in class, but this is getting you used to applying what you know to new situations for the exam.

Figure 3

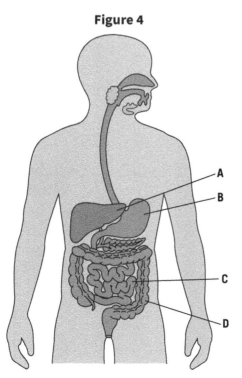

normal villi

villi affected by coeliac disease

normal villi

coeliac disease

Exam Tip

There is a clear difference in the picture. Think about how this difference may relate to the function of the digestive system.

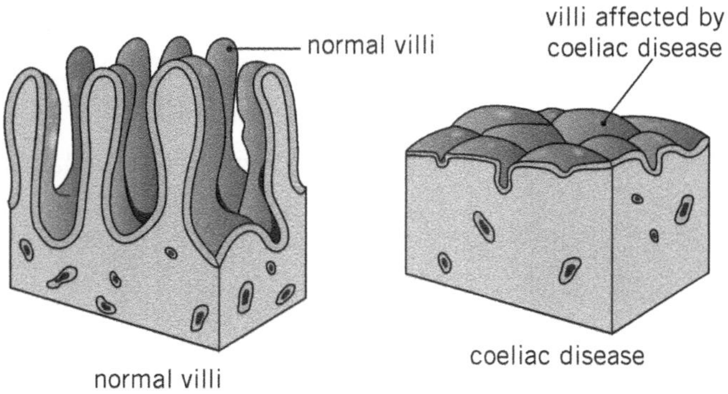

Use the information in the question and your own knowledge to suggest why a child with coeliac disease may not grow as tall as their peers. **[4 marks]**

04 **Figure 4** shows some organs from the digestive system.

04.1 Identify organs **A** and **C** from **Figure 4**. **[2 marks]**

04.2 Identify the organ from **Figure 4** that is responsible for absorbing water from undigested food. **[1 mark]**

Figure 4

A

B

C

D

04.3 The stomach is made up of a number of tissues. Draw **one** line from each type of stomach tissue to its function. **[3 marks]**

Stomach tissue   **Function**

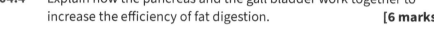

| muscular tissue |
| glandular tissue |
| epithelial tissue |

| churns the food and digestive juices of the stomach together |
| covers the inside and outside of the stomach |
| sends impulses to other areas of the body |
| produces the digestive juices |

04.4 Explain how the pancreas and the gall bladder work together to increase the efficiency of fat digestion. **[6 marks]**

05 Multicellular organisms are organised into five levels.

05.1 Complete the missing level of organisation in the diagram below. **[1 mark]**

cell → tissue → _____ → organ system → organism

05.2 Define the term tissue. **[1 mark]**

05.3 Match the following organ systems to their function. **[3 marks]**

| respiratory system |
| circulatory system |
| excretory system |

| produces new offspring |
| transports materials around the body |
| removes waste products from the body |
| exchanges gases between the body and its environment |

06 A number of changes take place in the thorax when you breathe in and out.

06.1 Select the most appropriate words to complete **Table 1**, showing the changes which happen during exhalation. Choose one word for each structure. **[4 marks]**

Table 1

Structure	Change
intercostal muscles	relax / contract
ribcage	moves up / moves down
diaphragm muscles	relax / contract
diaphragm	flattens / returns to domed shape

06.2 Give **two** ways in which the composition of gases changes between exhaled air and inhaled air. **[2 marks]**

07 Oxygen diffuses into the blood stream through the alveoli. A single alveolus is shown in **Figure 5**.

Figure 5

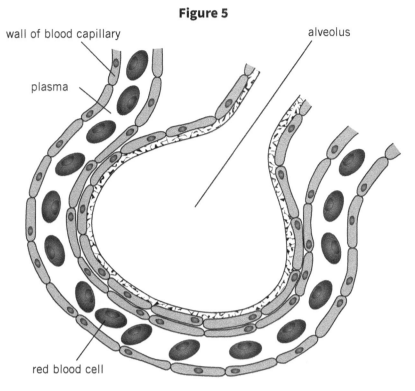

07.1 Explain how diffusion differs from active transport. **[2 marks]**

07.2 Explain how **two** features shown in **Figure 5** maximise the rate at which oxygen diffuses from the air into the blood. **[4 marks]**

07.3 Describe **two** ways in which a steep concentration gradient is maintained across the capillary wall to maximise diffusion. **[2 marks]**

08 Sleep apnoea is a condition where people stop breathing whilst they are asleep. This can be very dangerous. A positive pressure ventilation system can be used to help prevent this condition causing significant health issues.

08.1 Describe how a positive pressure ventilation system works. **[4 marks]**

08.2 Explain the differences between a positive pressure ventilation system and normal breathing. **[4 marks]**

08.3 Evaluate the use of a positive pressure ventilation system compared with a negative pressure ventilation system (iron lung) for the treatment of sleep apnoea. **[4 marks]**

> **! Exam Tip**
>
> This question asks you to refer to the figure, so the features you explain must be visible. Do not write about any features that you cannot see that affect diffusion such as concentration gradients.

09 This question is about water and nutrient transport in plants.

09.1 Explain why a household plant will start to wilt if you don't water it for several days. **[4 marks]**

09.2 Plants also need a supply of minerals to remain healthy, for example, nitrates. Nitrates are taken in through the roots. **Figure 6** shows the change over time in the mass uptake of nitrate ions for root cells with and without access to oxygen.

Figure 6

Describe the trends shown in the mass uptake of nitrate ions.
[4 marks]

09.3 Calculate the percentage difference in the mass of nitrate uptake for roots with and without access to oxygen after 210 seconds. **[2 marks]**

09.4 Explain why the plant had taken up a greater mass of nitrate ions at 210 seconds when a supply of oxygen was present. **[4 marks]**

10 **Figure 7** shows the typical lengths of some different structures.

Figure 7

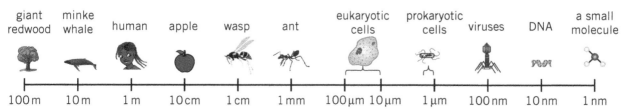

10.1 Deduce the difference in order of magnitude between an ant and a human. **[1 mark]**

10.2 Explain why humans need lungs whereas ants do not. **[2 marks]**

10.3 The resolution of a light microscope is 800 nm. Identify the smallest structure from **Figure 7** that can be viewed using the light microscope. **[2 marks]**

10.4 An angstrom (Å) is a unit of length used to measure small distances. $1\text{Å} = 1\times10^{-10}\text{m}$.

Hydrogen atoms have a diameter of 1 Å. Calculate how many hydrogen atoms, placed end to end, would be the same width as a virus cell. **[3 marks]**

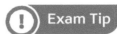

Exam Tip

This may be a new unit to you, but don't let that distract you or put you off. Just treat it like you would any other calculation question.

11 A student investigated the effect of different salt solutions on stalks of celery. They placed the celery stalks into different concentrations of salt solution and measured the change in their mass. **Table 2** shows their results.

Table 2

Concentration of salt solution in mol/dm³	Starting mass of celery stalk in g	Final mass of celery stalk in g	Change of mass of celery stalk in g
0.0	1.40	1.60	0.20
0.1	1.42	1.56	0.14
0.2	1.39	1.45	
0.3	1.36	1.28	−0.08
0.4	1.44	1.28	−0.16

11.1 Describe an investigation method the student could use to get the results in **Table 2**.

Include the following in your answer:
- independent, dependent, and control variables
- apparatus used **[4 marks]**

11.2 Calculate the change of mass for the 0.2 mol/dm³ concentration of salt solution in **Table 2**. **[1 mark]**

11.3 Calculate the percentage change for this concentration of salt solution. Give your answer to **three** significant figures. **[3 marks]**

11.4 Explain the reasons for the change of mass for the 0.0 and 0.4 mol/dm³ salt solutions. **[3 marks]**

11.5 Suggest **one** potential risk in this experiment and explain how to manage this risk. **[2 marks]**

12 A student measures the diameter of a capillary on an electron micrograph (**Figure 8**).

Figure 8

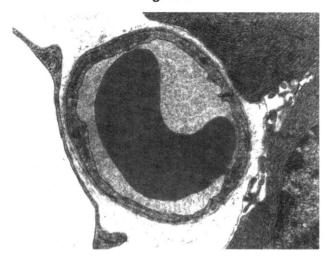

The image was produced from looking at a capillary through an electron microscope at a magnification of ×1250.

12.1 The student measured the diameter of the capillary to be 10 mm. Calculate the actual diameter of the capillary. Give your answer in micrometres. **[3 marks]**

12.2 Compare how the resolution and magnification differ between light and electron microscopes. **[2 marks]**

12.3 **Table 3** shows the average lengths of different cells.

Table 3

Component	Average length in μm
small animal cell	10
large plant cell	100
prokaryotic cell	1

Calculate the order of magnitude comparison between the small animal cell and the large plant cell. **[2 marks]**

B4 Circulatory system

The circulatory system is made of the heart and blood vessels. It transports material in the blood all over the body.

Blood is a tissue made up of four main components	
	• **Red blood cells** – transport oxygen around the body when the haemoglobin binds with oxygen to form oxyhaemoglobin.
	• **Plasma** – transports substances (such as carbon dioxide, glucose, and urea) and blood cells around the body.
	• **Platelets** – small fragments of cells that form blood clots at the site of a wound creating barriers to infections.
	• **White blood cells** – part of the immune system to defend the body against pathogens.

Blood clotting

Blood clotting involves a series of enzyme controlled reactions. The protein fibrinogen is converted to fibrin which forms a network of fibres. The fibres traps blood cells forming a clot.

Blood vessels

The structure of each blood vessel relates to its functions.

Vessel	Function	Structure	Diagram
artery	carries blood *away from* the heart (high pressure)	• thick, muscular, and elastic walls • the walls can stretch and withstand high pressure • small lumen	thick wall, small lumen, thick layer of muscle and elastic fibres
vein	carries blood *to* the heart (low pressure)	• have valves to stop blood flowing the wrong way • thin walls • large lumen	relatively thin wall, large lumen, often has valves
capillary	• carries blood to tissues and cells • connects arteries and **veins**	• one cell thick – short diffusion distance for substances to move between the blood and tissues (e.g., oxygen into cells and carbon dioxide out) • very narrow lumen	wall one cell thick, tiny vessel with narrow lumen

The heart

The heart is the organ that pumps blood around your body. It is made from cardiac muscle tissue, which is supplied with oxygen by the coronary **artery**.

Blood enters the atria of the heart. The atria contract and force blood into the **ventricles**. The ventricles contract and force blood out of the heart.

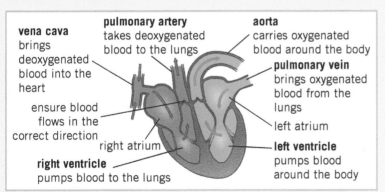

vena cava brings deoxygenated blood into the heart

pulmonary artery takes deoxygenated blood to the lungs

aorta carries oxygenated blood around the body

pulmonary vein brings oxygenated blood from the lungs

ensure blood flows in the correct direction

left atrium

right atrium

left ventricle pumps blood around the body

right ventricle pumps blood to the lungs

Heart rate is controlled by a group of cells in the right **atrium** that generate electrical impulses, acting as a **pacemaker**.

Double circulatory system

The human circulatory system is described as a double circulatory system because blood passes through the heart twice for every circuit around the body:

• the right ventricle pumps blood to the lungs where gas exchange takes place

• the left ventricle pumps blood around the rest of the body.

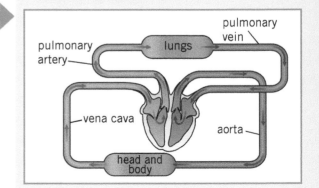

pulmonary artery

lungs

pulmonary vein

vena cava

aorta

head and body

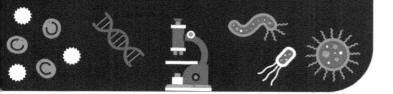

Coronary heart disease

Coronary heart disease (CHD) occurs when the coronary arteries become narrowed by the build-up of layers of fatty material within them.

This reduces the flow of blood, resulting in less oxygen for the heart muscle, which can lead to heart attacks.

Types of human blood

Antigens are proteins found on the surface of cells. The antigens contained in your red blood cells determine your blood group.

Blood group	Antigen on red blood cells	Antibody in plasma
A	A	b
B	B	a
AB	A and B	none
O	none	a and b

Before a transfusion, donor and recipient blood groups are checked. If they are mixed incorrectly, the antigen may stick to its complementary antibody and cause the blood cells to stick together (agglutination). Blood group O is the universal donor – its cells have no antigens so it can be given to everyone.

Treating coronary heart disease

Treatment	Description	Advantages	Disadvantages
stent	inserted into blocked coronary arteries to keep them open	• widens the artery – allows more blood to flow, so more oxygen is supplied to the heart • less serious surgery	• can involve major surgery – risk of infection, blood loss, blood clots, and damage to blood vessels • risks from anaesthetic used during surgery
artificial pacemaker	small electrical device implanted into the chest that sends electrical signals to the heart to stimulate it to beat correctly	• minor surgical procedure • lasts a long time • sensitive – responds to exercise and causes heart to beat faster	• risk of infection from surgery • batteries need to be replaced
replace faulty heart valves	heart valves that leak or do not open fully, preventing control of blood flow to the heart, can be replaced with biological or mechanical valves	• allows control of blood flow to the heart • long-term cure for faulty heart valves	• can involve major surgery – risk of infection and blood loss • risks from anaesthetic used during surgery
transplants	if the heart fails a donor heart, or heart and lungs, can be transplanted artificial hearts can be used to keep patients alive whilst waiting for a heart transplant, or to allow the heart to rest during recovery	• long-term cure for the most serious heart conditions • treats problems that cannot be treated in other ways	• transplant may be rejected if there is not a match between donor and patient • lengthy process • major surgery – risk of infection and blood loss • risks from anaesthetic used during surgery • immunosuppressant drugs taken to reduce the risk of transplant rejection make the patient more prone to infection

Key Terms

Make sure you can write a definition for these key terms.

antigen   artery   atrium   capillary   coronary heart disease   pacemaker   plasma

platelet   red blood cell   stent   vein   ventricle   white blood cell

Retrieval

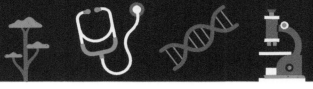

Learn the answers to the questions below then cover the answers column with a piece of paper and write as many as you can. Check and repeat.

B4 questions

Answers

	B4 questions	Answers
1	What is coronary heart disease?	occurs when a layer of fatty material builds up inside the coronary arteries, narrowing them – results in a lack of oxygen for the heart
2	What is a stent?	device inserted into a blocked artery to keep it open, allowing more blood and oxygen to the heart
3	What is an artifical pacemaker?	small electrical device that sends electrical signals to stimulate the heart to beat correctly
4	What is a faulty heart valve?	valve that doesn't open properly or leaks
5	How can a faulty heart valve be treated?	replace with a biological or mechanical valve
6	When do heart transplants take place?	in cases of heart failure
7	What are artificial hearts used for?	keep patients alive whilst waiting for a transplant, or allow the heart to rest for recovery
8	How does the structure of a vein relate to its function?	carries blood back to the heart at low pressure – doesn't need thick, elasticated walls, but has valves to prevent blood flowing the wrong way
9	How does the structure of a capillary relate to its function?	carries blood to cells and tissues – has a one-cell-thick wall to provide a short diffusion distance
10	Name the four main components of blood.	red blood cells, white blood cells, plasma, platelets
11	What is the function of platelets?	form blood clots – prevent the loss of blood and stop wounds becoming infected
12	Describe three adaptations of a red blood cell.	• bi-concave disc shape – large surface area to volume ratio for diffusion of oxygen • contains haemoglobin – binds to oxygen • no nucleus – more space for oxygen
13	How do white blood cells protect the body?	• engulf pathogens • produce antitoxins to neutralise toxins, or antibodies
14	Name the substances transported in the blood plasma.	hormones, proteins, urea, carbon dioxide, glucose
15	Why is the human circulatory system a double circulatory system?	blood passes through the heart twice for every circuit around the body – deoxygenated blood is pumped from the right side of the heart to the lungs, and the oxygenated blood that returns is pumped from the left side of the heart to the body
16	How does the structure of an artery relate to its function?	carries blood away from the heart under high pressure – has a small lumen and thick, elasticated walls that can stretch
17	Name the four main blood groups.	A, B, AB, O

Put paper here

Now use the questions below to check your knowledge from previous chapters.

B4

Previous questions

Answers

	Previous questions	Answers
1	What is an organ system?	a group of organs working together to perform a similar function
2	Give three examples of animal tissues.	muscular, glandular, and epithelial tissue
3	Give two functions of glandular tissue.	producing enzymes and hormones
4	Name two structures in the digestive system that produce digestive juices.	pancreas and salivary glands
5	What is the function of ribosomes?	enable the production of protein (protein synthesis)
6	Name three factors that affect the rate of diffusion.	concentration gradient, temperature, membrane surface area
7	Describe the structural changes that take place during inhalation.	intercostal muscles and diaphragm muscles contract, pulling the ribcage upwards and causing the diaphragm to flatten

Put paper here

 # Maths Skills

Practise your maths skills using the worked example and practice questions below.

Calculating rate of blood flow

The rate of blood flow in the body changes in response to things like exercise and illnesses.

Blood flow increases during exercise to deliver oxygen to working muscles and to remove waste products.

The rate of blood flow can be reduced by non-communicable diseases such as coronary heart disease.

To calculate rate of blood flow:

rate of blood flow (ml/min)

$$= \frac{\text{volume of blood (ml)}}{\text{time (min)}}$$

Remember to add units to your answer. Rate of blood flow can be measured in ml/min or l/hr – check the question to see which units you need to use.

Worked example

1660 ml of blood is pumped through a vein in 4 min.

Calculate the rate of blood flow through the vein in ml/min.

$$\frac{1660}{4} = 15 \text{ ml/min}$$

You may have to convert millilitres to litres if given a large volume.

To do this, divide the volume in ml by 1000.

Practice

1 3540 ml of blood is pumped through an artery in 3.5 min.

   Calculate the rate of blood flow through the artery in ml/min.

2 11540 ml of blood is pumped through an artery in 12.5 minutes.

   Calculate the rate of blood flow through the artery in ml/min.

3 670 l of blood is pumped through the heart in 1 hr.

   Calculate the rate of blood flow through the heart in ml/min.

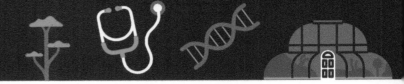

Exam-style questions

01 **Figure 1** shows the main causes of death in the UK in 2012 for people under the age of 75. The total number of deaths recorded in this period was 150 000.

Figure 1

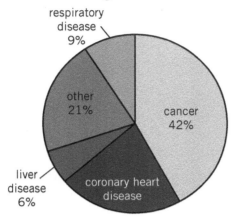

01.1 Give **one** cause of coronary heart disease. **[1 mark]**

_____

01.2 Calculate the percentage of people under the age of 75 who died in 2012 due to coronary heart disease. **[1 mark]**

_____ %

01.3 Calculate the number of people under the age of 75 who died in 2012 due to coronary heart disease. **[2 marks]**

_____ people

01.4 Suggest **three** ways a person could reduce their risk of coronary heart disease. **[3 marks]**

1 _____

_____

2 _____

_____

3 _____

_____

> **Exam Tip**
>
> The total number of people is given in the first part of the question.

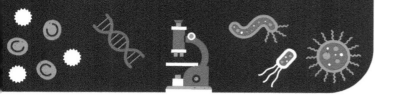

02 If a patient has a blocked blood vessel they may be treated using a stent or by undergoing bypass surgery. This is where another piece of blood vessel is used to replace the damaged vessel.

02.1 Describe how stents are used to treat blocked blood vessels. **[4 marks]**

_____

_____

_____

_____

02.2 Evaluate the use of stents to treat blocked blood vessels by explaining the risks and benefits of having a stent. **[4 marks]**

_____

_____

_____

_____

02.3 **Figure 2** shows the proportion of patients suffering complications following surgery to treat coronary heart disease. This information was collected by analysing the health records of 2500 patients, half of whom received a stent and half of whom received a bypass operation.

Figure 2

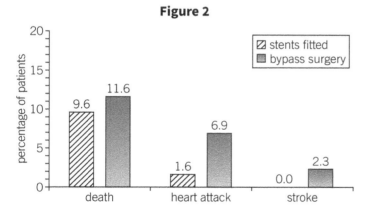

Calculate how many more patients died following a bypass operation compared to those who received a stent. **[3 marks]**

_____ patients

03   **Figure 3** shows a cross-section through the human heart.

Figure 3

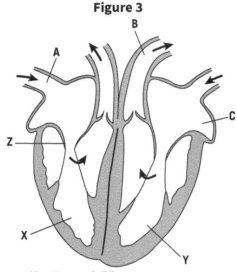

magnification: × 0.75

Exam Tip

The first thing you should do when you see a diagram of a heart is mark down your right (on the left-hand side) and left (on the right-hand side).

03.1   Identify which label is pointing to the left atrium.   **[1 mark]**

03.2   Name the blood vessels labelled **A** and **B**.   **[2 marks]**

03.3   Identify and describe the function of part **Z**.   **[2 marks]**

03.4   Humans have a double circulatory system. Describe what this means.   **[2 marks]**

04   **Figure 4** represents cross-sectional areas through the three main types of blood vessel.

Figure 4

A   B   C

04.1   Identify which blood vessel in **Figure 4** represents an artery.   **[1 mark]**

Exam Tip

Use **Figure 4** to help with this question!

04.2   Explain **one** way arteries are adapted for their function.   **[2 marks]**

04.3   Blood in the arteries is usually bright red because it is full of oxygen. Identify the artery where this is not true.   **[1 mark]**

aorta   vena cava   pulmonary artery   coronary artery

04.4   Give a reason for your answer to **04.3**.   **[1 mark]**

04.5   Describe **two** reasons why it is important that blood is transported to every cell in the body.   **[2 marks]**

05   Every year many patients need to have heart valve replacements.

05.1   Describe the function of the heart valve labelled **X** in **Figure 5**.

[2 marks]

Figure 5

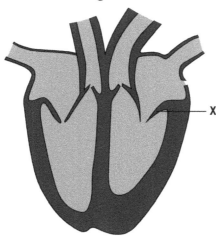

05.2   Over time valves can become leaky. Explain how this can cause
health issues. **[3 marks]**

05.3   **Table 1** gives information about two types of heart valve.

Table 1

	Mechanical heart valve	Biological heart valve
Material	titanium	usually cow or pig tissue, but can be from a human donor
Lifespan	20 years	10–15 years
Additional medication	anti-coagulation medication to prevent blood clotting around the valve	not required

A 20-year-old patient requires a heart valve replacement. Using
Table 1 and your own knowledge, evaluate the advantages and
disadvantages of each type of heart valve.   **[6 marks]**

06 Whilst waiting for a heart transplant some patients are fitted with artificial hearts to keep them alive.

Figure 6 shows one example of an artificial heart. It is connected to an external power supply.

Figure 6

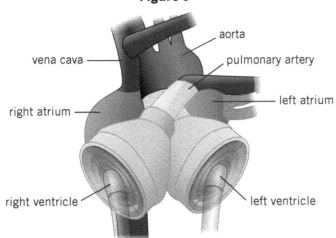

06.1 Use the information in **Figure 6** and your own knowledge to identify **two** differences between a real heart and an artificial heart.

[2 marks]

06.2 Suggest **two** advantages and **two** disadvantages of treating patients with this artificial heart. **[4 marks]**

>
> **Exam Tip**
>
> You can use a table to answer this question, making it clear what goes with what.

06.3 Suggest **one** reason why artificial hearts are not widely used in the treatment of heart disease. **[1 mark]**

07 **Table 2** shows the number of red blood cells present in people living at different altitudes above sea level.

Table 2

Height above sea level in m	Mean number of red blood cells in millions per mm³ of blood
0	4.9
1000	5.5
2000	6.2
3000	6.8
4000	7.2
5000	7.6

07.1 Explain how a red blood cell is adapted to perform its function. **[6 marks]**

07.2 Using **Table 2**, calculate the percentage change between the number of red blood cells present in a person living at 2000 m above sea level, and 4000 m above sea level. **[2 marks]**

>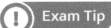
> **Exam Tip**
>
> Percentage change is how different they are from each other as a percentage.

07.3 As altitude increases, the amount of oxygen in the air decreases. Using information in **Table 2**, explain how differences in a person's blood composition enable them to live at different altitudes.

[3 marks]

08 **Figure 7** shows a section of blood vessels in the upper arm.

Figure 7

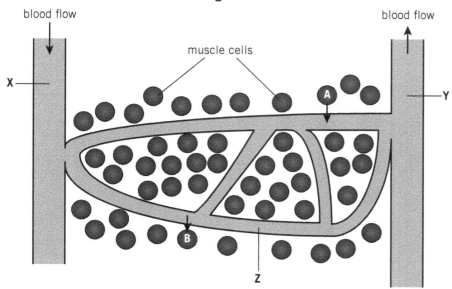

08.1 Name the blood vessel represented by label **Z**. **[1 mark]**

08.2 Describe **two** ways structure **Z** is adapted to maximise the rate of diffusion of carbon dioxide. **[2 marks]**

08.3 Identify which arrow shows the direction of transport of carbon dioxide. **[1 mark]**

09 Atherosclerosis is one form of coronary heart disease. Patients with this form of the disease have a build-up of fatty material on the inner walls of their arteries.

09.1 Explain how atherosclerosis increases the risk of a heart attack. **[2 marks]**

09.2 Describe **one** mechanical technique doctors can use to lower the risk of a heart attack for a patient with atherosclerosis. **[3 marks]**

09.3 Patients with coronary heart disease are often advised to take aspirin daily. An effect of aspirin is to reduce the ability of platelets to stick together.

Suggest and explain the benefits to a person with atherosclerosis taking this drug. **[4 marks]**

10 **Figure 8** shows the changes in blood pressure of a person at rest. Their blood pressure was measured in an artery and a vein at the same time.

! **Exam Tip**

Thinking about how structure relates to function might give you a clue here.

Figure 8

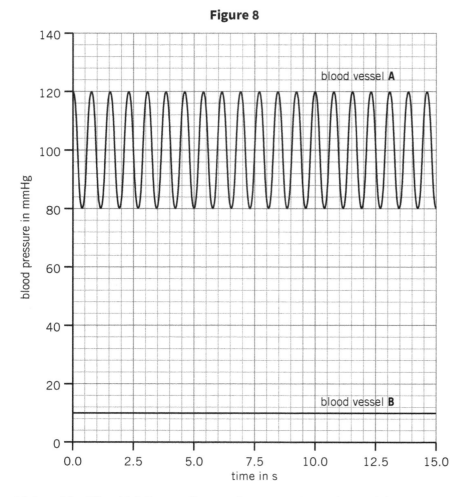

10.1 Identify which line on the graph represents a vein. Explain your answer. **[3 marks]**

10.2 Explain how a vein is adapted to transporting blood back to the heart. **[4 marks]**

10.3 Draw a line on **Figure 8** to suggest the pressure you would find in a capillary. **[1 mark]**

10.4 Calculate the person's heart rate. **[2 marks]**

! **Exam Tip**

Measuring the number of beats in 15 seconds then multiplying by four will give a more accurate result.

11 **Figure 9** shows a simple diagram of a human heart.

Figure 9

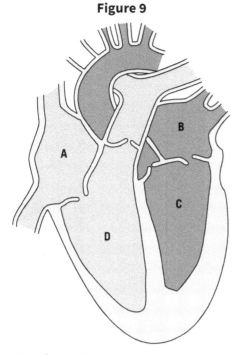

11.1 Name part **A** in **Figure 9**. [1 mark]

11.2 Compare and contrast the functions of parts **C** and **D** in **Figure 9**. [3 marks]

11.3 There are different rates of blood flow through the heart at rest and during exercise. A student has a heart rate during exercise of 125 beats per minute with a stroke volume (the volume of blood pumped out during each contraction of the heart) of 70 ml. Use the equation below to calculate their cardiac output. [3 marks]

cardiac output = stroke volume × heart rate
   (l/minute)   (l)   (beats per minute)

> **! Exam Tip**
>
> Although this is not an equation you may have seen before, just plug the numbers given to you in the question into the equation.

11.4 A patient has an appointment with their doctor. The doctor gave the patient an ultrasound scan, which confirmed that fatty materials had deposited in the coronary arteries. The doctor considers three treatment options: inserting a stent, prescribing a statin medication, or both of these. Statins are drugs that reduce blood cholesterol, slowing down the deposit of fatty materials in the arteries. Suggest which treatment option(s) the doctor should use to treat the patient at this stage. [6 marks]

12 The circulatory system transports a number of materials around the body. This includes glucose and oxygen needed for respiration.

12.1 Name **two** other substances transported by the blood. [2 marks]

12.2 Blood contains red and white blood cells. Name **one** other component of blood and describe its function. [2 marks]

12.3 Blood travels around the body in blood vessels. Describe the function of arteries. [1 mark]

B5 Organisation in plants

Tissues in leaves

Leaves are organs because they contain many tissues that work together to perform photosynthesis. The surface area to volume ratio of leaves is increased by their flattened shape and internal air spaces.

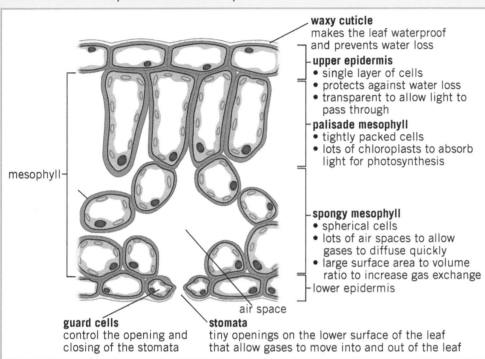

waxy cuticle
makes the leaf waterproof and prevents water loss

upper epidermis
- single layer of cells
- protects against water loss
- transparent to allow light to pass through

palisade mesophyll
- tightly packed cells
- lots of chloroplasts to absorb light for photosynthesis

spongy mesophyll
- spherical cells
- lots of air spaces to allow gases to diffuse quickly
- large surface area to volume ratio to increase gas exchange

lower epidermis

mesophyll

guard cells
control the opening and closing of the stomata

air space

stomata
tiny openings on the lower surface of the leaf that allow gases to move into and out of the leaf

Tissues in the stem and roots

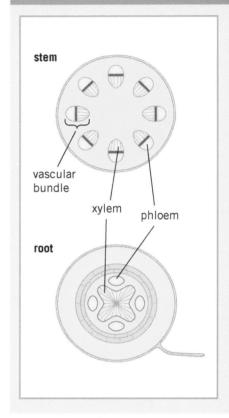

stem

vascular bundle

xylem   phloem

root

Stomata

Stomata are tiny openings in the undersides of leaves – this placement reduces water loss through evaporation.

They control gas exchange and water loss from leaves by:

- allowing diffusion of carbon dioxide into the plant for photosynthesis
- allowing diffusion of oxygen out of the plant.

Guard cells are used to open and close the stomata.

When a plant has plenty of water, the guard cells become turgid. The cell wall on the inner surface is very thick, so it cannot stretch as much as the outer surface. So as the guard cells swell up, they curve away from each other, opening the stoma.

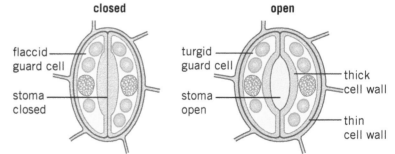

closed

flaccid guard cell

stoma closed

open

turgid guard cell

stoma open

thick cell wall

thin cell wall

 **Key Terms**

Make sure you can write a definition for these key terms.

| cuticle | epidermis | flaccid | guard cell | mesophyll | phloem | stomata |

| translocation | transpiration | transpiration stream | turgid | xylem |

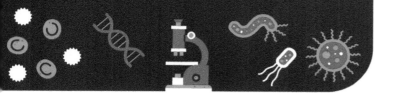

Transpiration

Water is lost through the stomata by evaporation. This pulls water up from the roots through the **xylem** and is called **transpiration**. The constant movement of water up the plant is called the **transpiration stream**.

- provides water to cells to keep them **turgid**
- provides water to cells for photosynthesis
- transports mineral ions to leaves

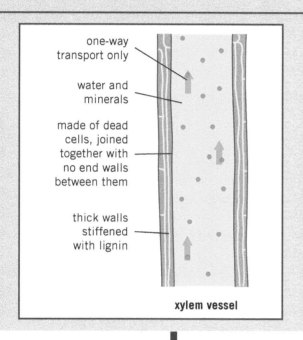

one-way transport only

water and minerals

made of dead cells, joined together with no end walls between them

thick walls stiffened with lignin

xylem vessel

Translocation

The movement of dissolved sugars from the leaves to the rest of the plant through the **phloem** is called **translocation**.

- moves dissolved sugars made in the leaves during photosynthesis to other parts of the plant
- this allows for respiration, growth, and glucose storage

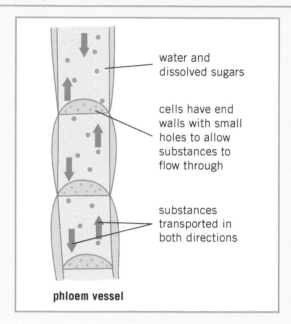

water and dissolved sugars

cells have end walls with small holes to allow substances to flow through

substances transported in both directions

phloem vessel

Factors affecting the rate of transpiration

Factor	Effect on transpiration	Because...
temperature	higher temperatures *increase* the rate of transpiration	water evaporates faster in higher temperatures
humidity	lower humidity *increases* the rate of transpiration	the drier the air, the steeper the concentration gradient of water molecules between the air and leaf
wind speed	more wind *increases* the rate of transpiration	wind removes the water vapour quickly, maintaining a steeper concentration gradient
light intensity	higher light intensity *increases* the rate of transpiration	stomata open wider to let more carbon dioxide into the leaf for photosynthesis

Root hair cells

- increase absorption of water and mineral ions into the root by increasing the root surface area
- contain lots of mitochondria to transfer energy, which is used to take in mineral ions by active transport

 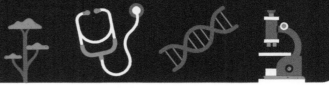

Learn the answers to the questions below then cover the answers column with a piece of paper and write as many as you can. Check and repeat.

B5 questions	Answers
1 Why is a leaf an organ?	there are many tissues inside the leaf that work together to perform photosynthesis
2 How is the upper epidermis adapted for its function?	• single layer of transparent cells allows light to pass through • cells secrete a waxy substance that makes leaves waterproof
3 How is the palisade mesophyll adapted for its function?	tightly packed cells with lots of chloroplasts to absorb as much light as possible for photosynthesis
4 How is the spongy mesophyll adapted for its function?	air spaces increase the surface area and allow gases to diffuse quickly
5 What is the function of the guard cells?	control the opening and closing of the stomata
6 What is the function of the xylem?	transport water and mineral ions from the roots to the rest of the plant
7 Give three adaptations of the xylem.	• made of dead cells • no end wall between cells • walls strengthened by a chemical called lignin to withstand the pressure of the water
8 What is the function of the phloem?	transport dissolved sugars from the leaves to the rest of the plant
9 What is the purpose of translocation?	transport dissolved sugars from the leaves to other parts of the plant for respiration, growth, and storage
10 Define the term transpiration.	movement of water from the roots to the leaves through the xylem
11 What is the purpose of transpiration?	• provides water to keep cells turgid • provides water to cells for photosynthesis • transports mineral ions to leaves
12 Name four factors that affect the rate of transpiration.	temperature, light intensity, humidity, and wind speed
13 What effect does temperature have on the rate of transpiration?	higher temperatures increase the rate of transpiration
14 What effect does humidity have on the rate of transpiration?	higher levels of humidity decrease the rate of transpiration
15 Why does increased light intensity increase the rate of transpiration?	stomata open wider to let more carbon dioxide into the leaf for photosynthesis
16 What is the function of the stomata?	allow diffusion of gases into and out of the plant
17 Where are most stomata found?	underside of leaves
18 What is the advantage to the plant of having a high number of stomata at this location?	reduces the amount of water loss through evaporation

Put paper here

Now use the questions below to check your knowledge from previous chapters.

Previous questions / Answers

	Previous questions	Answers
1	List the structures air passes through when breathing in.	mouth/nose → trachea → bronchi → bronchioles → alveoli
2	What is a stent?	device inserted into a blocked artery to keep it open, allowing more blood and oxygen to the heart
3	How does the structure of a vein relate to its function?	carries blood back to the heart at low pressure – doesn't need thick, elasticated walls, but has valves to prevent blood flowing the wrong way
4	Name the four main components of blood.	red blood cells, white blood cells, plasma, platelets
5	How are villi adapted for exchanging substances?	• long and thin – increases surface area • one-cell-thick membrane – short diffusion pathway • good blood supply – maintains a steep concentration gradient

Put paper here

Put paper here

Working Scientifically

Practise your working scientifically skills using the worked example and practice questions below.

Risk assessments

When planning an investigation you need to

- identify possible hazards – what may cause an injury
- identify any associated risks – how you may be injured and its likelihood
- suggest control measures – ways of minimising the risks.

This information is normally summarised in a risk assessment.

Worked example

The following is a risk assessment for heating water in a beaker using a Bunsen burner:

Hazard	Risk	Control measure
Bunsen burner	burns from naked flame	• leave on visible yellow flame when not used for heating
	setting hair alight	• tie hair back
glass beaker	cuts from broken glass	• place beaker away from edge of bench • use dustpan and brush to clear any breakages
	burns from hot glass	• do not handle beaker until cool

Practice

A student used a swab to collect some of their own cheek cells. They rubbed them onto a slide and observed them under a microscope.

Design a risk assessment for this activity, including at least two risks.

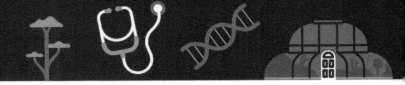

Exam-style questions

01 Four leaves of approximately the same size were removed from an oak tree.

Petroleum jelly was spread over the surface of leaves **A–C**. This acts as a waterproof agent to prevent water loss from the leaves.

All four leaves were then hung from a piece of string.

Figure 1

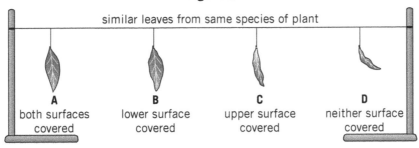

similar leaves from same species of plant

A	**B**	**C**	**D**
both surfaces covered	lower surface covered	upper surface covered	neither surface covered

01.1 Suggest why no petroleum jelly was spread over the surface of leaf **D**.   **[1 mark]**

_____

_____

01.2 The mass of each leaf was measured at regular intervals.

Name the apparatus used to measure the mass of each leaf.   **[1 mark]**

_____

01.3 The results of the investigation are shown in **Figure 2**.

Figure 2

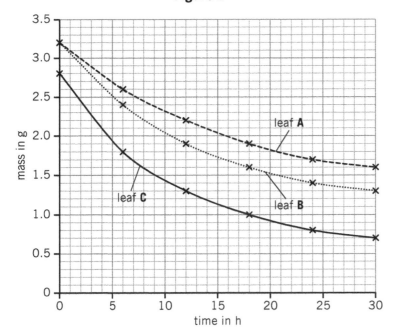

Exam Tip

You can use the points already plotted as a guide to find 6 and 12 hours.

The values for leaf **D** are shown in **Table 1**.

Table 1

Leaf	Mass in g					
	Start	After 6 h	After 12 h	After 18 h	After 24 h	After 30 h
D	2.7	1.6	1.0	0.6	0.4	0.3

Plot this data on **Figure 2**. Draw a line of best fit. **[3 marks]**

01.4 Identify which leaf lost water most quickly. Give a reason for your answer. **[2 marks]**

_____

_____

_____

02 **Figure 3** shows a cross-section through a leaf.

Figure 3

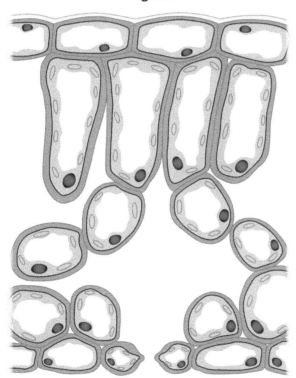

02.1 Identify and label a stoma on the diagram. **[1 mark]**

02.2 Describe the role of guard cells in controlling water loss from a leaf. **[2 marks]**

_____

_____

_____

03 A group of students were studying the factors that affect the rate of transpiration in a plant. They used a potometer (**Figure 4**) to measure the rate of water uptake by a plant. The rate of water uptake can be used as an approximation of the rate of transpiration in a plant.

Figure 4

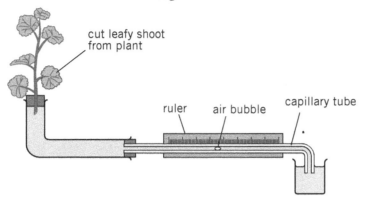

cut leafy shoot from plant

ruler   air bubble   capillary tube

(!) Exam Tips

You may not have seen a practical set up like this before, but don't panic!

This question is testing if you can apply your practical skills.

03.1 Define the term transpiration. **[2 marks]**

03.2 The students studied the rate of water uptake of the plant by measuring the distance travelled by an air bubble at 5-minute intervals over 30 minutes. Explain why the rate of water uptake and the rate of transpiration are different. **[2 marks]**

03.3 The students' results are shown in **Table 2**.

Plot a graph of the water uptake of the plant on **Figure 5** below. Draw a suitable line of best fit. **[3 marks]**

Table 2

Time in min	Distance moved by bubble from start point in mm
0	0
5	4
10	8
15	11
20	16
25	19
30	25

Figure 5

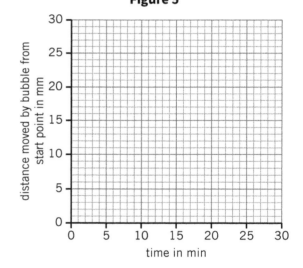

distance moved by bubble from start point in mm

time in min

03.4 Describe the relationship between the distance moved by the bubble and time. **[1 mark]**

03.5 Use your graph to determine how long it took the bubble to move 10 mm. **[1 mark]**

03.6 Calculate the rate of water uptake by the plant between 10 and 20 min. **[4 marks]**

03.7 The experiment was carried out at room temperature. Explain how you would expect the graph to differ if the experiment was repeated at 35 °C. **[2 marks]**

04 Plants use transport systems to move materials around inside them.

04.1 Name the structure found in stems that contains the xylem and phloem tissue. **[1 mark]**

04.2 Define the term translocation. **[1 mark]**

04.3 Describe the main structural differences between xylem and phloem tissue. **[4 marks]**

04.4 Suggest why plant pests such as greenfly bite into the phloem tissue in a plant. **[1 mark]**

05 A student carried out an investigation on beech leaves to compare the number of stomata present on the upper and lower surfaces of the leaf.

05.1 Describe how the student could take samples from the leaf to count the number of stomata present. **[3 marks]**

05.2 The student's results are shown in **Table 3**.

Table 3

Surface	Number of stomata present					Mean
	Sample 1	Sample 2	Sample 3	Sample 4	Sample 5	
Upper	1	2	2	3	2	2
Lower	36	42	35	41	37	

Calculate the mean result for the lower surface of the leaf. Give your answer to **two** significant figures. **[2 marks]**

05.3 The student concluded that most stomata are found on the lower surface of a beech leaf. Explain why this is an advantage for a beech tree. **[2 marks]**

Exam Tip

Use data from the graph.

Exam Tip

Show your working on the graph.

Exam Tip

Calculating rate is a maths skill you might use more often in chemistry, but you should be prepared for it to come up anywhere in science.

Exam Tip

You might not have covered greenfly in class, but apply what you know from your lessons to this new context.

Exam Tip

Remember significant figures and decimal places are different things. Don't get them confused!

06 **Figure 6** shows a plant cell.

Figure 6

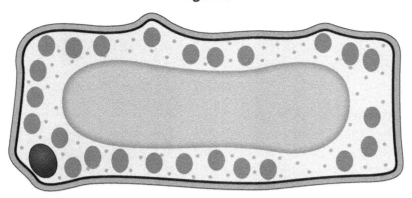

06.1 Identify which part of a plant the cell has been taken from. Choose **one** answer. **[1 mark]**

palisade mesophyll   phloem tissue   root   xylem tissue

06.2 Give a reason for your answer to **06.1**. **[1 mark]**

06.3 Describe how water moves between cells in a leaf. **[2 marks]**

06.4 The main function of a leaf is to perform photosynthesis to provide food for the plant. Describe how the tissues inside a leaf are organised to maximise photosynthesis. **[6 marks]**

Exam Tips

This is a six-mark question, so make sure you write enough.

Think about how the cells in a plant differ depending on their location and function.

07 As well as anchoring a plant into the ground, roots are also responsible for the uptake of water and mineral ions from the soil.

07.1 Explain how a root hair cell is adapted for the uptake of water and mineral ions. **[3 marks]**

Exam Tips

'Explain' questions are asking *why*.

An answer describing what a root hair cell looks like won't get marks.

07.2 **Figure 7** represents the movement of water and mineral ions into the root hair cell.

Figure 7

outside cell   inside cell

cell membrane

high concentration of substance A   **process X**   low concentration of substance A

low concentration of substance B   **process Y**   high concentration of substance B

Identify and name the process in **Figure 7** that represents the uptake of mineral ions. Give a reason for your answer. **[2 marks]**

07.3 Name the vessel that transports mineral ions around the plant. **[1 mark]**

07.4 Describe **one** use of mineral ions in a plant. **[1 mark]**

Exam Tips

Try to get into the mind of the examiner.

This is a two-mark question – the first mark will be for identifying the process and the second mark will be for the reason.

08 Scientists can use sampling and counting techniques to investigate the distribution of stomata on leaves. **Figure 8** is an observational diagram produced by a scientist when looking at a lower leaf epidermis. For each sample observed, the scientist calculated the density of stomata present in the form: *number of stomata per mm²*. Partially visible stomata were counted as present.

Figure 8

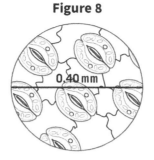

0.40 mm

08.1 Calculate the density of stomata for the sample shown in **Figure 8**. **[5 marks]**

! Exam Tip

You'll need to work out the area of the circle first.

08.2 The scientist then estimated the total surface area of the leaf from which the sample was taken. Suggest how the scientist estimated the leaf surface area. **[2 marks]**

08.3 The scientist measured the leaf's surface area to be approximately 8 cm². Estimate the number of stomata that would be found on the surface of this leaf. **[3 marks]**

08.4 Suggest and explain how the scientist's results may have been different if the sample was taken from the upper surface of the leaf. **[3 marks]**

Figure 9

09 Marram grass grows on sand dunes. Sand dunes are generally very dry and windy habitats. The leaves of marram grass are specially adapted to reduce water loss by transpiration. Some of these features are shown in **Figure 9**.

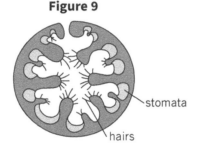

— stomata

— hairs

09.1 Define the term transpiration. **[2 marks]**

09.2 Identify which property of the waxy cuticle reduces the rate of transpiration. Choose **one** answer. **[1 mark]**

impermeable   large surface area   reflective   thermal insulator

! Exam Tip

You'll need to refer to rolled leaves, stomata, and leaf hairs if you want to get full marks on this question.

09.3 Using **Figure 9**, suggest and explain how the rolled leaves, stomata, and leaf hairs work together to reduce the rate of transpiration. **[3 marks]**

10 The photograph in **Figure 10** was taken through a microscope. It shows a vascular bundle in a leaf. Vascular bundles contain both xylem and phloem tissue.

Figure 10

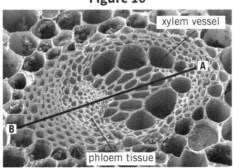

xylem vessel

A

B

phloem tissue

10.1 Describe **one** difference between the structure of the xylem vessel and the phloem tube in **Figure 10**. [1 mark]

10.2 Name the chemical present in xylem vessel walls that provides the strength to withstand the pressure of the movement of water in the plant. [1 mark]

10.3 The chemical named in **10.3** can be seen using a stain. Use this information to plan how you could find the position of the vascular bundles in a stem. [3 marks]

Exam Tip

You can still answer this question if you haven't identified the chemical.

10.4 Deer are a concern in managed woodlands. They eat tree bark and new tree shoots, and rub their antlers on tree trunks to leave a scent marker to warn other deer away from the area. Explain the reasons why protective collars are placed around tree saplings in areas of managed woodland. [6 marks]

Exam Tip

The question has given you a description of the problem. Take each part of the problem and explain what protective collars can do to solve it.

11 **Figure 11** shows a bacterial cell.

Figure 11

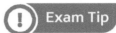

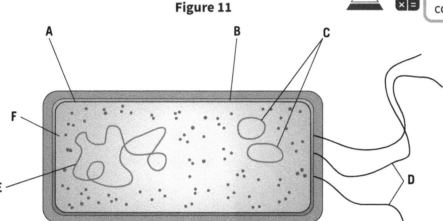

11.1 Identify which part of the cell (**A**–**F**) is the cell membrane. [1 mark]

11.2 Describe the function of structure **D**. [1 mark]

11.3 Use **Figure 11** to explain how you can tell that this is a prokaryotic cell. [2 marks]

12 A group of students were asked to investigate the effect of sugar solutions of different concentrations on samples of strawberry tissue.

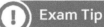

Figure 12

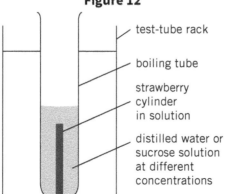

test-tube rack

boiling tube

strawberry cylinder in solution

distilled water or sucrose solution at different concentrations

Exam Tip

This is one of the required practicals in a slightly different context. You need to get used to applying what you know to new situations.

12.1 Using the apparatus in **Figure 12** and other standard laboratory equipment, suggest a method the students could have used to accurately determine the concentration of sucrose in the strawberry samples. **[6 marks]**

12.2 To increase the size of strawberries from their plants, growers provide the plants with lots of water. Discuss the potential economic advantages and disadvantages to the grower of providing excess water to strawberry plants. **[6 marks]**

13 Fish and single-celled amoebas are both examples of living organisms found in water.

13.1 Explain which of these organisms has a specialised transport system. **[3 marks]**

13.2 Humans have a double circulatory system to transport materials around the body. Frogs have only a partial double circulatory system as shown in **Figure 13**.

Figure 13

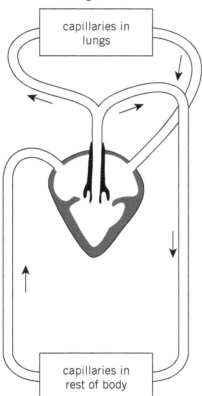

capillaries in lungs

capillaries in rest of body

Using **Figure 13** and your own knowledge, give **two** similarities and **two** differences between the frog and human circulatory systems. **[4 marks]**

13.3 Suggest and explain why the frog transport system is less effective in supplying body tissues with oxygen. **[3 marks]**

B6 Enzymes and digestion

Enzymes

Enzymes are large proteins that **catalyse** (speed up) reactions. Enzymes are not changed in the reactions they catalyse.

Lock and key theory

This is a simple model of how enzymes work:

1 The enzyme's **active site** (where the reaction occurs) is a specific shape.
2 The enzyme (the lock) will only catalyse a specific reaction because the **substrate** (the key) fits into its active site.
3 At the active site, enzymes can break molecules down into smaller ones or bind small molecules together to form larger ones.
4 When the products have been released, the enzyme's active site can accept another substrate molecule.

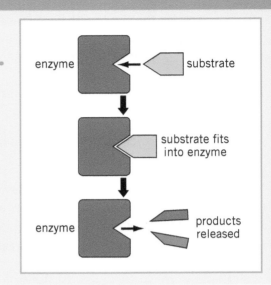

The effect of temperature on enzymes

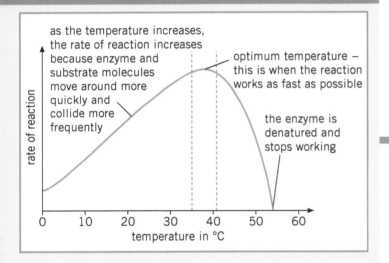

as the temperature increases, the rate of reaction increases because enzyme and substrate molecules move around more quickly and collide more frequently

optimum temperature – this is when the reaction works as fast as possible

the enzyme is denatured and stops working

Denaturation

At extremes of pH or at very high temperatures the shape of an enzyme's active site can change.

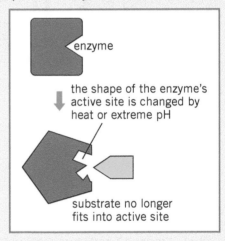

enzyme

the shape of the enzyme's active site is changed by heat or extreme pH

substrate no longer fits into active site

The substrate can no longer bind to the active site, so the enzyme cannot catalyse the reaction – the enzyme has been **denatured**.

> **Revision Tip**
>
> This is one area where biology and chemistry overlap.
>
> The first part of the graph can be explained by the collision theory you have learnt in your chemistry lessons.

Key Terms

Make sure you can write a definition for these key terms.

| active site | amylase | catalyse | denatured | enzyme |
| lipase | optimum | protease | substrate | |

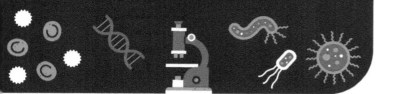

Digestive enzymes

Digestive enzymes are produced in glands and the lining of the gut. They are released into the gut, where they come into contact with food molecules. Digestive enzymes catalyse the breakdown of large, insoluble food molecules into small, soluble molecules that can then be absorbed into the bloodstream. For example, carbohydrases break down carbohydrates into simple sugars.

These products of digestion can be used to build new carbohydrates, lipids, and proteins.

Some of the glucose produced is used in respiration.

Enzyme	Sites of production	Reaction catalysed	Site of reaction
amylase	salivary glands pancreas small intestine	starch → glucose	mouth and small intestine
proteases	stomach pancreas small intestine	proteins → amino acids	stomach and small intestine
lipases	pancreas small intestine	lipids → fatty acids and glycerol	small intestine

The effect of pH on enzymes

Different enzymes have different **optimum** pH values.

This allows enzymes to be adapted to work well in environments with different pH values. For example, the stomach produces hydrochloric acid. Enzymes in the stomach work most effectively in acid conditions.

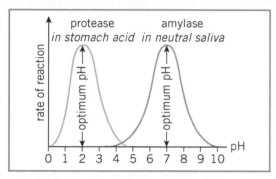

Bile

Bile is produced in the liver and stored in the gall bladder. From there, it is released into the small intestine.

Bile has two main roles in digestion:

- It creates alkaline conditions – to allow small intestine enzymes to work effectively.

- It emulsifies fats – increasing the surface area of fats for lipase enzymes to act on.

Use of enzymes in the home and industry

Some microorganisms produce useful enzymes that we can use in our homes or in industry, for example:

Use	Enzymes used	Advantages
biological detergents	proteases and lipases	work best at low temperatures, saving electricity
baby food	proteases	pre-digest some of the protein in the food, making it easier for the baby to digest
lower-calorie foods	isomerases (convert glucose syrup into fructose syrup)	fructose is much sweeter than sugar so less needs to be added to food products

 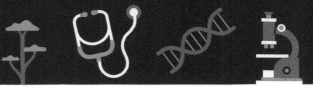

Retrieval

Learn the answers to the questions below then cover the answers column with a piece of paper and write as many as you can. Check and repeat.

B6 questions		Answers
1	What are enzymes?	protein molecules that catalyse specific reactions in organisms
2	Why are enzymes described as specific?	each enzyme only catalyses a specific reaction, because the active site only fits together with certain substrates (like a lock and key)
3	Describe the function of amylase.	to break down starch into glucose
4	Where is amylase produced?	salivary glands, pancreas, and small intestine
5	Describe the function of proteases.	to break down proteins into amino acids
6	Where are proteases produced?	stomach, pancreas, and small intestine
7	Describe the function of lipases.	to break down lipids into fatty acids and glycerol
8	Where are lipases produced?	pancreas and small intestine
9	What are two factors that affect the rate of activity of an enzyme?	temperature and pH
10	What does denatured mean?	shape of an enzyme's active site is changed by high temperatures or an extreme pH, so it can no longer bind with the substrate
11	Describe the effect of temperature on enzyme activity.	as temperature increases, rate of reaction increases until it reaches the optimum for enzyme activity – above this temperature enzyme activity decreases and eventually stops
12	Describe the effect of pH on enzyme activity.	different enzymes have a different optimum pH at which their activity is greatest – at a pH much lower or higher than this, enzyme activity decreases and eventually stops
13	Why do different digestive enzymes have different optimum pHs?	different parts of the digestive system have very different pHs – the stomach is strongly acidic and the pH in the small intestine is close to neutral
14	Describe the role of bile in digestion.	creates alkaline conditions needed for small intestine enzymes and emulsifies fats
15	Give three commercial uses of enzymes.	biological detergents, baby foods, lower-calorie food production

Put paper here

B6

Now use the questions below to check your knowledge from previous chapters.

Previous questions | Answers

	Previous questions	Answers
1	What is the function of saliva in digestion?	lubrication to help swallowing; contains amylase to break down starch
2	Why is active transport needed in plant roots?	concentration of mineral ions in the soil is lower than inside the root hair cells – the mineral ions must move against the concentration gradient to enter the root hair cells
3	What is the function of the guard cells?	control the opening and closing of the stomata
4	Define the term transpiration.	movement of water from the roots to the leaves through the stomata
5	How does the structure of an artery relate to its function?	carries blood away from the heart under high pressure – has a small lumen and thick, elasticated walls that can stretch
6	What is the function of a nerve cell?	carries electrical impulses around the body
7	Name four factors that affect transpiration.	temperature, light intensity, humidity, and wind speed
8	Name the five levels of organisation.	cells → tissues → organs → organ systems → organisms

(Put paper here)

Required Practical Skills

Practise answering questions on the required practicals using the example below. You need to be able to apply your skills and knowledge to other practicals too.

Rate of enzyme reaction	Worked example	Practice
This practical tests your ability to accurately measure and record time, temperature, volume, and pH.	A class carried out an investigation into the effect that pH has on the ability of amylase to break down carbohydrates. They timed how long it took for the amylase to break down starch at different pH values between 5 and 11. Suggest the results the class would observe.	1 A student wanted to repeat the experiment on the following day to compare their results. Suggest why using the same enzyme solution on two different days would not give comparable results.
You will need to know how to find the rate of a reaction by using a continuous sampling technique to measure the time taken for an indicator to change colour.	**Answer:**	2 Suggest how the class might have timed how long it took for the amylase to break down the starch.
You will be familiar with measuring the effect of pH on the rate of reaction of amylase digesting starch, using iodine as an indicator. This method can also be used to investigate the effect of temperature by placing the enzyme and substrate solutions in different temperature water baths.	The optimum pH of amylase is around 7, so the time taken to break down starch will be shortest at pH 7. At pH values lower than 7 it will take longer to break down the starch – it will take the longest time at pH 5, decreasing in time taken until pH 7. Above pH 7 it will take a longer time to break down the starch, and the amylase may stop breaking down the starch entirely at pH 11.	3 Give one variable the class must control for this experiment to be valid.

 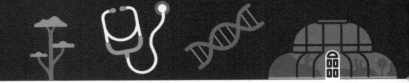

Practice

Exam-style questions

01 Lipase is an enzyme that breaks down lipids.

01.1 Name the products when a lipid is broken down. **[1 mark]**

_____

! Exam Tip

Can you think of another name for a lipid that will point you towards the answer?

01.2 Name **one** organ in the body where lipase is made. **[1 mark]**

_____

01.3 A group of students investigated the effect of temperature on the action of the enzyme lipase.

They used the following method in their investigation:

1 Add 10 cm³ of lipid solution to a test tube.

2 Add 2 cm³ of lipase solution to a second test tube.

3 Place both test tubes into a water bath set at 20 °C.

4 Leave in the water bath for five minutes.

5 Add the lipid solution to the lipase solution and mix.

6 Remove a sample of the mixture every five minutes and test for the presence of lipids. Continue until no lipid is detected.

7 Repeat the experiment every 5 °C between temperatures of 20 °C and 50 °C.

Name the independent variable in the students' investigation. **[1 mark]**

_____

01.4 Suggest why the lipase solution and lipid solution were left in the water bath for five minutes before mixing. **[1 mark]**

_____

_____

01.5 The students' results are shown in **Table 1**.

Table 1

Temperature in °C	Mean time taken until no lipid remained in min
20	20
25	15
30	10
35	5
40	10
45	20
50	lipid still present after 30 minutes of testing

Describe the effect on the breakdown of the lipid when the temperature is increased between 20 °C and 35 °C. **[1 mark]**

_____

_____

01.6 Explain the result that was observed at 50 °C. **[2 marks]**

_____

_____

_____

02 **Figure 1** demonstrates the lock and key theory of enzyme action.

Figure 1

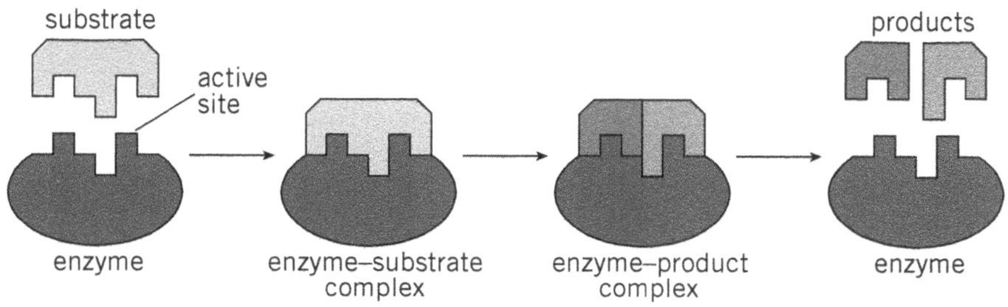

substrate   products
active
site

enzyme   enzyme–substrate   enzyme–product   enzyme
                complex   complex

02.1 Using **Figure 1** and your own knowledge, explain what is meant by enzyme specificity. **[3 marks]**

_____

_____

_____

_____

02.2 Explain why you only need a small volume of an enzyme to catalyse a reaction. **[2 marks]**

_____

_____

_____

02.3 Describe **one** example of an enzyme-controlled reaction where small molecules are joined together to form larger ones. **[1 mark]**

_____

_____

02.4 Measles is an infectious disease caused by a virus. It causes sufferers to have a raised body temperature. Using your knowledge of enzymes, suggest and explain **one** way in which this may be damaging to the body and **one** way in which this may be beneficial to the body. **[4 marks]**

_____

_____

_____

_____

_____

(!) **Exam Tip**

When you're talking about enzymes, it's really important that you use the correct terms.

When the active site breaks down, an enzyme becomes denatured – lots of students write that the enzyme has died or has been killed.

This is incorrect and will lose you marks in the exam.

03 A group of students investigated the effect of pH on the action of the enzyme amylase.

03.1 Name the substance that is broken down by amylase. **[1 mark]**

03.2 The students placed starch solutions of known volume and concentration in a water bath at 30 °C. They then added a buffer solution, at one of five different pH values, to each starch solution. Give **two** variables that the students controlled. **[2 marks]**

(!) **Exam Tip**

Go through the text with a highlighter and pick out anything that was kept the same.

03.3 The students then took each sample of starch solution, one at a time, and mixed it with a fixed volume and concentration of amylase. They used the equipment in **Figure 2** to test for the presence of starch every 30 seconds.

Figure 2

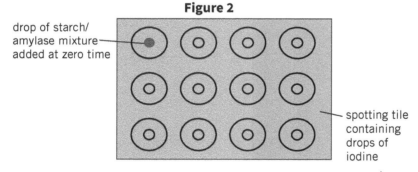

drop of starch/ amylase mixture added at zero time

spotting tile containing drops of iodine

Describe how you would monitor the reaction to identify when all of the starch has been broken down. **[3 marks]**

03.4 The students' results are shown in **Table 2**.

Table 2

pH of buffer solution	Time taken for amylase to break down starch solution in s			
	Repeat 1	Repeat 2	Repeat 3	Mean
5	112	120	119	117
6	33	30	27	30
7	33	28	29	30
8	55	65	60	60
9	129	120	135	

Calculate the mean time taken for the action of amylase at pH 9. **[1 mark]**

03.5 Plot the students' mean results on **Figure 3**.
[3 marks]

03.6 Use **Figure 3** to calculate the optimum pH for amylase to catalyse the breakdown of starch. [1 mark]

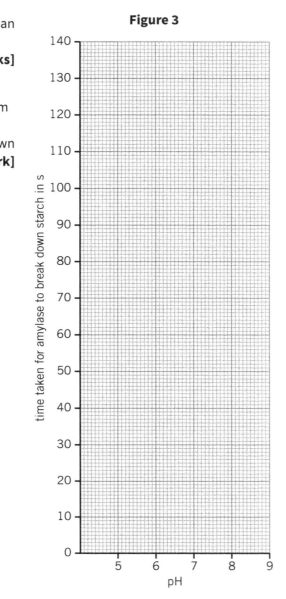

Figure 3

y-axis: time taken for amylase to break down starch in s
x-axis: pH

04 **Figure 4** shows how pH affects the activity of two different types of protease enzyme – enzyme **A** and enzyme **B**.

Figure 4

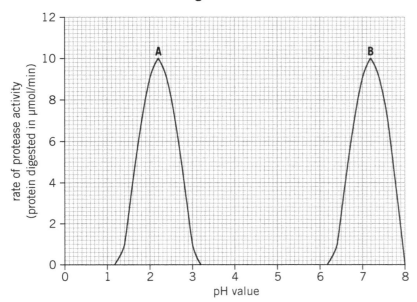

y-axis: rate of protease activity (protein digested in μmol/min)
x-axis: pH value

04.1 Name the substance that proteases break down into amino acids.
[1 mark]

04.2 Describe the role of amino acids in the body. [2 marks]

04.3 Use **Figure 4** to identify the optimum pH of enzyme **A**. [1 mark]

04.4 Suggest and explain where enzymes **A** and **B** are found in the body. [4 marks]

04.5 Explain the advantage of adding enzymes to biological washing powders. [4 marks]

04.6 Explain why many biological washing powders recommend not washing clothes on a 60 °C cycle. [2 marks]

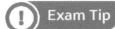

05 A student was studying the effect of pH on the enzyme activity of an unknown carbohydrase. They were provided with the following apparatus:

- test tubes and rack
- spotting tiles
- 10 cm³ measuring cylinder
- 3 cm³ pipettes
- glass stirring rod
- stopwatch

- safety goggles
- starch solution
- carbohydrase solution
- iodine solution
- thermometer
- pH buffer solutions

Explain how the student could investigate the effect of pH on the rate of reaction of the enzyme. [6 marks]

06 Biological washing powders contain enzymes. A scientist carried out an investigation to determine if a new type of protease enzyme should be included in washing powder.

06.1 Describe the function of proteases. [1 mark]

06.2 Protease function can be studied by looking at the time it takes to digest cooked egg white.

- The scientist placed a 2 cm³ piece of egg white into a test tube.
- They then added a fixed volume of the protease enzyme to the test tube and timed how long it took for the egg white to halve in length.
- The experiment was repeated at temperatures between 10 °C and 60 °C.
- A control was also set up using water instead of protease at each temperature. The egg white in the control samples remained undigested after two hours.

Name the equipment the scientist should have used to change the temperature. [1 mark]

06.3 **Figure 5** shows the scientist's results.

Figure 5

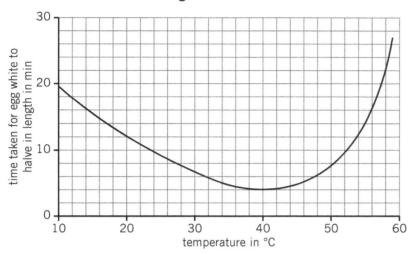

Identify the optimum temperature for protease activity. **[1 mark]**

06.4 Calculate the rate of reaction for the enzyme to break down the egg white at 20 °C. Give the unit of rate. **[3 marks]**

06.5 Using information in **Figure 5** and your own knowledge, suggest and explain **one** advantage and **one** disadvantage of using this enzyme in a biological washing powder. **[4 marks]**

Exam Tip

You may be surprised to see this question in biology, but we know the exam is going to be full of surprises! It's the same method we use in chemistry to find the gradient.

07 The small intestine is covered in villi. A diagram of a villus is shown in **Figure 6**.

Figure 6

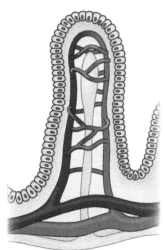

07.1 Identify which type of structure a villus is classified as. **[1 mark]**

cell   organ   tissue   organ system

07.2 Use information in **Figure 6** and your own knowledge to explain how a villus is adapted to its function. **[3 marks]**

07.3 Explain why villi cells have a large number of mitochondria. **[2 marks]**

08 Trypsin is an example of a protease enzyme.

08.1 Name the type of molecule broken down by trypsin. **[1 mark]**

08.2 Trypsin is produced in the pancreas and released into the small intestine. Identify the optimum pH for trypsin activity. Choose **one** answer. **[1 mark]**

pH 2   pH 4   pH 8   pH 9

08.3 Trypsin is specific for catalysing one type of reaction. Using the lock and key theory, explain what is meant by enzyme specificity. **[3 marks]**

Exam Tip

Key words are important for this question.

09 Cryophilic bacteria are a group of bacteria capable of growing and reproducing at low temperatures, ranging from −20 °C to +10 °C. They are found in permanently cold environments, such as polar regions and the deep sea. They are able to survive because their enzymes are able to work at low temperatures.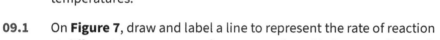

09.1 On **Figure 7**, draw and label a line to represent the rate of reaction at different temperatures of an enzyme found in humans. **[2 marks]**

Figure 7

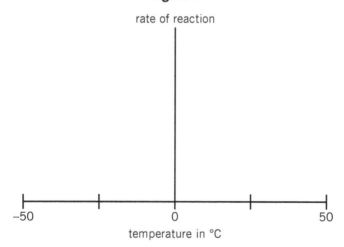

Exam Tip

Don't worry if you've never heard of cryophilic bacteria before. This is just about applying the science you know to a new context.

Exam Tip

Your line needs to be bell-shaped!

Exam Tip

This graph may look a bit confusing, but that's just because the y-axis is in the middle. Treat it like any other graph.

09.2 Draw and label a second line on **Figure 7** to represent the rate of reaction at different temperatures of an enzyme found in cryophilic bacteria. **[2 marks]**

10 Living cells could not function without enzyme-controlled reactions.

10.1 Explain how changing pH affects the rate of an enzyme-controlled reaction. **[3 marks]**

10.2 The enzyme trypsin breaks down casein (a form of protein) in milk. Give the name of the group of digestive enzymes that trypsin belongs to. **[1 mark]**

Exam Tip

Use example pHs: "at low pH…" and "at high pH…"

10.3 Trypsin breaks down casein, changing its colour from white to clear. Some scientists took a range of milk samples and mixed them with trypsin at different temperatures. They measured the rate at which trypsin breaks down casein using a spectrophotometer.

A spectrophotometer measures the amount of light transmitted through the liquid.

Suggest a method, using the spectrophotometer, to determine the optimum temperature for trypsin action. **[4 marks]**

10.4 The scientists noticed that the glass of the test tube containing the milk solution was cloudy.

Suggest and explain the effect of the clouded glass on the scientists' results. **[3 marks]**

11 LPL deficiency is an inherited condition that prevents the digestive enzyme lipase from working efficiently.

11.1 Identify the products that will not be formed as easily in a patient with LPL deficiency. **[2 marks]**

11.2 Explain why protease cannot break down fats. **[2 marks]**

11.3 **Figure 8** shows the impact of pH on the rate of reaction of lipase.

Figure 8

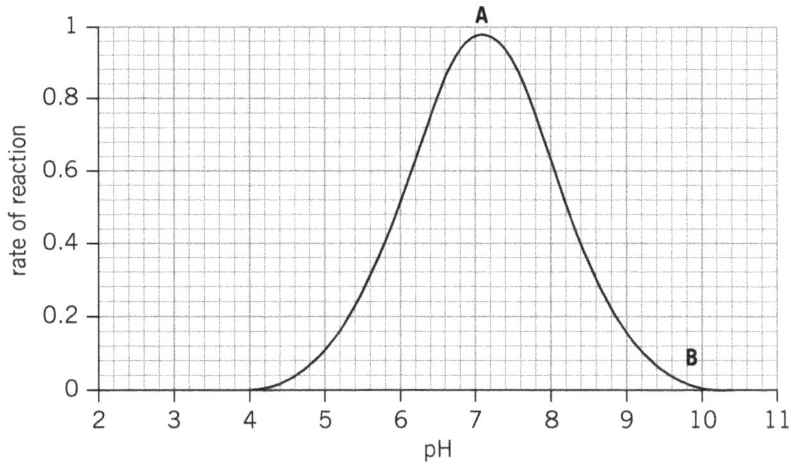

Explain the difference between points **A** and **B** in **Figure 8**.
[3 marks]

11.4 Suggest what piece of equipment could be used to ensure that the temperature was kept constant throughout the investigation that produces the results in **Figure 8**. **[1 mark]**

Knowledge

B7 Photosynthesis

Photosynthetic reaction

Photosynthesis is a chemical reaction in which energy is transferred from the environment as light from the Sun to the leaves of a plant. It is performed by plants, algae, and some bacteria.

Chlorophyll, the green pigment in **chloroplasts** in the leaves, absorbs the light energy. Leaves are well-adapted to ensure high rates of photosynthesis.

Limiting factors

A **limiting factor** is anything that limits the rate of a reaction when it is in short supply.

The main limiting factors for photosynthesis are:
- temperature
- carbon dioxide concentration.
- light intensity

$$\text{carbon dioxide} \quad + \quad \text{water} \quad \xrightarrow{\text{light}} \quad \text{glucose} \quad + \quad \text{oxygen}$$

$$6CO_2 \quad + \quad 6H_2O \quad \xrightarrow{\text{light}} \quad C_6H_{12}O_6 \quad + \quad 6O_2$$

Photosynthesis rate

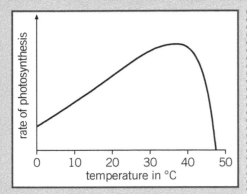

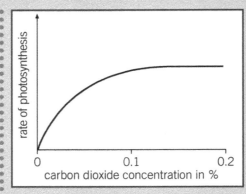

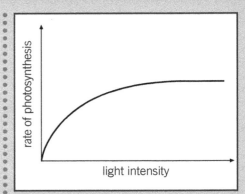

- At low temperatures the rate of photosynthesis is low because the reactant molecules have less kinetic energy.
- Photosynthesis is an enzyme-controlled reaction, so at high temperatures the enzymes are denatured and the rate quickly decreases.

- Carbon dioxide is used up in photosynthesis, so increasing the carbon dioxide concentration increases the rate of photosynthesis.
- At a certain point, another factor becomes limiting.
- Carbon dioxide is often the limiting factor for photosynthesis.

- Light energy is needed for photosynthesis, so increasing the light intensity increases the rate of photosynthesis.
- At a certain point, another factor becomes limiting.
- Photosynthesis will stop if there is little or no light.

 **Key Terms**   **Make sure you can write a definition for these key terms.**

| chlorophyll | chloroplast | glucose |
| inverse square law | limiting factor | photosynthesis |

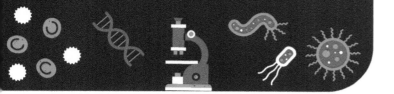

Interaction of limiting factors

Limiting factors often interact, and any one may be limiting photosynthesis.

For example, on the graph the lowest curve has both carbon dioxide and temperature limiting photosynthesis. Temperature is limiting for the middle curve, and the highest curve shows how rate increases when both temperature and carbon dioxide are increased until another factor becomes limiting.

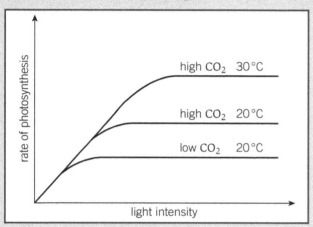

Uses of glucose

Photosynthesis produces **glucose**. Glucose is used to provide energy for lots of processes in plants.

For example, glucose is used:

- for respiration, to release energy
- to produce cellulose, which strengthens cell walls
- to produce fat or oil (lipids) for storage
- to produce amino acids for protein synthesis – plants also need nitrate ions from the soil for this
- to make insoluble starch, which is stored in the leaves, tubers, and bulbs to be used for energy later.

Inverse square law

As the distance of a light source from a plant increases, the light intensity decreases – an inverse relationship. This is not linear, as light intensity varies in inverse proportion to the square of the distance:

$$\text{light intensity} \propto \frac{1}{\text{distance}^2}$$

For example, if you double the distance between a light source and a plant, light intensity falls by a quarter.

Greenhouse economics

Commercial greenhouses control limiting factors to get the highest possible rates of photosynthesis so they can grow plants as quickly as possible or produce the highest yields, whilst still making profit.

For example, light intensity can be increased with artificial lights that provide the optimum wavelengths of light for photosynthesis and lengthen a plant's growing season.

Carbon dioxide levels can be increased by using liquid carbon dioxide or paraffin heaters.

Irrigation systems can be used to provide water and temperature is carefully controlled through the use of heaters and opening windows.

 Revision Tip

Make sure you learn the shapes of the graphs on these pages.

In an exam you may be asked to sketch them (the axes and shape of line), describe them (use words to show the shape), or explain them (say *why* the shape is how it is).

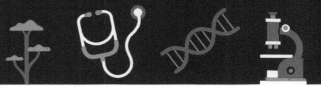
Learn the answers to the questions below then cover the answers column with a piece of paper and write as many as you can. Check and repeat.

	B7 questions	Answers
1	Where does photosynthesis occur?	chloroplasts in the leaves of a plant
2	What is the name of the green pigment in the leaves?	chlorophyll
3	What type of energy is absorbed in photosynthesis?	light energy
4	Give the word equation for photosynthesis.	carbon dioxide + water → glucose + oxygen
5	Give the balanced symbol equation for photosynthesis.	$6CO_2 + 6H_2O \rightarrow C_6H_{12}O_6 + 6O_2$
6	Define the term limiting factor.	anything that limits the rate of a reaction when it is in short supply
7	Give the limiting factors of photosynthesis.	temperature, carbon dioxide concentration, light intensity
8	Describe how light intensity affects the rate of photosynthesis.	increasing the light intensity increases the rate of photosynthesis until another factor becomes limiting
9	Describe how carbon dioxide concentration affects the rate of photosynthesis.	increasing the carbon dioxide concentration increases the rate of photosynthesis until another factor becomes limiting
10	Describe how temperature affects the rate of photosynthesis.	increasing the temperature increases the rate of photosynthesis as the reaction rate increases – at high temperatures enzymes are denatured so the rate of photosynthesis quickly decreases
11	Why are limiting factors important in the economics of growing plants in greenhouses?	greenhouses need to produce the maximum rate of photosynthesis whilst making profit
12	How do plants use the glucose produced in photosynthesis?	• respiration • convert it into insoluble starch for storage • produce fat or oil for storage • produce cellulose to strengthen cell walls • produce amino acids for protein synthesis

Put paper here

Now use the questions below to check your knowledge from previous chapters.

Previous questions

Answers

	Previous questions	Answers
1	How do white blood cells protect the body?	• engulf pathogens • produce antitoxins to neutralise toxins or antibodies
2	What three functions do white blood cells have?	phagocytosis, producing antibodies, producing antitoxins
3	Why is the human circulatory system a double circulatory system?	blood passes through the heart twice for every circuit around the body – deoxygenated blood is pumped from the right side of the heart to the lungs, and the oxygenated blood that returns is pumped from the left side of the heart to the body
4	What are enzymes?	protein molecules that catalyse specific reactions in organisms
5	Why do different digestive enzymes have different optimum pHs?	different parts of the digestive system have very different pHs – the stomach is strongly acidic, and the pH in the small intestine is close to neutral
6	What is a stent?	device inserted into a blocked artery to keep it open, allowing more blood and oxygen to the heart

Put paper here

Put paper here

Put paper here

Required Practical Skills

Practise answering questions on the required practicals using the example below. You need to be able to apply your skills and knowledge to other practicals too.

Rate of photosynthesis	Worked example	Practice
You should be able to accurately measure changes in the rate of photosynthesis of a plant, and how the rate changes in response to changes in the environment. This requires being able to describe how to measure the rate of a reaction or biological process by collecting a gas produced. For example, collecting bubbles of oxygen produced by pondweed to compare the volume of gas produced at different light intensities. It is important to understand how different factors affect rates of photosynthesis, including light intensity, temperature, and carbon dioxide concentration.	A student used an inverted test tube to investigate the number of bubbles released from a piece of pondweed in a beaker of water in a 10-minute period. They repeated each measurement five times. **1** Identify the dependent variable in this experiment. Number of bubbles released. **2** Explain how the student could use this set up to investigate how light intensity affects the rate of photosynthesis. Carry out the experiment described above with a switched-on lamp placed exactly 10 cm from the pondweed. Record the number of bubbles produced over the 10 mins, repeating the experiment five times. Move the lamp 10 cm further away from the pondweed, and repeat the same experiment. Calculate the mean number of bubbles produced for each light intensity, and compare the results.	**1** Suggest how the student could change the experiment to give a more accurate measurement of the gas released. **2** Explain how temperature affects the rate of plant photosynthesis. **3** Name a piece of equipment that could be used to investigate how temperature affects the amount of gas released by the pondweed.

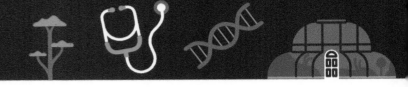

Exam-style questions

01   A student set up the apparatus in **Figure 1** to investigate the effect of light intensity on photosynthesis in pondweed.

Figure 1

LED light source

pondweed in sodium hydrogen carbonate solution

distance from light source in cm

> **Exam Tip**
>
> Figures can give you lots of information that you may not have thought of. For example, why is it an LED light source in **Figure 1**? Why is the pondweed not just in water?

01.1   Identify the independent variable in this investigation.   **[1 mark]**

_____

01.2   Give the reason the pondweed was placed in a solution of sodium hydrogen carbonate.   **[1 mark]**

_____

01.3   The student measured the rate of photosynthesis of the pondweed by counting the number of oxygen bubbles produced in one minute. Describe how you could test the bubbles to show they contained oxygen.   **[2 marks]**

_____

_____

> **Exam Tip**
>
> You'll need a little bit of chemistry here!

01.4   The student's results are shown in **Table 1**.

Plot the data on **Figure 2**.   **[4 marks]**

Table 1

Distance from light source in cm	Number of bubbles produced per minute
10	15
20	8
30	4
40	2
50	0

Figure 2

number of bubbles produced per minute

distance from light source in cm

01.5 Describe the trend shown by your graph in **Figure 2**.　　[1 mark]

_____

_____

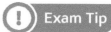

Exam Tip

For a one-mark question you only need to give a simple answer, such as an increase or decrease.

01.6 Use **Figure 2** to determine the rate of photosynthesis at 25 cm.　　[1 mark]

_____

01.7 The student stated that counting bubbles was not an accurate way of measuring the volume of oxygen produced.

Write down **one** reason why the student is correct.　　[1 mark]

_____

_____

01.8 Suggest **one** improvement the student could make to improve the accuracy of this investigation.　　[1 mark]

_____

02 Plants produce glucose by the process of photosynthesis.

02.1 Complete the following chemical equation that describes the process of photosynthesis.　　[2 marks]

$$6CO_2 + \underline{\hspace{2cm}} \rightarrow \underline{\hspace{2cm}} + 6O_2$$

Exam Tip

Balancing this equation can seem tricky – the easiest thing to do is to learn the numbers.

02.2 Explain why a shortage of carbon dioxide is a limiting factor in photosynthesis.　　[2 marks]

_____

_____

_____

02.3 Describe how a carbon atom from the atmosphere can become part of a starch molecule inside a leaf.　　[6 marks]

_____

_____

_____

_____

_____

_____

_____

03 **Figure 3** shows a cross-section through a leaf.

03.1 Identify the structures labelled **A** and **B**. [2 marks]

03.2 Explain **two** ways the leaf is adapted to absorb light for photosynthesis. [4 marks]

03.3 Explain **two** ways the leaf is adapted to take in carbon dioxide for photosynthesis. [4 marks]

Figure 3

> **!** **Exam Tip**
>
> You'll need to refer to specific parts of the leaf and how they act in this answer.

04 A tomato grower wants to know which growing conditions lead to the highest growth rate of tomato plants. They set up three experiments to measure the rate of photosynthesis in the tomatoes. **Figure 4** shows the results. All of the plants were given an adequate supply of water.

Figure 4

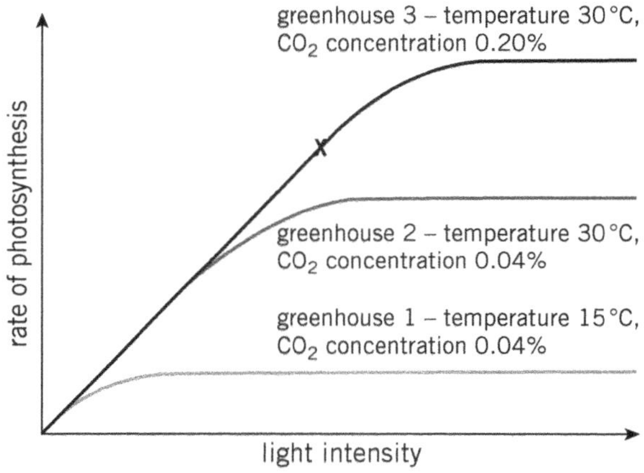

greenhouse 3 – temperature 30 °C, CO_2 concentration 0.20%

greenhouse 2 – temperature 30 °C, CO_2 concentration 0.04%

greenhouse 1 – temperature 15 °C, CO_2 concentration 0.04%

rate of photosynthesis

light intensity

> **!** **Exam Tip**
>
> Start this question by looking at the data on the graph and highlighting the differences between the conditions.

04.1 Identify the limiting factor at the point labelled **X** on the graph. [1 mark]

light intensity   volume of soil added

carbon dioxide concentration   temperature

04.2 The tomato grower sets up a fourth greenhouse at a temperature of 40 °C and a carbon dioxide concentration of 0.2%. Explain what will happen to the rate of photosynthesis under these conditions. [2 marks]

04.3 The tomato grower concludes from their investigation that increasing the temperature, light intensity, and carbon dioxide concentration maximises the rate of growth of tomato plants. Evaluate the validity of the tomato grower's conclusions. [3 marks]

> **!** **Exam Tip**
>
> For an 'evaluate' question you need to give a justified opinion.

04.4 Explain why the tomato grower should not raise the temperature of the greenhouses above 40 °C. [2 marks]

05 A number of factors affect the rate of photosynthesis. Two of these factors include carbon dioxide and temperature.

05.1 Name **one** other factor that limits the rate of photosynthesis. **[1 mark]**

05.2 **Figure 5** shows the effect of carbon dioxide on the rate of photosynthesis. Describe and explain the shape of the graph. **[4 marks]**

05.3 Explain how temperature affects the rate of photosynthesis. **[4 marks]**

Figure 5

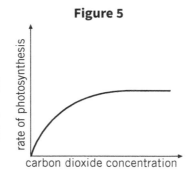

> **(!) Exam Tip**
>
> This answer needs to have the *what* and the *why*.

06 Light intensity, carbon dioxide concentration, and temperature are three of the factors that affect the rate of photosynthesis. Design an investigation to study the effect of light intensity on the rate of photosynthesis. **[6 marks]**

Here is a list of some of the apparatus you might use:

- desk lamp
- metre rule
- funnel
- pondweed
- beaker

> **(!) Exam Tip**
>
> This is a required practical, so you should know this method really well!

07 Plants produce glucose through the process of photosynthesis. Some of this is used immediately in respiration. The remainder is converted into starch molecules.

07.1 Explain why plants convert glucose into starch. **[3 marks]**

07.2 Onions store starch in bulbs. Suggest how you could demonstrate that an onion contains starch. **[2 marks]**

07.3 Some of the glucose produced in respiration is also used to produce proteins. Explain how glucose is used to make proteins. **[4 marks]**

08 A group of students investigated the effect of temperature on the rate of photosynthesis. They carried out their investigation using pondweed. **Figure 6** shows how they set up their apparatus. The experiment was repeated using water baths set at different temperatures.

Figure 6

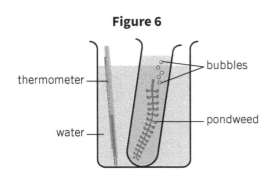

08.1 Write down **one** factor the students must control. **[1 mark]**

08.2 Explain why the students should leave the test tube in the water bath for five minutes before taking their measurements. **[1 mark]**

08.3 Bubbles of oxygen gas are released when the pondweed photosynthesises. Describe **one** way the students could calculate the rate of photosynthesis. **[2 marks]**

08.4 At 60 °C no bubbles of gas were produced. Explain why. **[2 marks]**

09 A scientist investigated how light intensity affected the rate of photosynthesis of pondweed. The scientist placed the pondweed in a beaker of water at different distances from a table lamp. They calculated the rate of photosynthesis by counting how many bubbles were produced in one minute. The scientist's results are shown in **Table 2**.

Table 2

Distance of lamp from pondweed in m	Light intensity in arbitrary units	Bubbles produced per minute
0.20		60
0.30	11	28
0.40	6	17
0.50	4	12
0.60	3	9

Light intensity can be calculated using the inverse square law:

$$\text{light intensity} \propto \frac{1}{\text{distance}^2}$$

09.1 Calculate the light intensity when the lamp is 20 cm from the pondweed. **[1 mark]**

09.2 Plot a graph of light intensity against rate of photosynthesis on **Figure 7**. **[4 marks]**

Figure 7

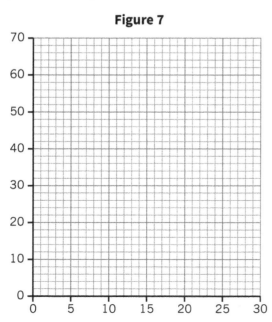

> **! Exam Tip**
> This is the same as the inverse square law in maths.

> **! Exam Tip**
> Always use crosses to plot points, and remember to draw a line of best fit.

> **! Exam Tip**
> Don't worry if you've never come across arbitrary units before, it just means it doesn't really matter what the units are.

09.3   Describe the trends shown in the data collected.   **[2 marks]**

09.4   The scientist concluded that during this experiment, light intensity was a limiting factor for photosynthesis. Write down the evidence used by the scientist to form this conclusion.   **[1 mark]**

(!) **Exam Tip**

Use data from the graph in your answer.

09.5   When the light is placed a distance of 0.10 m from the pondweed, carbon dioxide becomes the limiting factor. Sketch a second graph of light intensity against rate of photosynthesis to show this effect for lamp distances of 0.10–0.60 m.   **[3 marks]**

10   Plants make their own food by the process of photosynthesis.

10.1   Write down the word equation for photosynthesis.   **[2 marks]**

10.2   **Figure 8** shows the effect of temperature on the rate of photosynthesis.

Figure 8

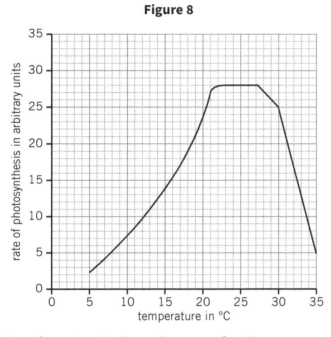

Using **Figure 8**, write down the range of optimum temperatures for photosynthesis.   **[1 mark]**

(!) **Exam Tip**

Draw lines on the graph to show your working.

10.3   Suggest why the rate of photosynthesis stays the same between these temperatures.   **[2 marks]**

10.4   A farmer decides to use this information to set their greenhouse to the optimum conditions. Identify the best temperature to heat the farmer's greenhouse to. Give reasons for your answer.   **[3 marks]**

(!) **Exam Tip**

The question has asked for reasons for your answer. This means the only way to get full marks on this is by giving data from the graph.

11 Plants make their own food by respiration.

11.1 Complete the chemical reaction for photosynthesis. **[1 mark]**

$$6CO_2 + 6H_2O \rightarrow \underline{\hspace{2cm}}$$

11.2 Describe the role of chloroplasts in photosynthesis. **[3 marks]**

11.3 Large-scale commercial growers maximise the rate of photosynthesis in condition-controlled greenhouses. A farmer investigates how increasing the carbon dioxide concentration in a greenhouse affects their crop yield. The results are shown in **Table 3**. Carbon dioxide in the atmosphere is at 0.05%.

Table 3

% carbon dioxide	Lettuce yield in kg/m²	Tomato yield in kg/m²
0.05	0.9	4.4
0.10	1.2	6.4
0.15	1.4	7.0
0.20	1.5	7.4

Explain how changing the carbon dioxide concentration changes the yield of lettuce and tomato crops. **[4 marks]**

11.4 To increase the carbon dioxide concentration by 0.05%, it costs the farmer £0.64 per m². The farmer sells their lettuce for £0.50/kg and their tomatoes for £1.60/kg. Evaluate the economic benefits of increasing carbon dioxide to 0.10%. **[6 marks]**

> **! Exam Tip**
>
> For an 'evaluate' question you'll need to give advantages and disadvantages, and end your answer with your opinion and a reason supporting it.
>
> Most of the answer is going to be using data from the table, so as long as you've backed up your answer with evidence then don't worry about your opinion.

12 Enzymes have a number of commercial uses. One use is in the preparation of sugar solution, a widely used ingredient in food production. Enzymes convert starch into sweet sugar syrup.

12.1 Name the type of digestive enzyme that would be used in syrup production. **[1 mark]**

12.2 Suggest **one** advantage of using enzymes in this way. **[1 mark]**

12.3 Suggest and explain **two** possible disadvantages of this technique. **[4 marks]**

13 After severe blood loss, patients often require a blood transfusion.

13.1 Name the **four** main blood groups. **[1 mark]**

13.2 Blood cells from different blood groups have different antigens. Describe what is meant by an antigen. **[1 mark]**

13.3 If blood groups are incorrectly matched, it can result in agglutination. Describe what this means. **[1 mark]**

13.4 A patient has blood group A. Name the blood groups from which they can receive a blood transfusion. **[1 mark]**

14 *Cabomba* is an aquatic plant that undergoes photosynthesis.

14.1 Write down the word equation for photosynthesis. **[2 marks]**

14.2 **Figure 9** shows the volume of gas produced by *Cabomba* with a light intensity of 1000 lux.

Figure 9

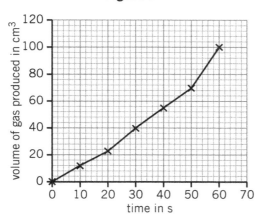

Suggest an appropriate piece of equipment to measure the volume of gas produced by *Cabomba*. **[1 mark]**

14.3 Give **one** control variable for this investigation. **[1 mark]**

14.4 Calculate the rate of photosynthesis in the first 30 seconds. Give your answer to **three** significant figures. **[3 marks]**

14.5 **Figure 10** shows how increasing light intensity affects the rate of photosynthesis.

Figure 10

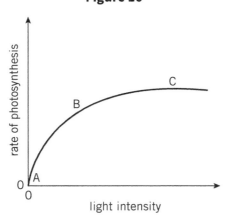

Explain the differences in the rate of photosynthesis between **A** and **B** with the rate of photosynthesis at **C** in **Figure 10.** **[3 marks]**

Exam Tip

The steeper the curve, the faster the rate. The flatter the curve, the slower the rate.

B8 Respiration

Cellular respiration

Cellular **respiration** occurs continually in the **mitochondria** of living cells to supply the cells with energy. It can take place aerobically (using oxygen) or anaerobically (without oxygen) to transfer energy to the cell.

The energy released during respiration is needed for all living processes, including:

- chemical reactions to build larger molecules, for example, making proteins from amino acids
- muscle contraction for movement
- keeping warm.

Type of respiration	Oxygen required?	Relative amount of energy transferred
aerobic	✓	complete **oxidation** of glucose – large amount of energy is released
anaerobic	✗	incomplete oxidation of glucose – much less energy is transferred per glucose molecule

Revision Tip

You need to learn the balanced symbol equations for the different types of respiration as well as the word equations.

Aerobic respiration

glucose $\quad+\quad$ oxygen $\quad\rightarrow\quad$ carbon dioxide $\quad+\quad$ water

$$C_6H_{12}O_6 \quad + \quad 6O_2 \quad \rightarrow \quad 6CO_2 \quad + \quad 6H_2O$$

Anaerobic respiration in muscles

glucose $\quad\rightarrow\quad$ lactic acid

$$C_6H_{12}O_6 \quad \rightarrow \quad 2C_3H_6O_3$$

Fermentation

Anaerobic respiration in plant and yeast cells is represented by the equation:

glucose $\rightarrow$ ethanol + carbon dioxide

Anaerobic respiration in yeast cells is called **fermentation**.

The products of fermentation are important in the manufacturing of bread and alcoholic drinks.

Cell components involved in respiration

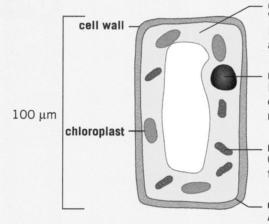

cell wall

cytoplasm
Where enzymes are made. Location of reactions in anaerobic respiration.

nucleus
Holds genetic code for enzymes involved in respiration.

mitochondrion
Contains the enzymes for aerobic respiration.

cell membrane
Allows gases and water to pass freely into and out of the cell. Controls the passage of other molecules.

chloroplast

100 µm

Typical plant cell

Typical animal cell

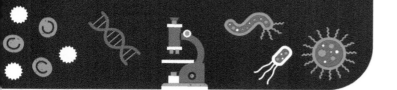

Response to exercise

During exercise the human body reacts to the increased demand for energy by:

- increasing the heart rate, increasing blood flow to the muscles
- increasing the rate and depth of breathing
- converting glycogen stored in the muscles back to glucose.

These changes increase the supply of glucose and oxygen to the muscles and the removal of carbon dioxide from the muscles.

If insufficient oxygen is supplied, anaerobic respiration takes place instead, leading to the build-up of **lactic acid**.

During long periods of vigorous exercise, muscles become fatigued and stop contracting efficiently. One cause of fatigue is the build-up of lactic acid in the muscles.

Removal of lactic acid

lactic acid in the muscles

transported to the liver in the blood

lactic acid is converted back to glucose

After exercise, the lactic acid accumulated during anaerobic respiration needs to be removed. **Oxygen debt** is the amount of oxygen needed to react with the lactic acid to remove it from cells.

 Revision Tip

A question on respiration could be easily linked to one on enzyme action and breakdown of carbohydrates, proteins, or lipids.

Don't expect questions in the exam to cover only one topic, as they can link a few topics together within one question.

Oxygen and lactic acid in the blood

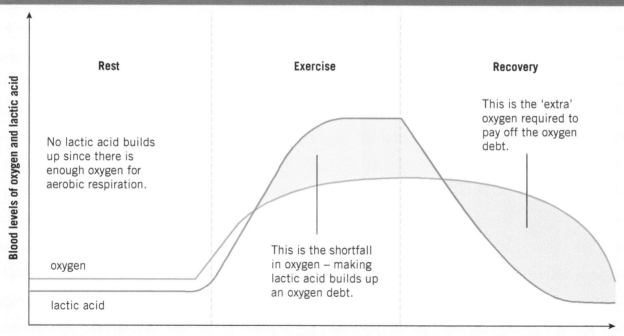

Rest | Exercise | Recovery

No lactic acid builds up since there is enough oxygen for aerobic respiration.

This is the 'extra' oxygen required to pay off the oxygen debt.

This is the shortfall in oxygen – making lactic acid builds up an oxygen debt.

Blood levels of oxygen and lactic acid

oxygen

lactic acid

Time in minutes

 **Key Terms**

Make sure you can write a definition for these key terms.

| aerobic | anaerobic | fermentation | lactic acid | mitochondria |
| | oxidation | oxygen debt | respiration | |

 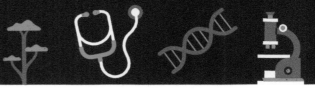

Learn the answers to the questions below then cover the answers column with a piece of paper and write as many as you can. Check and repeat.

B8 questions | Answers

	B8 questions	Answers
1	Define the term cellular respiration.	an exothermic reaction that occurs continuously in the mitochondria of living cells to release energy from glucose
2	What do organisms need energy for?	• chemical reactions to build larger molecules • muscle contraction for movement • keeping warm
3	What is the difference between aerobic and anaerobic respiration?	aerobic respiration uses oxygen, anaerobic respiration does not
4	Write the word equation for aerobic respiration.	glucose + oxygen $\rightarrow$ carbon dioxide + water
5	Write the word equation for anaerobic respiration in muscles.	glucose $\rightarrow$ lactic acid
6	Write the balanced symbol equation for aerobic respiration.	$C_6H_{12}O_6 + 6O_2 \rightarrow 6CO_2 + 6H_2O$
7	Write the balanced symbol equation for anaerobic respiration.	$C_6H_{12}O_6 \rightarrow 2C_3H_6O_3$
8	Why does aerobic respiration release more energy than anaerobic respiration?	oxidation of glucose is complete in aerobic respiration and incomplete in anaerobic respiration
9	What is anaerobic respiration in yeast cells called?	fermentation
10	Write the word equation for anaerobic respiration in plant and yeast cells.	glucose $\rightarrow$ ethanol + carbon dioxide
11	Give some uses of fermentation in food production.	beer and bread production
12	How does the body supply the muscles with more oxygenated blood during exercise?	heart rate, breathing rate, and breath volume increase
13	What substance builds up in the muscles during anaerobic respiration?	lactic acid
14	What happens to muscles during long periods of activity?	muscles become fatigued and stop contracting efficiently
15	What is oxygen debt?	amount of oxygen the body needs after exercise to react with the accumulated lactic acid and remove it from cells
16	How is lactic acid removed from the body?	lactic acid in muscles $\rightarrow$ transported to liver in blood $\rightarrow$ lactic acid converted back to glucose
17	Give two reasons why the body normally respires aerobically.	• more energy is transferred per glucose molecule • lactic acid is not produced

Put paper here

Now use the questions below to check your knowledge from previous chapters.

B8

Previous questions | Answers

	Previous questions	Answers
1	How are the lungs adapted for efficient gas exchange?	• alveoli – large surface area • moist membranes – increase rate of diffusion • one-cell-thick membranes – short diffusion pathway • good blood supply – maintains a steep concentration gradient
2	Describe the function of amylase.	to break down starch into glucose
3	Where are lipases produced?	pancreas and small intestine
4	What is the purpose of translocation?	transport dissolved sugars from the leaves to the rest of the plant
5	Give the word equation for photosynthesis.	carbon dioxide + water → glucose + oxygen
6	How do plants use the glucose produced in photosynthesis?	• respiration • convert it into insoluble starch for storage • produce fat or oil for storage • produce cellulose to strengthen the cell wall • produce amino acids for protein synthesis
7	Give the balanced symbol equation for photosynthesis.	$6CO_2 + 6H_2O \rightarrow C_6H_{12}O_6 + 6O_2$

Put paper here (×3)

Required Practical Skills

Practise answering questions on the required practicals using the example below. You need to be able to apply your skills and knowledge to other practicals too.

The effect of exercise on the body	Worked example	Practice
This practical tests your ability to measure your heart rate and breathing rate at regular intervals after exercise until they return to resting rates. To find your resting breathing rate and heart rate, you will need to take several readings of each variable and then calculate the mean. The mean is a calculated average of the numbers. Calculating a mean is a maths skill you will have to perform in many practicals. The mean is affected by outliers. If there are any outliers in your results you should repeat or remove these results before calculating the mean.	A student measured the number of times they took a breath in a certain amount of time when sitting and resting. Here are their results: 13, 18, 13, 14, 6, 13, 16, 14, 19, 15 **Step 1:** Check for any outliers. Six breaths is less than half the nearest value so this should be removed from your calculation. **Step 2:** Add all the values together: 13 + 18 + 13 + 14 + 13 + 16 + 14 + 19 + 15 = 135 **Step 3:** Divide by the total number of values. $\frac{135}{9} = 15$ The student's mean resting breathing rate = 15	A student took five measurements of their resting heart rate in beats per minute (bpm). Their results are shown below: 78, 82, 83, 79, 84 1 Describe how the student would measure their heart rate. 2 Calculate their mean resting heart rate. 3 The student took a sixth measurement of 90 bpm. Explain how a measurement of 90 bpm would affect the mean result if included in the calculation.

 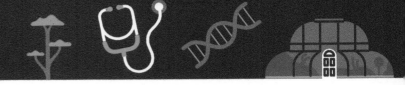

Practice

Exam-style questions

01 Animals transfer energy into a form that cells can use by the process of respiration.

01.1 Complete the following balanced chemical equation to summarise the process of aerobic respiration in animal cells. **[2 marks]**

$$6 O_2 + \underline{\hspace{4cm}} \longrightarrow \underline{\hspace{3cm}} + 6 CO_2 + energy$$

! Exam Tip

Instead of remembering the chemical formulae and then trying to balance this equation, it's easier to remember the numbers needed to balance it.

01.2 Explain why fat cells do not have as many mitochondria as muscle cells. **[3 marks]**

_____

_____

_____

_____

! Exam Tip

Think about the differences in function between muscle and fat cells.

01.3 Plants do not move or maintain a certain body temperature.

Describe **two** ways plants use energy from respiration. **[2 marks]**

1 _____

_____

2 _____

_____

02 A group of students investigated the effect of temperature on the rate of aerobic respiration in earthworms.

They placed the equipment shown in **Figure 1** into a water bath.

Figure 1

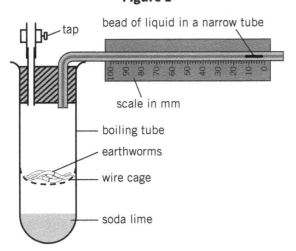

tap

bead of liquid in a narrow tube

scale in mm

boiling tube

earthworms

wire cage

soda lime

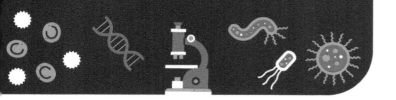
02.1 Identify the function of the soda lime. **[1 mark]**
Tick **one** box.

to absorb carbon dioxide ☐

to absorb oxygen ☐

to provide the earthworms with water ☐

to provide the earthworms with nutrients ☐

02.2 Explain how this equipment can be used to measure the rate of respiration at different temperatures. **[6 marks]**

_____

_____

_____

_____

_____

_____

_____

_____

> **Exam Tip**
>
> You'll need a safe way to heat the boiling tube that can be controlled and measured.

02.3 Write down **one** ethical consideration needed in this experiment. **[1 mark]**

_____

_____

02.4 The students' results at 10 °C and 20 °C are shown in **Figure 2**.

Figure 2

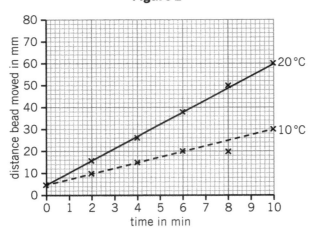

Compare the rate of respiration of earthworms at 10 °C and 20 °C. **[5 marks]**

_____

_____

_____

_____

! **Exam Tip**

This question is worth five marks, so you need to include data from both lines on the graph, and talk about the differences between the lines.

02.5 Draw a line on **Figure 2** to show what you predict the rate of respiration would be for earthworms at 25 °C.

Give reasons for your answer. **[3 marks]**

_____

_____

_____

_____

03 Yeast respires anaerobically. This reaction is called fermentation and it is used in the manufacture of some foods.

03.1 Write down the word equation for anaerobic respiration in yeast cells. **[2 marks]**

! **Exam Tip**

Both of the products of this reaction are used in the food industry.

03.2 To make food products efficiently, producers need to know the optimum conditions for yeast to respire. A food scientist set up the apparatus in **Figure 3** to study how temperature affects yeast respiration.

Figure 3

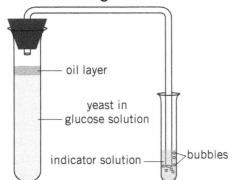

oil layer

yeast in glucose solution

indicator solution — bubbles

The indicator solution responds as follows:

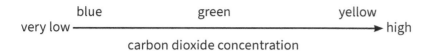

```
        blue              green            yellow
very low ─────────────────────────────────────→ high
              carbon dioxide concentration
```

Suggest which colour the indicator will turn when yeast is respiring at its maximum rate. **[1 mark]**

03.3 Explain the purpose of the layer of oil. **[1 mark]**

03.4 Explain how you would use this equipment to study the effect of temperature on the rate of respiration. **[4 marks]**

03.5 Suggest how you can adapt this investigation to obtain quantitative data on the rate of yeast respiration. **[3 marks]**

04 **Figure 4** shows the concentration of lactic acid in a person's blood. The concentration of lactic acid was measured before, during, and after ten minutes of vigorous exercise.

Figure 4

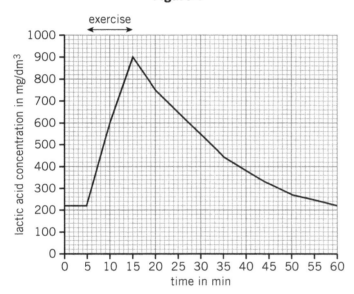

04.1 Identify the level of lactic acid in the person's blood before exercise. **[1 mark]**

04.2 Explain why lactic acid was produced between 5 and 15 minutes. **[2 marks]**

04.3 Calculate the rate at which lactic acid was produced during the period of exercise. **[2 marks]**

04.4 Describe and explain the trend shown by the graph between 15 and 60 minutes. **[6 marks]**

05 Respiration takes place in all living plant and animal cells.

05.1 Describe the purpose of respiration. **[2 marks]**

! Exam Tip

The important thing about the oil is that it is sitting on top of the mixture.

! Exam Tip

Don't forget to give the units!

! Exam Tip

The clue to this answer is in the question.

! Exam Tip

Draw a large triangle on the graph to help you calculate this. Remember to write down your working out.

05.2 Organisms can respire both aerobically and anaerobically. **Table 1** summarises the similarities and differences between these processes. Complete the table. **[4 marks]**

Table 1

Type of respiration	aerobic	anaerobic	
Organism it occurs in	plants and animals	plants	animals
Oxygen required?	yes	no	
Glucose required?	yes		yes
Carbon dioxide produced?	yes	yes	
Other products produced	water		lactic acid

05.3 Describe **two** ways yeast is used to produce food products using anaerobic respiration. **[4 marks]**

06 **Figure 5** shows the main components in an animal cell as seen under a light microscope.

Figure 5

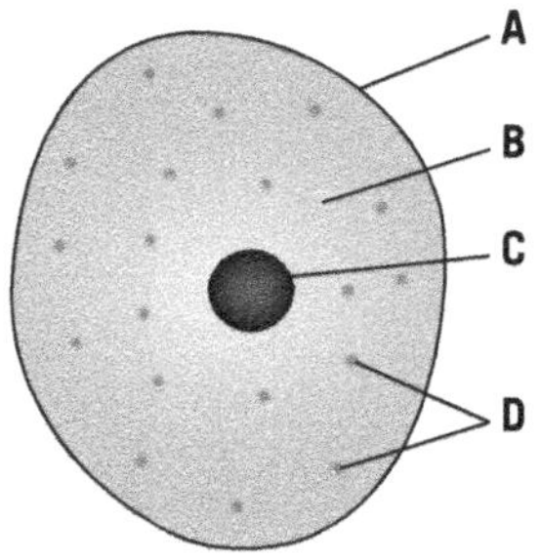

06.1 Identify the part of the cell where aerobic respiration occurs. **[1 mark]**

06.2 What are the products of respiration? Choose **one** answer. **[1 mark]**

glucose + oxygen   carbon dioxide + water

glucose + carbon dioxide   water + oxygen

Exam Tip

The equation for respiration is the opposite to photosynthesis, so if you have trouble write down the one you remember and reverse it.

06.3 When a person is exercising vigorously, body cells can switch to anaerobic respiration. Give **two** reasons why animal cells normally respire aerobically. **[2 marks]**

07 As part of a fitness test, an athlete ran as fast as possible for 15 minutes on a treadmill. The glucose and lactic acid concentrations of the athlete's blood were measured. **Figure 6** shows the results.

Figure 6

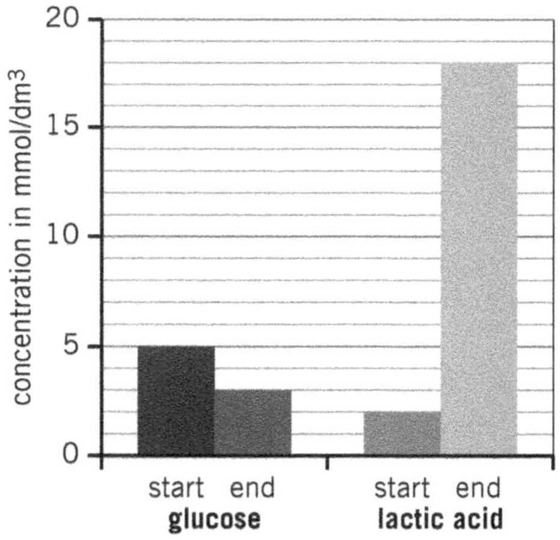

07.1 Using **Figure 6**, explain how the athlete respired over the 15 minutes of their fitness test. **[4 marks]**

Exam Tip

You'll need to use data from the graph to get full marks on this question.

07.2 Calculate the percentage change in the athlete's lactic acid concentration between the start and end of the exercise. **[2 marks]**

Exam Tip

Show all of your working out.

07.3 Explain why the athlete's heart and breathing rates increased during the fitness test. **[6 marks]**

08   A student investigated how their heart and breathing rate changed after exercise. They measured their breathing rate and heart rate at rest, and then immediately after running on the spot for two minutes.

08.1   Explain why they first took both measurements at rest.   **[1 mark]**

08.2   Heart rate is usually measured in beats per minute (bpm). The three measurements for heart rate at rest were 68 bpm, 65 bpm and 65 bpm Calculate the student's mean resting heart rate.   **[1 mark]**

08.3   **Table 2** shows the mean heart rate and breaths per minute when the student is resting and after exercise.

Table 2

Measurement	Mean heart rate in bpm	Breathing rate in breaths per minute
resting level		15
after exercise	96	40

Explain the differences shown in **Table 2**.   **[3 marks]**

09   Endurance athletes wish to avoid lactic acid build-up in their muscle cells.

09.1   Lactic acid build-up is a concern for marathon runners, but is not an important consideration for sprinters. Explain why.   **[4 marks]**

> ⓘ **Exam Tip**
>
> Marathons take many hours whilst sprints are generally over in under a minute.

09.2   To increase the blood's oxygen-carrying capability, many marathon runners train at high altitudes. This encourages the body to produce more red blood cells. Explain why high-altitude training can improve the performance of an athlete.   **[4 marks]**

09.3   Blood doping is an illegal practice that mimics altitude training. An athlete provides up to two litres of blood several weeks before a competition, which is then stored. The blood is then re-infused into the athlete one week before the competition. Explain why blood doping would produce a performance enhancement for an athlete similar to the effect produced through high-altitude training.   **[3 marks]**

> ⓘ **Exam Tip**
>
> The advantage of high-altitude training is the increase in red blood cells. How could blood doping mimic this?

10   All living organisms respire.

10.1   Complete the chemical equation for aerobic respiration.   **[1 mark]**

$$C_6H_{12}O_6 + \underline{\hspace{3cm}} \rightarrow 6\,CO_2 + \underline{\hspace{3cm}}$$

10.2   Explain **two** reasons why animals usually respire aerobically.   **[4 marks]**

10.3   Cheetahs are able to sprint very fast. After sprinting a cheetah will puff and pant for several minutes. With reference to respiration, explain why this happens.   **[4 marks]**

> ⓘ **Exam Tip**
>
> Think about the different types of respiration that occur when running.

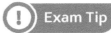

11 Variegated leaves are leaves with areas that do not contain chlorophyll. To show that chlorophyll is needed for a plant to photosynthesise, a scientist tested a leaf for the presence of starch.

11.1 Explain why the scientist first boiled the leaf in ethanol and then washed the leaf using water. **[3 marks]**

! Exam Tip

There are a few you could pick from, but only write about one safety procedure. You won't get extra marks for writing about two or three.

11.2 Describe and explain **one** safety procedure the scientist should follow when performing this experiment. **[2 marks]**

11.3 Predict and explain the results the scientist will observe when iodine is added to different areas of the leaf. **[4 marks]**

11.4 Explain how a plant produces starch. **[6 marks]**

12 **Figure 7** shows some of the main structures in the respiratory system.

Figure 7

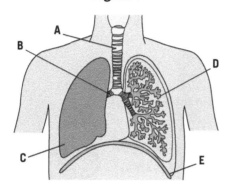

12.1 Identify the parts of the respiratory system labelled **A–E**. **[5 marks]**

12.2 Explain how the alveoli are adapted for gas exchange. **[3 marks]**

12.3 Emphysema is an example of a lung disease. The walls of the alveoli break down, forming larger air spaces than normal. A doctor measured the volume of air in the lungs of two people over a period of 8 seconds. The measurements were taken at rest.

Table 3

Time in seconds	Volume of air in lungs in dm³	
	Person 1	Person 2
0	6.8	7.2
1	4.0	6.2
2	2.8	5.8
3	2.3	5.3
4	2.0	5.0
5	1.8	4.8
6	1.5	4.5
7	1.5	4.2
8	1.5	3.9

Use evidence from **Table 3** to explain whether the doctor measured the two people inhaling or exhaling. **[2 marks]**

! Exam Tip

Look at the difference in the start and end values.

12.4 Compare the mean rate of change of lung volume in the two people over the 8 seconds of the test. **[5 marks]**

12.5 One person in the investigation had healthy lungs. The other person had emphysema. Identify which person has emphysema, giving reasons for your answer. **[2 marks]**

13 Organisms are made up of a number of organ systems. One example is the digestive system.

13.1 Give another example of an organ system and describe its function. **[2 marks]**

13.2 The main organs in the digestive system are labelled in **Figure 8**. Identify the label that shows the liver. **[1 mark]**

Figure 8

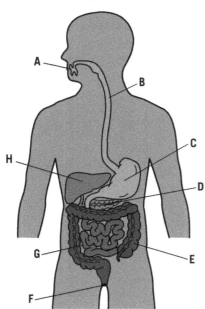

13.3 Describe the function of organ **E**. **[1 mark]**

13.4 Explain **two** reasons why organ **C** contains hydrochloric acid. **[2 marks]**

14 Many people donate blood. The donated blood can be used to treat a number of medical conditions or to replace blood lost in an accident.

14.1 Explain why blood is described as a tissue. **[1 mark]**

14.2 The largest single component of blood is blood plasma. Blood cells and platelets are transported around the body by the plasma. Name **two** other substances that are transported around the body in the plasma. **[2 marks]**

14.3 Explain the role of white blood cells in the body's defence against pathogens. **[6 marks]**

Exam Tip
Remember to give units for your answer.

Exam Tip
If you can't label all of these organs, now is a great time to practise!

Exam Tip
Plasma is the straw-coloured fluid in blood.

Knowledge

B9 Adaptation, competition, and interdependence

Ecosystem organisation

Individual organisms

↓

Population
the total number of organisms of the same species that live in one specific geographical area

↓

Community
group of two or more populations of different species living in one specific geographical area

↓

Ecosystem
the interaction of a community of living organisms with the non-living parts of their environment

A stable **community** is one where all the species and environmental factors are in balance so that **population** sizes remain fairly constant.

An example of this is the interaction between predator and prey species, which rise and fall in a constant cycle so that each remains within a stable range.

Competition

To survive and reproduce, organisms require a supply of resources from their surroundings and from the other living organisms there.

This can create competition, where organisms within a community compete for resources.

Animals often compete for:
- food
- mates
- territory.

Plants often compete for:
- light
- space
- water and mineral ions from the soil.

Interdependence

Within a community each species interacts with many others and may depend on other species for things like food, shelter, pollination, and seed dispersal.

If one species is removed it can affect the whole community – this is called **interdependence**.

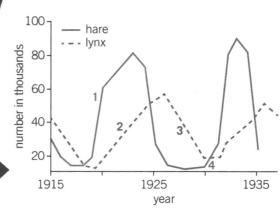

1 If the population of hares increases there is a larger food supply for the lynx.

2 This can therefore support more lynx, so more offspring survive.

3 The growing numbers of lynx eventually reduce the food supply. The number of predators starts to decrease.

4 The prey population starts to increase once more – the cycle then begins again.

Adaptations of organisms

Organisms (including microorganisms) have features – **adaptations** – that enable them to survive in the conditions in which they live. The adaptations of an organism may allow it to outcompete others, and provide it with an evolutionary advantage.

Structural adaptations
The physical features that allow an organism to successfully compete:
- sharp teeth to hunt prey
- colouring that may provide camouflage to hide from predators or hunt prey
- a large or small body surface area to volume ratio

Behavioural adaptations
The behaviour of an organism that gives it an advantage:
- migrating to find food
- courtship dances to attract a mate
- use of tools to obtain food
- working together in packs

Functional adaptations
Adaptations related to processes that allow an organism to survive:
- photosynthesis in plants
- production of poisons or venom to deter predators and kill prey
- changes in reproduction timings

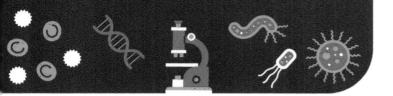

Examples of adaptations

You can work out how an organism is adapted to where it lives when given information on its environment and what it looks like.

For example, without the following adaptations the polar bear, camel and cactus below would be at a disadvantage in their environment.

Organism	Example adaptations
	• white fur for camouflage when hunting prey • feet with large surface area to distribute weight on snow • small ears to reduce heat loss • thick fur for insulation
	• feet with large surface area to distribute weight on sand • hump stores fat to provide energy when food is scarce • tough mouth and tongue to allow camel to eat cacti • long eyelashes to keep sand out of eyes
	• spines instead of leaves to reduce surface area and therefore water loss, and to deter predators • long roots to reach water underground • large, fleshy stem to store water

 Some organisms are **extremophiles**, which means they live in environments that are very extreme where most other organisms could not survive. For example, areas with:

- very high or low temperatures
- extreme pressures
- high salt concentrations
- highly acidic or alkaline conditions
- low levels of oxygen or water.

Bacteria that live in deep sea vents are extremophiles.

Deep sea vents are formed when seawater circulates through hot volcanic rocks on the seafloor. These environments have very high pressures and temperatures, no sunlight, and are strongly acidic.

Parasite adaptations

Parasites are organisms that live in or on a host organism. They feed off their host whilst it is alive, harming the host.

Fleas

Fleas live amongst the hairs of mammals and feed off blood.

Adaptations include:

- sharp mouthparts to pierce host skin
- chemicals in saliva to stop blood clotting and blocking mouthparts
- hard bodies that are not damaged when an animal scratches them.

Tapeworms

Tapeworms live inside the intestines of mammals and feed off digested food.

Adaptations include:

- hooks and/or suckers on the head to attach firmly to the gut wall
- long flattened shape to provide a large surface area for soluble food to diffuse through
- thick outer cuticle to protect them from the host's digestive enzymes.

Malarial parasites

Malarial parasites (*Plasmodium*) damage human liver and blood.

Adaptations include:

- huge reproductive rates
- using a very efficient vector – the protozoa is spread between hosts by female *Anopheles* mosquitoes
- rapid mutation, making it difficult to develop immunity or produce drugs against it.

 **Key Terms** Make sure you can write a definition for these key terms.

adaptation	community	ecosystem	extremophile
	interdependence	parasite	population

 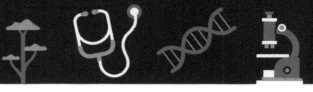

Retrieval

Learn the answers to the questions below, then cover the answers column with a piece of paper and write as many as you can. Check and repeat.

B9 questions

Answers

1	What is a population?	*Put paper here*	total number of organisms of the same species that live in a specific geographical area
2	What is a community?		group of two or more populations of different species living in a specific geographical area
3	What is an ecosystem?	*Put paper here*	the interaction of a community of living organisms with the non-living parts of their environment
4	What is competition?		contest between organisms within a community for resources
5	What is interdependence?	*Put paper here*	when species in a community depend on others for resources and shelter
6	What do animals often compete for?		food, mates, and territory
7	What do plants often compete for?		light, space, water, and mineral ions
8	What is a parasite?		organism that lives in or on a host organism
9	Give three examples of parasites.	*Put paper here*	tapeworms, fleas, and malarial parasites (*Plasmodium*)
10	Give some adaptations of a flea.		sharp mouthparts, chemicals in saliva that prevent blood clotting, hard bodies
11	What is a stable community?	*Put paper here*	when all species and environmental factors are in balance, so population sizes remain fairly constant
12	How do adaptations help an organism?		they enable the organism to survive in the conditions in which it lives
13	What are the three types of adaptations?	*Put paper here*	structural, behavioural, and functional
14	What is an extremophile?		an organism that lives in a very extreme environment
15	What makes an environment extreme?	*Put paper here*	• very high or low temperatures • extreme pressures • high salt concentrations • highly acidic or alkaline conditions • lack of oxygen or water

Now use the questions below to check your knowledge from previous chapters.

B9

Previous questions

Answers

1	What is an organ?	group of tissues working together to perform a specific function
2	Why is a leaf an organ?	there are many tissues inside the leaf that work together to perform photosynthesis
3	How do white blood cells protect the body?	• engulf pathogens • produce antitoxins to neutralise toxins, or antibodies
4	Write the word equation for aerobic respiration.	glucose + oxygen → carbon dioxide + water
5	Name four factors that affect the rate of transpiration.	temperature, light intensity, humidity, wind speed
6	Where is amylase produced?	salivary glands, pancreas, and small intestine

Put paper here

Put paper here

Maths Skills

Practise your maths skills using the worked example and practice questions below.

Estimations	Worked example	Practice
Estimates are often used in science before an exact calculation is done, such as when dealing with large numbers like population sizes. For example, if you work out how many snails live in $1\,m^2$, you can use this value to estimate how many snails live in an area of $10\,m^2$. You can also make estimates from sets of data. To make an estimate based on a graph, try drawing a line or curve of best fit through the data points. This will enable you to draw a straight line tangent between two points, from which you can make an estimate.	A grassy field on a farm measured 120 metres by 90 metres. A student wanted to estimate the number of daisies growing in the field. The student placed a $1\,m \times 1\,m$ quadrat in one position in an area that daisies were found in. 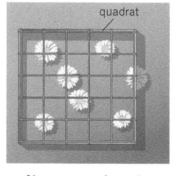quadrat To estimate the number of buttercup plants in the field: Number of buttercups in $1\,m \times 1\,m$ quadrat = 7 Area of the field $(120 \times 90) = 10\,800\,m^2$ $7 \times 10\,800 = 75\,600$ daisies estimated in the field	**1** The average number of dandelions in a 1 metre by 1 metre square of a park is 6. The park measures 230 metres by 350 metres. Estimate the number of dandelions in the park. **2** The average number of daisies in a 1 metre by 1 metre square of a field is 28. The field measures 180 metres by 80 metres. Estimate the number of daisies in the field.

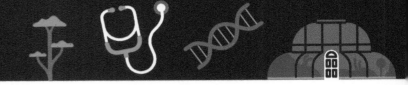
01 Over the past 50 years, scientists in Italy have been monitoring the populations of red and grey squirrels. Red squirrels are native to the Piedmont region; grey squirrels were introduced to the area in the mid 20th century.

To monitor the populations of these species, the scientists divided a map of the area into squares of equal size, known as cells. They then recorded the number of cells in which each species of squirrel was present.

01.1 Evaluate whether this technique provides data on population size.
[2 marks]

> ! **Exam Tip**
>
> For this question, you need to give your opinion and the reason you have that opinion.

_____

_____

_____

01.2 The results of the monitoring are shown in **Figure 1**.

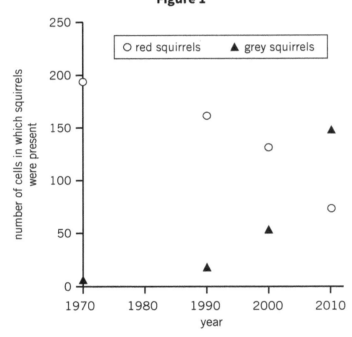

Figure 1

> ! **Exam Tip**
>
> Draw a line for the red squirrels and another for the grey squirrels to make the pattern more obvious.

Describe the trends shown in the graph. **[3 marks]**

_____

_____

_____

_____

01.3   **Table 1** provides information on the two squirrel species.

Table 1

	Red squirrel	Grey squirrel
Life expectancy	7 years	2–4 years
Reproduction	up to six young, twice a year	up to nine young, twice a year
Age of sexual maturity	12 months	12 months
Survival rate of offspring	15%	40%
Health	*Parapox* virus results in high levels of fatalities	carriers of *Parapox* virus

Using **Table 1**, suggest reasons for the changes seen in squirrel populations in Italy.   **[4 marks]**

_____

_____

_____

_____

_____

01.4   Five breeding pairs of red squirrels are introduced into a new area, where no squirrel populations currently exist. Using data from **Table 1**, estimate the maximum number of offspring that survive from the breeding pairs after four years.   **[4 marks]**

_____

_____

_____

_____

_____

01.5   Suggest reasons why the total population of red squirrels may be higher, or lower, than the value calculated in **01.4**.   **[3 marks]**

_____

_____

_____

_____

02 Common seals are found in the Atlantic and Pacific Oceans.

Figure 2

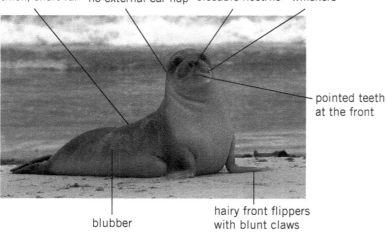

thick, short fur | closable ears with no external ear flap | closable nostrils | whiskers

pointed teeth at the front

blubber

hairy front flippers with blunt claws

02.1 Using **Figure 2** and your own knowledge, explain **two** ways seals are adapted for swimming. **[4 marks]**

1 _____

_____

2 _____

_____

02.2 Suggest why seals have closable ears and nostrils. **[1 mark]**

_____

_____

02.3 Arctic seals are another species of seal, which is adapted to live in cold regions of the world.

Suggest and explain **two** ways in which Arctic seals may differ from the common seal. **[4 marks]**

1 _____

_____

2 _____

_____

03 Parasites live on or in a host organism.

03.1 Write down what is meant by a parasitic relationship. **[1 mark]**

03.2 Give **one** example of an external parasite. **[1 mark]**

03.3 Explain **two** ways a tapeworm is adapted for living in a human's small intestine. **[4 marks]**

04 Blackberry bushes are found in hedgerows. They are often referred to as brambles as they have long, thorny, arching stems, which can grow up to several metres tall.

04.1 Suggest **two** ways a blackberry bush is adapted to its environment. **[2 marks]**

04.2 Blackberry seeds are found within the blackberry fruit. These berries are eaten by a number of hedgerow birds. Describe how blackberry seeds are dispersed. **[2 marks]**

04.3 Explain the advantages to the blackberry bush of dispersing its seeds. **[2 marks]**

05 Within a community, each species depends on other species in order to survive. This is called interdependence.

05.1 Explain the interdependence that occurs between bees and cereal crops. **[4 marks]**

05.2 Fields of cereal are fairly unstable communities. This means that the population number of each species living within the community can fluctuate significantly.

Suggest and explain **two** ways a farmer could increase the stability of communities in their farmland, whilst still maximising crop yields. **[4 marks]**

06 Living organisms can be found almost everywhere on the planet.

06.1 Give the term that describes an organism that can live in an extreme environment. **[1 mark]**

06.2 Some species of fish are adapted to live at the bottom of the ocean. One example is the angler fish. Suggest **two** conditions that can be found at the bottom of the ocean. **[2 marks]**

06.3 The angler fish gets its name from an elongated spine that supports a light-producing organ known as a photophore. The photophore contains bacteria that can emit light through a chemical process known as bioluminescence. The photophore produces a blue-green light similar to that of a firefly on land. Give the type of relationship that exists between the bacteria and the angler fish. **[1 mark]**

06.4 Angler fish are blind. Suggest how their photophore helps them to survive. **[2 marks]**

07 Marram grass (**Figure 3**) is adapted to live in very dry conditions, such as sand dune systems. The leaves of the marram grass are adapted to survive when water is limited. In very dry conditions, the leaves of the marram grass roll up to form long tubes. This helps drain any water down towards the roots of the plant.

Figure 3

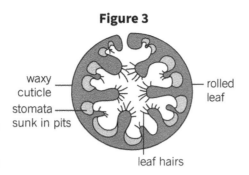

waxy cuticle
stomata sunk in pits
rolled leaf
leaf hairs

! Exam Tips

Look at **Figure 3** – does the shape of the inside of the leaf look similar to anything?

For this question, you need to take your biology knowledge and apply it differently!

Using **Figure 3** and your own knowledge, explain how the leaves of marram grass are adapted to survive with very limited water availability. **[6 marks]**

08 Deer can be found living in the wild in large areas of woodland.

08.1 Which of the following describes a woodland in which deer live? Choose **one** answer. **[1 mark]**

a community　　a population　　an ecosystem　　a habitat

08.2 Intraspecific competition is competition within a species. Identify and explain **two** factors that deer compete with each other for. **[4 marks]**

08.3 Some factors can affect a population indirectly. For example, temperature can indirectly affect the population of starfish. This is because rising temperatures kill coral, which is the food source of the starfish. Explain how light intensity indirectly affects the size of a deer population. **[3 marks]**

! Exam Tip

Think about what factors light intensity affects. How might this affect deer?

09 The zebra mussel is a small mussel originally native to the Caspian Sea.

A small population of these mussels was transferred to North America in the mid 1980s. One of the largest colonies exists in the Hudson River area. By the early 1990s, the biomass of the zebra mussel population exceeded the combined biomass of all other consumers in the Hudson River area.

Mussels are filter feeders; this means that they filter small organisms and organic particles out of the water. This has significantly increased the river water clarity.

Suggest and explain the positive and negative effects of the invasive species on the native populations of organisms in the Hudson River area. **[6 marks]**

! Exam Tips

There is a large block of text in this question.

This is very common in exams, which is why reading books (any books) is great exam preparation.

10   Desert foxes and Arctic foxes show both similarities and differences in their appearance.

These are summarised in **Table 2**.

Table 2

	Desert fox	Arctic fox
Habitat	desert	ice sheets
Fur colour	pale yellow	white
Ears	large	small
Feet	covered in hairs on both surfaces	covered in hairs on both surfaces
Body features	specialised kidneys that reduce water loss from the body	have a thick layer of fat underneath the skin
Average height of males	20 cm	30 cm
Average mass of males	1.0 kg	6.0 kg

10.1   Explain why the two species of fox are different colours.   **[2 marks]**

10.2   Suggest **two** reasons why the feet of the Arctic fox are covered in hairs.   **[2 marks]**

> **! Exam Tip**
>
> Think about where each species lives.

10.3   The surface area to volume ratio of the foxes can be estimated by modelling their shape as a cube. Using this approach, the desert fox has a surface area to volume ratio of 3:10.

Estimate the surface area to volume ratio of an Arctic fox. **[3 marks]**

10.4   Explain why the two species of fox have different surface area to volume ratios.   **[3 marks]**

> **! Exam Tips**
>
> For the desert fox we can assume each length is 20 cm.
>
> So the volume would be $20 \times 20 \times 20 = 8000 \text{ cm}^3$, with a surface area of $6 \times (20 \times 20) = 2400$.

11   A scientist carried out an investigation to study the effect of pH on enzyme action.

11.1   Give the type of enzyme that catalyses the breakdown of protein.   **[1 mark]**

> **! Exam Tip**
>
> Enzymes generally sound like the thing they are breaking down.

11.2   Give the product that is formed when protein is broken down.   **[1 mark]**

11.3 The scientist's results are shown in **Table 3**.

Table 3

pH	Mean rate of product formed in mmol/min
1	18
2	24
3	11
4	3
5	0

Plot a graph of the scientist's results on **Figure 4**.   **[4 marks]**

Figure 4

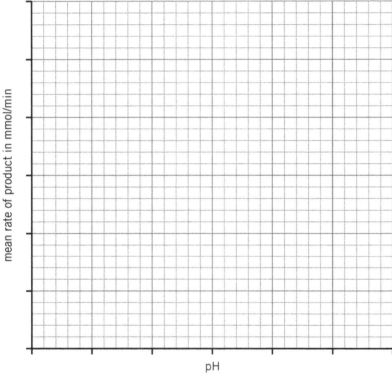

mean rate of product in mmol/min

pH

! Exam Tip

Make sure you use crosses to plot your points clearly, and draw a line of best fit.

11.4 Use your graph to determine the optimum pH of the enzyme.   **[1 mark]**

11.5 Explain what has happened to the enzyme at pH 5.   **[3 marks]**

11.6 Suggest where in the body the enzyme is secreted.   **[1 mark]**

! Exam Tip

Draw construction lines on your graph – they will help to prevent you from making mistakes!

12 Fresh cow's milk is a mixture containing water, lipids, protein, and lactose sugar. It also contains some vitamins and minerals.

12.1 Describe the chemical test that could be used to show that there is protein present in milk. **[2 marks]**

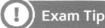

12.2 Lactose cannot be absorbed into the body. It must be digested by the enzyme lactase into the sugars glucose and galactose, which can then be absorbed.

Suggest why lactose cannot be absorbed into the blood. **[1 mark]**

12.3 Lactase can be added to fresh milk to predigest the lactose. This makes 'lactose-free' milk, which is suitable for people who do not produce enough lactase of their own.

A company that produces lactose-free milk investigated the effect of temperature on lactase. Their results are shown in **Table 4**.

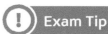

Table 4

Temperature in °C	Time taken to digest lactose in min
25	20
30	14
35	11
40	11
45	29
50	no digestion

Explain why no digestion occurred at 50 °C. **[3 marks]**

12.4 Using the information provided, suggest the optimum temperature for the company to heat milk to, prior to adding the lactase enzyme. Give a reason for your answer. **[2 marks]**

13 Yeast is a microorganism used in the brewing industry to make alcoholic drinks such as beer.

13.1 Write down the type of respiration yeast carries out to produce ethanol. **[1 mark]**

13.2 Comple the word equation to describe this reaction. **[2 marks]**

_____ ⟶ ethanol + _____ (+ energy)

13.3 Describe how a scientist can test for the product you have named in **13.2**. **[2 marks]**

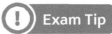

13.4 A group of students wanted to determine the optimum temperature for yeast to respire. Suggest which piece of equipment they should use to control the temperature. **[1 mark]**

13.5 The students decided to measure the respiration rate at five different temperatures between 10 °C and 50 °C, at 10 °C intervals. Describe what you would expect the students to find as the temperature in the investigation was increased. **[3 marks]**

Knowledge

B10 Organising an ecosystem

Levels of organisation

Feeding relationships within a community can be represented by **food chains**.

Photosynthetic organisms that synthesise molecules are the producers of all **biomass** for life on Earth, and so are the first step in all food chains.

all food chains begin with a **producer**, for example, a green plant or alga producing glucose through photosynthesis

slugs are **primary consumers** – they are **herbivores** that eat producers

sparrows are **secondary consumers** – they are **carnivores** that eat primary consumers

hawks are **tertiary consumers** – they are carnivores that eat secondary consumers

Organisms usually have more complex feeding relationships, with more than one predator or more than one food source. These can be shown in a **food web**.

Pyramids of biomass

The **trophic level** of an organism is the number of steps it is from the start of its food chain.

Pyramids of biomass represent the relative amount of biomass at each trophic level of a food chain.

Biomass is the amount of living or recently dead biological matter in an area. Biomass is transferred from each trophic level to the level above it in the food chain.

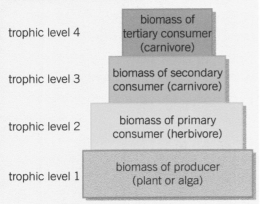

trophic level 4 — biomass of tertiary consumer (carnivore)

trophic level 3 — biomass of secondary consumer (carnivore)

trophic level 2 — biomass of primary consumer (herbivore)

trophic level 1 — biomass of producer (plant or alga)

How materials are cycled

All materials in the living world are recycled, which provides the building materials for future organisms. The constant cycling of carbon is called the **carbon cycle**.

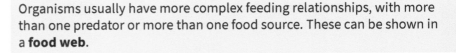
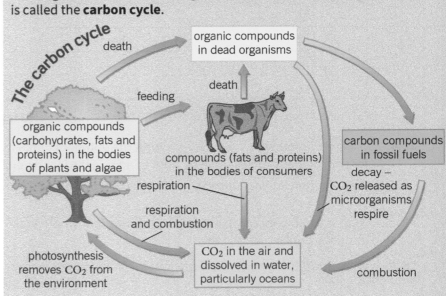

The carbon cycle

death

organic compounds in dead organisms

feeding

death

organic compounds (carbohydrates, fats and proteins) in the bodies of plants and algae

compounds (fats and proteins) in the bodies of consumers

carbon compounds in fossil fuels

decay – CO_2 released as microorganisms respire

respiration

respiration and combustion

photosynthesis removes CO_2 from the environment

CO_2 in the air and dissolved in water, particularly oceans

combustion

Loss of biomass

Radiation from the Sun is the source of energy for most communities. Producers transfer about 1% of the incident light energy used for photosynthesis to produce biomass. This energy is stored in substances that make up plant cells.

Approximately 10% of the biomass from each trophic level is transferred to the level above it.

The efficiency of food production can be improved by reducing the number of stages in a food chain.

This loss of biomass moving up the food chain is due to several factors:

- use in life processes, such as respiration. Respiration supplies all the energy needed for living processes
- not all of the matter eaten is digested, some is egested as waste products
- some absorbed material is lost as waste
- energy is used in movement and to keep animals warm.

Efficiency of food production

The efficiency of food production can be improved by reducing the number of stages in the food chain.

For example, by feeding chickens on purely plant material such as seeds rather than chicken pellets which can contain fish. Or, humans eating less meat. This removes at least one, but in many cases two stages in a food chain.

Decay

Decomposers, such as bacteria and fungi, break down dead plant and animal matter by secreting enzymes into the environment. The small soluble food molecules produced then diffuse into the decomposer.

These materials are cycled through an ecosystem by decomposers returning carbon to the atmosphere as carbon dioxide and mineral ions to the soil.

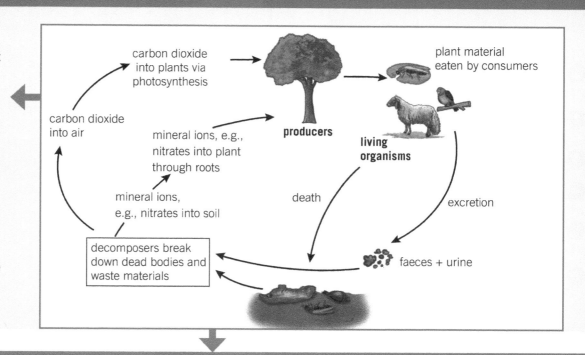

- carbon dioxide into plants via photosynthesis
- carbon dioxide into air
- mineral ions, e.g., nitrates into plant through roots
- mineral ions, e.g., nitrates into soil
- decomposers break down dead bodies and waste materials
- producers
- living organisms
- plant material eaten by consumers
- death
- excretion
- faeces + urine

Maximising decay

Materials **decay** because they are broken down by micoorganisms. Therefore decay occurs fastest under the following conditions:

- Warm – if it is too cold, chemical reactions in the microorganisms occur very slowly (if at all) and if it is too hot, the enzymes may be denatured.
- Moist – the moisture makes it easier for microorganisms to digest their food and prevents them drying out.
- Oxygen available – most decomposers respire aerobically.

Cycling of materials

Living organisms remove materials from the environment for growth and other processes. These materials are returned to the environment either in waste material or when living things die and decay.

 Revision Tip

When answering questions about the carbon or decay cycle, you may find it easier to sketch the cycle.

Don't worry about adding drawings – these won't gain marks. Just add a box stating the component, such as a factory or a tree.

Then add a description to each arrow, explaining that step.

 **Key Terms**

Make sure you can write a definition for these key terms.

| biomass | carbon cycle | carnivore | consumer | decay | decomposer |
| food chain | food web | herbivore | producer | trophic level |

 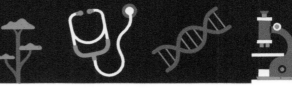

Retrieval

Learn the answers to the questions below, then cover the answers column with a piece of paper and write as many as you can. Check and repeat.

B10 questions

Answers

1	What is a producer?	organism that makes its own food, usually by photosynthesis
2	What is a food chain?	representation of the feeding relationships within a community
3	What is a consumer?	organism that eats other organisms for food
4	What is a herbivore?	organism that only eats producers (plants/algae)
5	What is the ultimate source of energy for most communities?	radiation from the Sun
6	What proportion of biomass is transferred from each trophic level to the one above?	approximately 10%
7	Why is biomass lost between trophic levels?	• some ingested material is egested • some material is lost as waste (carbon dioxide and water in respiration, water and urea in urine) • used in life processes, such as respiration • energy is used in movement and to keep animals warm
8	What is the carbon cycle?	process that returns carbon from organisms to the atmosphere as carbon dioxide, which can then be used by plants
9	Give three ways carbon dioxide is returned to the atmosphere.	respiration, combustion, and decay
10	Name the process by which plants take carbon dioxide out of the atmosphere.	photosynthesis
11	What is a decomposer?	microorganism that breaks down dead plant and animal matter
12	Give two examples of decomposers.	bacteria and fungi
13	What is the role of decay?	returns carbon to the atmosphere and mineral ions to the soil from dead matter
14	What factors affect the rate of decay by decomposers?	oxygen levels, moisture levels, temperature
15	What are the optimal conditions for decay?	warm, moist, and oxygen-rich

Put paper here

Now use the questions below to check your knowledge from previous chapters.

B10

Previous questions | Answers

1	What is the function of the cell wall?	strengthens and supports the cell
2	What is diffusion?	• net movement of particles from an area of high concentration to an area of low concentration along a concentration gradient • this is a passive process (does not require energy from respiration)
3	What is osmosis?	diffusion of water from a dilute solution to a concentrated solution through a partially permeable membrane
4	What is an ecosystem?	the interaction of a community of living organisms with the non-living parts of their environment
5	What do plants often compete for?	light, space, water, and mineral ions

Put paper here

Required Practical Skills

Practise answering questions on practical skills using the example below. You need to be able to apply your skills and knowledge to other practicals too.

Rate of decay	Worked example	Practice
In this practical the student investigated how changing the temperature changes the rate of decay of milk. You should be able to apply your knowledge to describe how an indicator solution can be used to measure the rate of a reaction. The indicator cresol red turns purple in alkaline conditions and yellow in solutions with a pH of less than 7.2.	A student collected data on the time taken for milk mixed with cresol red solution to turn from purple to yellow after adding lipase, at different temperatures.	1 Suggest a more accurate way to measure the colour change of the milk in the investigation. 2 The decay of milk is too slow to observe in a single lesson, so lipase is added to the milk to mimic natural decay. Identify the substance that the lipase breaks down, and give the name of the product that causes the milk pH to change.

Temperature in °C	Time taken in s
45	16
46	16
47	17
48	17
49	16

Evaluate the design of the experiment.

Answer:
The range in the independent variable is 45–49 °C, and the interval is 1 °C. This is not a wide enough range or interval to give a change in the dependent variable. This is supported by the data – the time taken is the same at 45 °C as at 49 °C, and the results only change by a maximum of 1 second. A bigger range in the independent variable would give more reliable results.

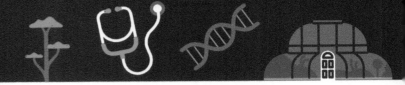
01 Scientists were studying the feeding relationships between organisms living on a tomato plant.

01.1 The scientist measured the dry biomass of organisms present. Explain how this could have been determined. **[2 marks]**

_____

_____

_____

01.2 Give **one** disadvantage of this technique. **[1 mark]**

_____

> **! Exam Tip**
>
> This question just asks for a disadvantage. You'll get no extra marks if you write an advantage as well. It's great that you know them but focus on just answering the question.

01.3 Their data is shown in **Table 1**.

Table 1

Organism	Dry biomass in g
tomato plant	300
aphids	25
ladybirds	2

Use the information in **Table 1** to construct a pyramid of biomass. **[3 marks]**

> **! Exam Tip**
>
> Use a ruler to get the scale roughly correct, but this isn't art so don't spend too much time making it look perfect.

01.4 Calculate the percentage biomass transfer between the tomato plants and the aphids. **[2 marks]**

_____%

01.5 Explain **two** reasons why not all of the aphid biomass is passed on to the ladybirds. **[4 marks]**

_____

_____

_____

_____

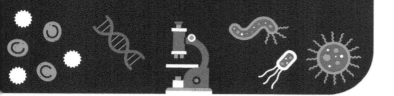

02 Materials are constantly cycled through organisms and the environment in which they live.

02.1 Name the organisms that break down dead plants and animals.

[1 mark]

_____

02.2 Describe the conditions in which decay occurs most quickly.

[3 marks]

_____

_____

_____

_____

03 Isle Royale is a large isolated island on Lake Superior, in the USA. It is home to populations of wolves and moose. The wolves are the only natural predators of the moose.

The populations of wolves and moose on the island have been monitored over a 60-year period (**Figure 1**).

Figure 1

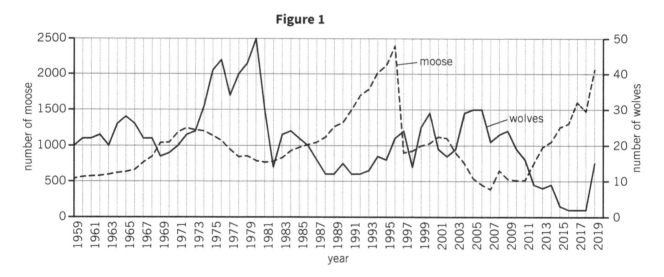

03.1 Identify the largest population of wolves on the island between 1959 and 2019. **[1 mark]**

03.2 The population of moose rose significantly between 1982 and 1996. Calculate the percentage increase in the moose population between 1982 and 1996. **[3 marks]**

03.3 Explain the general population size trends in **Figure 1**. **[4 marks]**

03.4 Other than availability of moose, suggest and explain **two** factors that may affect the wolf population. **[2 marks]**

04 **Figure 2** represents the main steps in the carbon cycle.

Figure 2

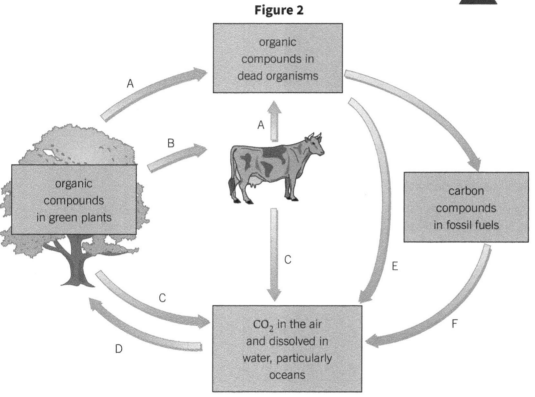

04.1 Write down the letter of the arrow that represents photosynthesis. **[1 mark]**

04.2 Name the process that arrow **F** represents. **[1 mark]**

04.3 Carbon is trapped inside the bodies of organisms. Name **one** other store of carbon. **[1 mark]**

04.4 Describe the role that microorganisms play in the carbon cycle. **[3 marks]**

05 **Figure 3** is a pyramid of biomass that represents a food chain in a woodland.

Figure 3

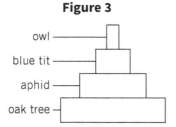

05.1 Name the organisms that are found in trophic level 3. **[1 mark]**

05.2 Describe the group of organisms that are found in trophic level 1 of any food chain. **[1 mark]**

05.3 Decomposers are missing from **Figure 3**. Explain the role that decomposers play in food chains. **[3 marks]**

06 When milk decays, bacteria convert lactose into lactic acid. A group of students investigated how temperature affects the rate of decay of milk. Milk may take several days to decay, so the students used the following method to model the process:

1 Prepare five water baths: 20 °C, 30 °C, 40 °C, 50 °C, and 60 °C.

2 Place 20 cm³ of alkaline solutions of milk into five separate conical flasks.

3 Place one conical flask in each water bath and leave to acclimatise.

4 Add a few drops of cresol red indicator to each beaker. Cresol red turns yellow when the pH drops below 7.2.

5 Add 2 cm³ of lipase to each beaker.

6 Time how long it takes for a colour change to take place in each beaker.

7 Repeat the entire experiment.

The students' results are shown in **Table 2**.

Table 2

Temperature in °C	Time until colour change in s			Rate of reaction in _____
	Test 1	Test 2	Mean	
20	240	280	260	0.004
30	64	58	61	0.016
40	38	44	41	
50	120	100	110	0.009
60	did not change	did not change	–	–

06.1 Complete the table heading by adding the correct unit to the rate of reaction column. **[1 mark]**

06.2 Calculate the rate of reaction at 40 °C. **[2 marks]**

06.3 Plot a graph of temperature versus rate of reaction on **Figure 4**.
Draw a line of best fit. **[3 marks]**

Figure 4

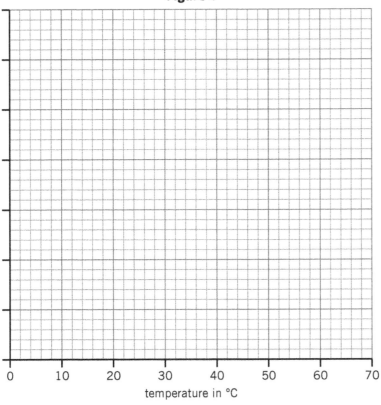

temperature in °C

Exam Tip

Always draw your graph using crosses to plot the points and add on a line of best fit.

06.4 Determine the optimum temperature for decay. **[2 marks]**

06.5 Explain why the students were unable to gain a result at a temperature of 60 °C. **[2 marks]**

06.6 Explain why the apparatus used by the students provides a model for the decay of milk. **[6 marks]**

07 Farmers are constantly looking at ways to increase the efficiency of food production.

The following food chain summarises the differences between eating wheat and eating meat products derived from pigs that have been fed on wheat.

wheat → humans   800 000 kJ per hectare of crop
wheat → pigs → humans   70 000 kJ per hectare of crop

07.1 Compare the amount of energy the two food chains transfer to humans. **[3 marks]**

07.2 Describe **two** reasons why the amount of energy the two food chains transfer to humans is different. **[2 marks]**

Exam Tip

In a question like this, use a maths calculation to support your answer.

07.3 Evaluate the advantages and disadvantages of rearing pigs indoors in controlled ambient conditions. **[6 marks]**

08 All materials in the living world are recycled to provide the building blocks for future organisms. Water is one example of a material that is recycled.

08.1 Describe the main steps in the water cycle. **[6 marks]**

08.2 Identify and explain **two** ways in which animals return water to the environment. **[4 marks]**

08.3 Explain the importance of the water cycle to living organisms. **[4 marks]**

08.4 Other than water, name **one** material that is recycled. **[1 mark]**

09 The carbon cycle is essential for life on Earth.

09.1 Describe the main processes in the carbon cycle. **[6 marks]**

09.2 Explain how **two** human activities are causing changes to the natural balance of the carbon cycle. **[4 marks]**

10 A group of students were asked to survey the number of daisies growing on their school field. They decided to take a series of samples using a 1 m × 1 m quadrat. Their results are in **Table 3**.

Table 3

Sample number	1	2	3	4	5	6	7	8
Number of daisies	11	14	14	2	14	15	11	15

10.1 Write down the median number of daisies from the students' samples. **[1 mark]**

10.2 Calculate the mean number of daisies from the students' samples. **[1 mark]**

10.3 Justify which value, from the median and the mean, gives the best estimate of the average number of daisies in the school field. **[2 marks]**

10.4 The school field measures 350 m × 200 m.

Estimate the number of daisies in the school field. **[3 marks]**

10.5 Suggest and explain **two** reasons for the difference in number of daisies measured in Sample 4. **[4 marks]**

> **! Exam Tip**
>
> Rewrite the data to help you find the median.

> **! Exam Tip**
>
> Whenever you are asked to find the mean, start by looking for anomalous results.

> **! Exam Tip**
>
> There is lots of information that is not specified in the main body of the question. This leaves you lots of space to suggest reasons. As long as you've got a good explanation you can easily pick up marks in **10.5**.

11 **Figure 5** shows the biomass of organisms required at each level of a food chain to support the next trophic level.

Figure 5

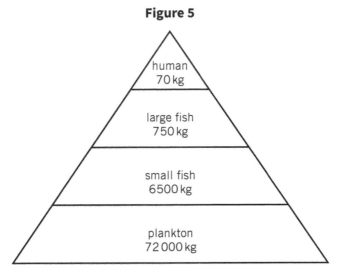

11.1 Write down the food chain represented by this diagram. **[1 mark]**

11.2 Calculate the percentage of biomass transferred between plankton and humans. **[2 marks]**

11.3 Explain why the efficiency of biomass transfer between trophic levels is much less than 100%. **[2 marks]**

11.4 The energy content of small fish is 6 kJ/g. Calculate the total energy transferred to the large fish in the food chain. **[5 marks]**

11.5 Lead is a metal linked to liver and brain damage in humans. Some industrial processes produce lead as a by-product, and this can contaminate water sources. Using **Figure 5**, suggest how eating a diet rich in fish could cause lead-related health disorders in humans. **[4 marks]**

> **! Exam Tip**
>
> You will need to carefully show your working. This will help you pick up marks even if you don't get the final answer correct.

12 Organisms have a number of adaptations that enable them to survive.

12.1 Match the specific examples of animal adaptions below to the type of adaption. **[2 marks]**

penguins huddling together for warmth	structural adaptation
snakes producing venom	behavioural adaptation
tigers having striped coats	functional adaptation

12.2 Plants are also adapted to their environment. Describe **two** ways desert plants prevent water loss. **[2 marks]**

12.3 Explain **one** way desert plant roots are adapted for collecting water. **[2 marks]**

13 To provide better yields many commercial growers plant tomatoes inside industrial greenhouses. The results of one scientist's research are shown in **Table 4**.

Table 4

Growing conditions	Yield of tomato plant in kg
outdoors	6.8
inside a greenhouse	11.3

13.1 Compare the yield of tomato plants grown in a greenhouse to those grown outside. **[2 marks]**

13.2 Explain how these increases in yield are likely to have been obtained. **[6 marks]**

14 Enzymes play an essential role in digestion.

14.1 Amylase is produced by the salivary glands. Describe the role of amylase. **[2 marks]**

14.2 Give **two** reasons why the stomach is acidic. **[2 marks]**

14.3 Explain why lipase enzymes cannot break down proteins. **[3 marks]**

15 Gorse plants have a number of adaptations to help them survive.

15.1 Draw **one** line between each adaptation and its function. **[3 marks]**

Adaptation	Function
flowers	reduce water loss
sharp spines	so herbivores do not eat the plant
small leaves	to attract insects to pollinate them

15.2 Gorse plants grow in sunny regions, usually in dry sandy soils. Suggest and explain how the roots of gorse plants may appear. **[2 marks]**

15.3 Other than water, give **two** factors that plants compete for. **[2 marks]**

15.4 Apart from competition with other gorse plants, a number of biotic factors can affect the population of gorse plants present in an area. Describe how **one** other biotic factor could reduce the population of gorse bushes in an area. **[2 marks]**

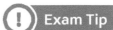

Exam Tip

The question has already given water, so you won't get any marks if you say that again.

⚙ Knowledge

B11 Humans and the environment

Biodiversity

Biodiversity is the variety of all the different species of organisms (plant, animal, and microorganism) on Earth, or within a specific ecosystem.

High biodiversity ensures the stability of an ecosystem, because it reduces the dependence of one species on another in the ecosystem for food or habitat maintenance.

The future of the human species depends on us maintaining a good level of biodiversity. Many human activities, such as **deforestation**, are reducing biodiversity, but only recently have measures been taken to try to prevent this.

Waste management

Rapid growth of the human population and increases in the standard of living mean humans are using more resources and producing more waste.

Waste and chemical materials need to be properly handled in order to reduce the amount of **pollution** they cause. Pollution kills plants and animals, and can accumulate in food chains, reducing biodiversity.

Pollution can occur:
- in water, from sewage, fertiliser run-off, or toxic chemicals (e.g., from factories)
- in air, from smoke and acidic gases
- on land, from landfill and toxic chemicals.

Acid rain

Sulfur dioxide (formed from burning coal and oil) and nitrogen oxides (for example from car engines) dissolve in rainwater and react with oxygen in the air to form dilute sulfuric acid and nitric acid. This produces **acid rain**.

Effects:
- kills the leaves, buds, flowers, and fruit of trees as it lands
- destroys plant roots as it soaks into the soil
- increases the acidity of lakes, rivers, and streams; if the concentration gets too high, plants and animals can no longer survive

Land use

Rapid population growth has led to humans using much more land for building, quarrying, farming, and dumping waste. This reduces the area in which animals can live and can further destroy habitats through pollution.

Deforestation

Large-scale deforestation in tropical areas has been carried out to provide timber, land for cattle and rice fields, and to grow crops for **biofuels**.

This has resulted in:
- large amounts of carbon dioxide being released into the atmosphere due to burning of trees
- extinctions and reductions in biodiversity as habitats are destroyed
- climate change, as trees absorb carbon dioxide and release water vapour.

Prevention:
- low-sulfur petrol and diesel used in vehicles
- catalytic converters fitted to cars which remove nitrogen oxides
- cleaner, low-sulfur fuels such as gas used in power stations
- more electricity generated using nuclear power
- desulfurisation processes used in power station chimneys to clean the flue gases before release

Toxin levels

Farmers often use **herbicides** to kill weeds and **pesticides** to kill pests, such as insects. These toxins can become part of food chains. The toxin level in the animals that consume affected plant material is small. However, if the toxin cannot be broken down by the body, toxin levels build up along the food chain. This is known as **bioaccumulation**. It can lead to dangerous levels of poisons building up in the top predators.

pesticide in lake water 0.002 ppb → small plants 1 ppm → small fish 2 ppm → cormorant 10 ppm → crocodile 34 ppm

Key
ppm parts per million
ppb parts per billion

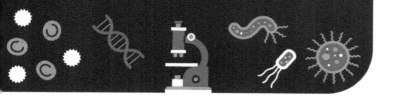

Eutrophication

If fertilisers or untreated sewage are washed into rivers, streams or lakes, **eutrophication** may occur.

> Fertilisers and sewage increase the concentration of mineral ions (particularly nitrates) in the water.

↓

> Mineral ions stimulate rapid growth of algae and/or plants.

↓

> Plants and algae die as too much competition for light so they cannot photosynthesise.

↓

> Increase in microorganisms (decomposers), which break down the dead plant material.

↓

> High levels of respiration by microorganisms decrease the oxygen levels in the water.

↓

> Aerobic organisms such as fish die as water oxygen levels are too low.

Greenhouse effect

The **greenhouse effect** is essential for maintaining the Earth's surface at a suitable temperature for life. Energy from the Sun reaches the Earth, warming it up, and much of it is radiated back out into space. However, greenhouse gases such as carbon dioxide and methane absorb some of the reflected energy. This keeps the Earth at a consistent warm temperature.

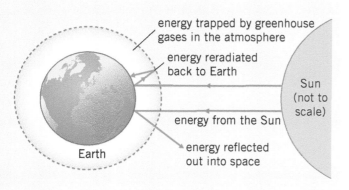

energy trapped by greenhouse gases in the atmosphere

energy reradiated back to Earth

Sun (not to scale)

energy from the Sun

energy reflected out into space

Earth

Global warming

Levels of carbon dioxide and methane in the atmosphere are increasing due to human activity, contributing to **global warming** and climate change as they trap more of the Sun's energy. Global warming is the gradual increase in the average temperature of the Earth.

This scientific consensus is based on systematic reviews of thousands of peer-reviewed publications.

Global warming has resulted in:

- large-scale habitat change and reduction, causing decreases in biodiversity
- climate change – increase in severe and unpredictable weather conditions
- rising sea levels – due to ice caps and glaciers melting
- migration of species to different parts of the world, affecting ecosystems
- changes in distribution – some animals may extend their range as climate change makes conditions more favourable; others may find their range shrinks.

 **Key Terms**   **Make sure you can write a definition for these key terms.**

acid rain   bioaccumulation   biodiversity   biofuel   deforestation   eutrophication
global warming   greenhouse effect   herbicide   pesticide   pollution

Retrieval

 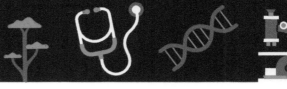

Learn the answers to the questions below, then cover the answers column with a piece of paper and write as many as you can. Check and repeat.

B11 questions

Answers

#	Question	Answer
1	What is biodiversity?	the variety of all the different species of organisms on Earth, or within an ecosystem
2	What is the advantage of high biodiversity?	ensures stability of ecosystems by reducing the dependence of one species on another
3	What is bioaccumulation?	build up of toxins along a food chain
4	Why are more resources being used, and more waste produced, by humans?	rapid growth in human population, and increase in the standard of living
5	Where does pollution occur?	water, air, and land
6	How are humans reducing the land available for other organisms?	building, quarrying, farming, and dumping waste
7	What are herbicides?	chemicals that kill weeds
8	Why have humans carried out large-scale deforestation in tropical areas?	• provide timber • provide land for cattle and rice fields • grow crops for biofuels
9	What are pesticides?	chemicals that kill insects
10	Which gases cause acid rain?	sulfur dioxide and nitrogen oxide
11	How does acid rain affect the environment?	kills trees and increases the acidity of waterways which can harm organisms present
12	Which gases are increasing in the atmosphere and contributing to global warming?	carbon dioxide and methane
13	What causes eutrophication?	untreated sewage or fertilisers being washed into lakes/rivers, increasing mineral concentrations
14	What is global warming?	increase in the average temperature of the Earth
15	What are some effects of global warming?	changes in Earth's climate, rising sea levels, changes in migration patterns, changes in the distribution of species

Put paper here

Now use the questions below to check your knowledge from previous chapters.

B11

Previous questions | Answers

	Previous questions	Answers
1	Why is biomass lost between trophic levels?	• some ingested material is egested • some material is lost as waste (carbon dioxide and water in respiration, water and urea in urine) • used in life processes, such as respiration • energy is used in movement and to keep animals warm
2	What is the carbon cycle?	process that returns carbon from organisms to the atmosphere as carbon dioxide, which can then be used by plants
3	What is interdependence?	when species in a community depend on others for resources and shelter
4	What do animals often compete for?	food, mates, and territory
5	Write the word equation for anaerobic respiration in plant and yeast cells.	glucose → ethanol + carbon dioxide
6	How does the body supply the muscles with more oxygenated blood during exercise?	heart rate, breathing rate, and breath volume increase

(Put paper here)

 ## Maths Skills

Practise your maths skills using the worked example and practice questions below.

Calculating percentage change

To calculate percentage change you need to work out the difference between the two numbers you are comparing.

Then, you divide the difference by the original number and multiply the answer by 100.

If your answer is a negative number, this equals a percentage decrease.

If your answer is a positive number, this equals a percentage increase.

percentage change =
$$\frac{\text{difference}}{\text{original number}} \times 100$$

Worked example

In 2016, the levels of methane in the atmosphere had risen to 1840 ppb from 1800 ppb 5 years earlier.

Calculate the percentage change in atmospheric methane levels between 2011 and 2016.

Work out the difference between the two numbers you are comparing:

1840 − 1800 = 40

Divide the difference (40) by the original number:

$$\frac{40}{1800} = 0.022$$

Multiply by 100: 0.022 × 100 = 2.2

Percentage change in methane levels = 2.2%

Practice

The table below gives information on the levels of carbon dioxide in the atmosphere between 1960 and 2000.

Year	Concentration in ppm
1960	316.9
1980	338.7
2000	369.4

1 Calculate the percentage change in carbon dioxide levels from 1960 to 1980.

2 Calculate the percentage change in carbon dioxide levels from 1980 to 2000.

3 Calculate the percentage change in carbon dioxide levels from 1960 to 2000.

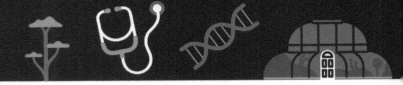

Exam-style questions

01 Large areas of the Amazon rainforest have been cleared for agriculture.

01.1 Choose the word that best describes this change in land use.
Tick **one** box. **[1 mark]**

afforestation ☐

deforestation ☐

eutrophication ☐

leaching ☐

01.2 Give **three** ways in which the removal of trees can lead to increasing carbon dioxide levels in the Earth's atmosphere. **[3 marks]**

1 _____

2 _____

3 _____

> **! Exam Tip**
>
> In **01.2** you will be awarded 1 mark per way, so don't write long sentences explaining why.

01.3 Explain why there is a difference in the level of biodiversity between rainforest regions and agricultural land. **[3 marks]**

_____

_____

_____

_____

01.4 Explain the long-term effects on the Earth's atmosphere of this change in land use. **[4 marks]**

_____

_____

_____

_____

_____

02 **Figure 1** shows how atmospheric carbon dioxide (CO_2) concentration and global mean temperature have changed since 1900.

Figure 1

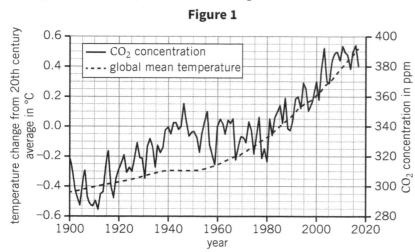

02.1 Describe the changes since 1900. **[4 marks]**

_____

_____

_____

_____

_____

! Exam Tip

You'll need to talk about both lines, give the general trend, and use data from the graph, for example, in 1900 the carbon dioxide concentration was ... since then it has ... and the level is now ... .

02.2 Name **two** activities that have led to the changes described in **02.1**. **[2 marks]**

1 _____

2 _____

02.3 The global mean temperature in the twentieth century was 13.9 °C. Calculate the global mean temperature in the year 2000. **[1 mark]**

Mean = _____

02.4 Calculate the mean rate of change of CO_2 concentration between the years 1910 and 2000. Include an appropriate unit with your answer. **[3 marks]**

! Exam Tip

To determine the units for rate of change, look at the units for the two values you are using and the calculation you did.

Mean = _____ Unit = _____

02.5 A student states that 'recent changes in global temperatures are caused by the changes in atmospheric carbon dioxide concentration'.

Discuss the extent to which **Figure 1** supports the student's statement. **[5 marks]**

_____

_____

_____

_____

_____

_____

_____

_____

! Exam Tip

02.5 refers to changes. You will need to be specific in your answer and give data from **Figure 1** to support what you say.

03 Air pollution is a significant problem in some cities.

03.1 Give **one** reason why air pollution is a concern for humans. **[1 mark]**

03.2 Describe what is meant by smog. **[1 mark]**

03.3 Nitrogen oxides (NO_x) are a type of air pollutant present in cities. Identify the main source of emission of NO_x. Choose **one** answer. **[1 mark]**

car exhausts   burning coal

burning wood   factories

! Exam Tip

NO_x is a way of referring to the different nitrous oxides that have different numbers of oxygen atoms in them.

03.4 **Table 1** shows how the concentration of NO_x varies over a one-week period in a particular city.

Table 1

NO_x concentration in µg/m³	125	110	120	123	130	85	70
Day	Monday	Tuesday	Wednesday	Thursday	Friday	Saturday	Sunday

Suggest **one** conclusion from this data. Give a reason for your answer. **[2 marks]**

03.5 Calculate the mean atmospheric concentration of NO_x. **[1 mark]**

03.6 Suggest and explain **one** way this figure could be reduced. **[2 marks]**

! Exam Tip

This data is from a city. To see any patterns in context think about the different activities that go on over a week and over a weekend.

04 Biodiversity is important in maintaining a stable ecosystem.

04.1 Define what is meant by the term biodiversity. **[1 mark]**

04.2 Identify the **two** factors that can reduce biodiversity. **[2 marks]**

breeding programmes   deforestation

monoculture farming   reintroduction of hedgerows

04.3 Describe why an area of woodland with multiple species of tree is more stable than an area containing only one tree species.

[3 marks]

05 **Table 2** shows the percentage recycling rate in the UK over five years.

Table 2

Year	Recycling rate in %
2010	40.4
2011	42.9
2012	43.9
2013	44.1
2014	44.9

05.1 Name **two** materials that can be recycled. **[2 marks]**

05.2 Explain **two** environmental benefits of recycling. **[4 marks]**

05.3 The UK was set a target to recycle at least 50% of household waste by 2020. Based on the data in **Table 2**, evaluate the likelihood that this target was met. **[4 marks]**

> **(!) Exam Tip**
>
> You'll have to back up what you say with a calculation based on data from **Table 2**.

06 Air pollution can lead to the formation of acid rain.

06.1 Name the **two** main gases responsible for the formation of acid rain. **[2 marks]**

06.2 Describe **one** negative effect of acid rain on living organisms. **[1 mark]**

06.3 Explain **one** way in which the production of acid rain from car engines has been reduced. **[2 marks]**

06.4 Explain why countries with low levels of air pollution can still suffer from the effects of acid rain. **[2 marks]**

07 **Figure 2** shows the change in the human population since the year 1800.

Figure 2

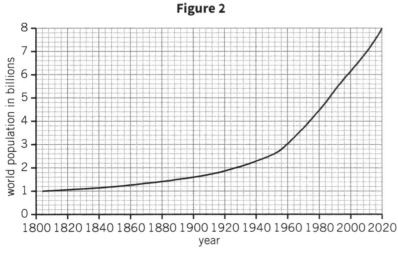

07.1 Describe the change in population in **Figure 2**. **[3 marks]**

> **(!) Exam Tip**
>
> The y-axis has the population in billions. Be careful that you use the correct unit.

07.2 Describe **three** ways the change in population has led to an increase in pollution. **[3 marks]**

07.3 Other than increases in pollution, suggest and explain **two** environmental issues that this change in human population could cause. **[4 marks]**

08 The article in **Figure 3** was published in an online magazine.

Figure 3

> **Stop biodiversity loss – or face human extinction**
>
> The United Nations' biodiversity chief warned today that the human race faces a biodiversity crisis.
>
> At a recent conference, it was reported that 'All countries need to draw up ambitious plans to protect the insects, birds, and animals upon which the human race relies as raw materials for its survival. Without these materials the human race faces a potential mass extinction event.'
>
> Many prominent environmental groups were quick to support this position, one adding that 'Around 1000 species per year are becoming extinct. These species could be hugely beneficial to the human race – but now we will never know.'

08.1 Define the term biodiversity. **[1 mark]**

08.2 Describe **two** examples of human activity that cause a decrease in biodiversity. **[2 marks]**

08.3 Suggest a project that scientists could plan to increase biodiversity. **[1 mark]**

08.4 Suggest and explain **two** ways in which a loss of biodiversity could lead to a mass extinction event for the human race. **[6 marks]**

Exam Tip

This is a large block of text. Read the questions first, then read the block of text. This way you can pick out key bits of information as you read the text. For example:

- **08.2** wants examples of human activity that decrease biodiversity, so highlight anything that decreases biodiversity in one colour.

- **08.3** wants projects carried out by scientists, so highlight any project in another colour.

09 The overuse of fertilisers on farms can lead to eutrophication in nearby lakes.

09.1 Describe why farmers use fertilisers. **[1 mark]**

09.2 Give **one** other cause of eutrophication. **[1 mark]**

09.3 Explain why the water oxygen level drops in lakes polluted with fertiliser. **[6 marks]**

Exam Tip

You may find it easier to use a flow diagram to answer a question like **09.3** that involves a series of steps.

10 Scientists are gathering increasing evidence for global warming.

10.1 State what is meant by global warming. **[1 mark]**

10.2 Name **one** gas released through human activity that is associated with global warming. **[1 mark]**

10.3 One effect of global warming is a rise in sea levels. Explain **one** effect of rising sea levels. **[2 marks]**

10.4 Give **one** other change caused by global warming. **[1 mark]**

11 Mercury compounds used to be common components of insecticides. They are very useful in killing insects, however they can damage the nervous systems and reproductive systems of mammals, including humans.

The food chain below represents the feeding relationships of tuna living in the ocean.

plankton → small fish → medium fish → tuna → humans

To prevent mercury poisoning people are advised not to eat more than two pieces of tuna each week. Explain how eating tuna could result in mercury poisoning. **[6 marks]**

12 The populations of lynx and snowshoe hare in Canada were studied over a number of years. The data collected are summarised in **Table 3**.

Table 3

Year	Hare numbers	Lynx numbers
1895	85 000	48 000
1900	18 000	6000
1903	65 000	18 000
1905	40 000	61 000
1908	28 000	28 000
1909	25 000	4000
1910	51 000	10 000
1912	70 000	32 000
1915	30 000	42 000

12.1 Using **Table 3**, describe the relationship between the snowshoe hare and lynx populations. **[2 marks]**

12.2 Explain whether the data provide evidence for a stable community. **[4 marks]**

12.3 Calculate the percentage change in the lynx population between 1909 and 1912. **[3 marks]**

12.4 Suggest and explain **two** factors that may be responsible for the unusually large hare population in 1895. **[2 marks]**

12.5 Suggest and explain what would happen to the forest environment if lynx started being hunted for their fur. **[3 marks]**

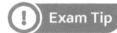

! Exam Tip

You will have to include data from **Table 3** in your answer.

B12 Nervous system and homeostasis

The nervous system

Function

The nervous system enables humans to react to their surroundings and to coordinate their behaviour – this includes both voluntary and involuntary actions.

Structure

The nervous system is made up of the **central nervous system** (CNS) and a network of nerves. The CNS comprises the **brain** and **spinal cord**.

Nervous system responses

Stimulus	**Receptor**	**Coordinator**	**Effector**	**Response**
a change in the environment is detected by **receptors**	information passes along **neurones** to the CNS as electrical impulses	the CNS coordinates the body's response to the stimulus	effectors bring about a response, such as glands secreting hormones	the body responds to the stimulus

Reflex arcs

Reflex actions of the nervous system are automatic and rapid – they do not involve the conscious part of the brain. Reflex actions are important for survival because they help prevent damage to the body. One example is the pain withdrawal reflex.

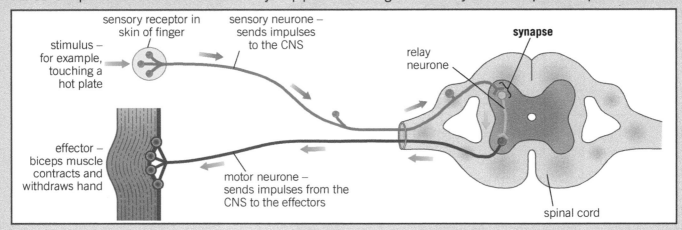

stimulus – for example, touching a hot plate

sensory receptor in skin of finger

sensory neurone – sends impulses to the CNS

relay neurone

synapse

effector – biceps muscle contracts and withdraws hand

motor neurone – sends impulses from the CNS to the effectors

spinal cord

Reflex arc structures

Neurones

carry electrical impulses around the body – relay neurones connect sensory neurones to motor neurones

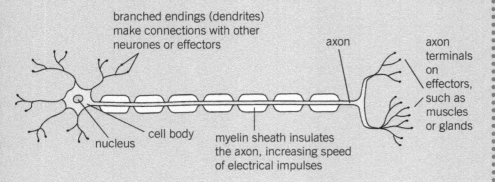

branched endings (dendrites) make connections with other neurones or effectors

axon

axon terminals on effectors, such as muscles or glands

nucleus

cell body

myelin sheath insulates the axon, increasing speed of electrical impulses

Synapses

are gaps between neurones, which allow electrical impulses in the nervous system to cross between neurones by transferring chemicals

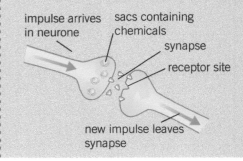

impulse arrives in neurone

sacs containing chemicals

synapse

receptor site

new impulse leaves synapse

Homeostasis

Homeostasis is the regulation of internal conditions (of a cell or whole organism) in response to internal and external changes, to constantly maintain optimum conditions for functioning.

In the human body, this includes control of:

- blood glucose concentration
- body temperature
- water and ion levels.

The automatic control systems of homeostasis may involve nervous responses or chemical responses.

All control systems involve:

- receptor cells, which detect **stimuli** such as light sensitive cells in the eyes, balance and sound receptors in the ear, and chemical receptors in the tongue and nose.
- **coordination centres** (such as the brain, spinal cord, and pancreas), which receive and process information from receptors
- **effectors** (muscles or glands), which produce responses to restore optimum conditions.

Control of body temperature

The skin also contains temperature receptors and sends nervous impulses to the thermoregulatory centre.

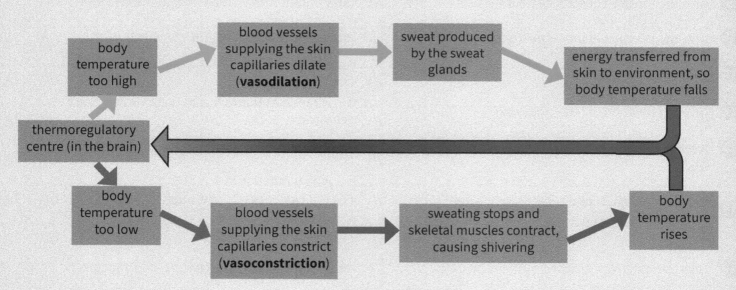

Body temperature is monitored and controlled by the **thermoregulatory centre** in the brain. The centre contains receptors sensitive to the blood temperature.

 **Key Terms**

Make sure you can write a definition for these key terms.

| brain | central nervous system | coordination centre | effector | homeostasis |

neurone   receptor   reflex action   spinal cord   stimulus   synapse

thermoregulatory centre   vasoconstriction   vasodilation

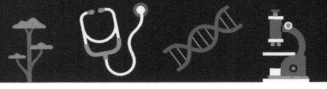

Retrieval

Learn the answers to the questions below then cover the answers column with a piece of paper and write as many as you can. Check and repeat.

	B12 questions	Answers
1	What is the function of the nervous system?	it enables organisms to react to their surroundings and coordinates behaviour
2	What are the two parts of the central nervous system?	brain and spinal cord
3	Why are reflex actions described as rapid and automatic?	they do not involve the conscious part of the brain
4	Why are reflex actions important?	for survival and to prevent damage to the body
5	Give the pathway of a nervous response.	stimulus → receptor → coordinator → effector → response
6	What is a stimulus?	a change in the internal or external environment
7	Name two types of effectors.	muscles and glands
8	Give the function of sensory neurones.	carry impulses from receptors to the CNS
9	Give the function of motor neurones.	carry impulses from the CNS to effectors
10	What is a synapse?	gap between two neurones, allowing impulses to cross
11	Give the function of relay neurones.	carry impulses from sensory neurones to motor neurones
12	What is homeostasis?	maintenance of a constant internal environment
13	Give four internal conditions controlled in homeostasis.	• body temperature • blood glucose concentration • water levels • ion levels
14	Give three things all control systems include.	receptors, coordination centres, and effectors
15	Name some organs that contain receptor cells.	eyes, brain, skin, pancreas
16	Why is homeostasis important?	maintains optimal conditions for cell and organ function, and enzyme activity
17	Where is body temperature monitored and controlled?	thermoregulatory centre in the brain
18	What happens if body temperature is too high?	blood vessels dilate (vasodilation) and sweat is produced
19	What happens if body temperature is too low?	blood vessels constrict (vasoconstriction), sweating stops, and shivering takes place

Put paper here

Now use the questions below to check your knowledge from previous chapters.

Previous questions

Answers

	Question	Answer
1	Define the term cellular respiration.	reaction that occurs continuously in the mitochondria of living cells to release energy from glucose
2	What factors affect the rate of decay by decomposers?	oxygen levels, moisture levels, temperature
3	How is lactic acid removed from the body?	lactic acid in muscles → transported by blood to the liver → lactic acid converted back to glucose
4	How does the body supply the muscles with more oxygenated blood during exercise?	heart rate, breathing rate, and breath volume increase
5	Describe how light intensity affects the rate of photosynthesis.	increasing light intensity increases the rate of photosynthesis until another factor becomes limiting
6	How does acid rain affect the environment?	kills trees and increases the acidity of waterways, which can harm organisms present
7	What causes eutrophication?	untreated sewage or fertilisers being washed into lakes/rivers, increasing mineral concentrations

Put paper here

Put paper here

Put paper here

Working Scientifically

Practise your working scientifically skills using the worked example and practice questions below.

Collecting data

Results tables should have the following features:

- column heading, including units of measurement when relevant
- independent variable in the left-hand column
- values of the independent variable listed from smallest to largest
- dependent variable in the right-hand column(s) (a separate column should be added for each repeat measurement)
- a final column to calculate the mean when relevant
- measurements within a column should be recorded to a consistent number of decimal places
- measurements should not be smaller than the precision of the measuring instrument

Worked example

Construct a results table for the following investigation:

A group of students investigated the effect of temperature on the rate of photosynthesis by calculating the number of bubbles produced per minute by a pond plant. The range of temperatures was 10 °C to 50 °C, in 10 °C increments. They repeated the experiment three times.

	Number of bubbles per minute			
Temperature in °C	**1st result**	**2nd result**	**3rd result**	**Mean**
10				
20				
30				
40				
50				

Practice

A student investigates how caffeine affects a person's reaction time. They ask a volunteer to consume different volumes of coffee (0 cm^3 to 200 cm^3, in 50 cm^3 intervals), before measuring their reaction time using a phone app.

They complete three repeats for each result. Construct a results table to record this data.

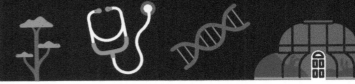
Exam-style questions

01   The nervous system allows humans to respond to their surroundings. **Figure 1** shows two different nerve pathways joining a big toe to the central nervous system. A touch to the big toe causes an impulse to travel through the nerve pathway.

Figure 1

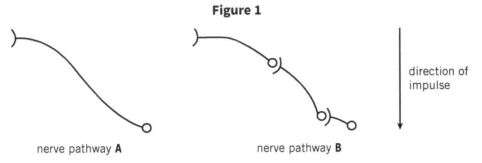

direction of impulse

nerve pathway **A**   nerve pathway **B**

01.1   Identify the type of neurone involved in these pathways.
        Choose **one** answer.   **[1 mark]**

sensory neurone   motor neurone   relay neurone

01.2   Nerve pathway **A** is 90 cm long. A nerve impulse travels along this pathway at 76 m/s.

        Calculate how long it takes for the nerve impulse to travel the length of the pathway.

        Give your answer to **two** significant figures.   **[3 marks]**

Exam Tips

The equation you need for this question is more often found in maths or physics, but there's no reason a question like this can't come up in biology.

Watch out for the non-standard units here.

_____

01.3   Nerve pathways **A** and **B** are the same total length. The nerve impulse takes longer to travel along pathway **B** than pathway **A**. Use your knowledge and information in **Figure 2** to explain why.   **[4 marks]**

Exam Tip

Look at the differences in structure.

_____

_____

_____

_____

_____

02 To keep an organism healthy both the nervous system and the hormonal system need to work together.

02.1 Define the term homeostasis. **[1 mark]**

_____

_____

02.2 One purpose of homeostasis is to provide optimal conditions for enzymes to work in.

Name **two** factors that can affect the rate of enzyme action. **[2 marks]**

1 _____

2 _____

02.3 Homeostasis involves a number of automatic control systems.

Explain why they are described as automatic systems. **[1 mark]**

_____

_____

02.4 Describe the main components of a control system. **[6 marks]**

_____

_____

_____

_____

_____

_____

_____

_____

_____

_____

03 Reflex actions are an important part of the nervous system.

03.1 Explain why the reflex arc is essential for survival. **[1 mark]**

03.2 Given **one** example of a body function that can be controlled both consciously and unconsciously. **[1 mark]**

03.3 Describe and explain the reflex action that would occur if you placed your hand on a hot radiator. **[6 marks]**

04 A student carried out an investigation to determine whether a person's reaction time was quicker with their dominant hand.

The student used the following steps:

1 The student investigator (Student **A**) held a ruler just above a second student's hand (Student **B**).

2 Student **A** let go of the ruler. Student **B** caught it as quickly as possible.

3 The experiment was then repeated with Student **B**'s opposite hand.

Exam Tip

Your dominant hand is the one you write with.

04.1 Identify the dependent variable in this investigation. **[1 mark]**

04.2 Identify **one** variable that should be controlled in this investigation. **[1 mark]**

04.3 Student **A** chose ten right-handed students to test. The results are shown in **Table 1**.

Table 1

	Student	1	2	3	4	5	6	7	8	9	10	Mean
Reaction time in s	Left hand	0.25	0.23	0.39	0.26	0.27	0.22	0.25	0.27	0.25	0.25	
	Right hand	0.28	0.24	0.25	0.27	0.26	0.22	0.26	0.24	0.23	0.25	0.25

Identify the anomalous result from the experiment. **[1 mark]**

04.4 Complete **Table 1** by calculating the mean reaction time for the left hand results. **[1 mark]**

Exam Tip

Whenever you're asked to calculate a mean, look out for any anomalous results and exclude them.

04.5 Student **A** reached the following conclusion: 'Right-handed people's reaction times are more rapid when using their dominant (right) hand.'

Explain the extent to which you agree or disagree with this conclusion. **[3 marks]**

04.6 Which type of reaction time did the experiment measure?

Choose **one** answer. **[1 mark]**

reflex reaction time

voluntary reaction time

Exam Tip

Think about examples of reflexes.

04.7 Give a reason for your answer to **04.6**. **[1 mark]**

04.8 The fastest measured reaction time of a human is approximately 0.1 s. Explain why a person's reaction time cannot be more rapid than this. **[3 marks]**

05 It is important that the body's core temperature remains constant.

Exam Tip

To help with this question imagine the pathway that a signal takes – is it the same the whole way?

05.1 Give the name of the process which maintains constant internal conditions inside the body. **[1 mark]**

05.2 Name **one** organ that contains temperature receptors. **[1 mark]**

05.3 Explain **two** changes that occur in the skin when you become too hot, to help reduce body temperature. **[4 marks]**

06 Automatic control systems in the body have three main components.

06.1 Complete the following flow chart showing the components of an automatic control system.

receptors ⟶ _____ ⟶ effectors **[1 mark]**

06.2 Receptors respond to stimuli. Complete **Table 2**, which shows examples of organs and the stimuli they detect. **[2 marks]**

Table 2

Organ	Receptors
eye	light
skin	
	blood glucose concentration

06.3 Explain why the control of body temperature is essential for enzyme reactions. **[4 marks]**

07 A student shouted loudly behind their friend. The friend jumped in reaction to the noise.

Explain in detail how the friend responded to the noise through the actions of their nervous system. **[6 marks]**

> (!) **Exam Tip**
>
> You need to include the path the signal took and what happened at each stage.

08 As a car driver approached a set of traffic lights, the lights turned red. This caused the driver to press the brake pedal with their foot, slowing the car down.

08.1 In this response, what is the changing traffic light? Choose **one** answer. **[1 mark]**

the coordinator   the effector   the receptor   the stimulus

08.2 In this response, what is the coordination centre? Choose **one** answer. **[1 mark]**

the eye   the brain   a synapse   the spinal cord

08.3 Whilst the driver is waiting at the traffic lights, an insect flies close to their eye. The driver's eye closes in response.

Explain how the driver's response to the insect is different to their response to the changing traffic lights. **[3 marks]**

09 The nervous system controls the body's response to changes in its external environment.

09.1 Complete the following flow chart to name the main steps in a nervous response. **[1 mark]**

stimulus ⟶ _____ ⟶ sensory neurone ⟶
CNS ⟶ motor neurone ⟶ _____

09.2 Name the part of the nervous system that the vertebral column protects. **[1 mark]**

09.3 Describe **two** differences between a motor neurone and a sensory neurone. **[2 marks]**

09.4 Many sports require good reactions. In relation to the nervous system, explain what reaction time depends on. **[2 marks]**

10 If a person needs to have a dental procedure, such as a filling, a dentist will often inject the gum with an anaesthetic so the person does not feel any pain. Procaine is an example of an anaesthetic drug used by a dentist. **Figure 2** shows what happens at one of the synapses in your gum.

Figure 2

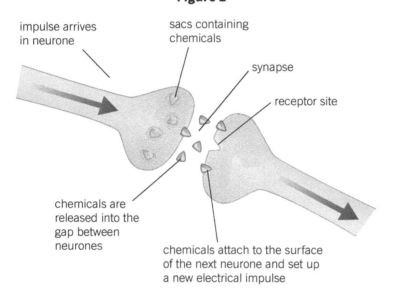

10.1 Name the type of neurone that transmits the electrical impulse from the pain receptor. **[1 mark]**

10.2 Procaine is a competitive inhibitor. It is very similar to the chemical that is released between neurones. Using your own knowledge and information from **Figure 2**, suggest how the drug procaine may work. **[6 marks]**

11 Multiple sclerosis (MS) is a disease that affects the nervous system. The disease causes the fatty layer surrounding the axon of a neurone to become damaged.

11.1 Name the lipid layer that surrounds the axon. **[1 mark]**

11.2 Symptoms of MS vary between individuals, but often the disease causes difficulty in movement and feelings of numbness or tingling. Suggest, with reasons, why people with MS experience these symptoms. **[6 marks]**

12 The small intestine is lined with millions of villi.

12.1 Describe **three** ways villi are adapted to their function. **[3 marks]**

12.2 Glucose is absorbed into the small intestine by active transport. Explain what is meant by active transport. **[2 marks]**

12.3 Amoeba are organisms that are one cell thick. Explain why they do not need specialised exchange surfaces. **[2 marks]**

13 A human's body temperature remains almost constant despite changes in external temperatures. When you walk outside on a cold day, your body is able to maintain an internal temperature of 37 °C.

13.1 Suggest what would happen if your body temperature dropped by 2 °C. **[2 marks]**

13.2 Explain how the body would detect and respond to a decrease in body temperature. **[6 marks]**

> **! Exam Tip**
> Think about the molecules needed to keep the body's chemical reactions happening.

13.3 If the air is dry, an athlete can run for two hours in temperatures of 35 °C without overheating. However, in humid conditions, if the temperature rises above 35 °C, the athlete's body will overheat. Suggest an explanation for the athlete overheating in humid conditions. **[3 marks]**

14 Leaves are specially adapted for photosynthesis.

14.1 Write the balanced chemical equation for photosynthesis. **[2 marks]**

14.2 Explain **two** ways in which leaves are adapted to maximise the absorption of sunlight. **[4 marks]**

14.3 Stomata play an important role in the movement of gases involved in photosynthesis.

Compare and explain the net movement of carbon dioxide through the stomata at midday and midnight. **[6 marks]**

> **! Exam Tip**
> At midday and midnight different chemical reactions are happening. How do these differ in relation to carbon dioxide?

14.4 Stomata are usually found on a leaf's lower surface. This is not the case for many aquatic plants, such as water lilies, whose leaves float on the surface of the water.

Explain why the stomata of many aquatic plants are found on the upper surface of the leaf. **[4 marks]**

B13 Hormonal coordination

Human endocrine system

The **endocrine system** is composed of glands that secrete chemicals called **hormones** into the bloodstream.

The blood carries hormones to a target organ, where an effect is produced.

Compared to the nervous system, the effects caused by the endocrine system are usually slower but act for longer and over a larger area.

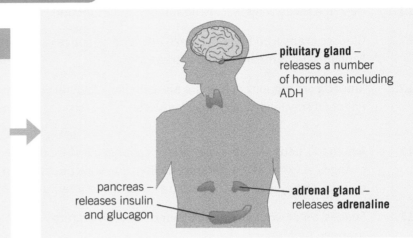

pituitary gland – releases a number of hormones including ADH

pancreas – releases insulin and glucagon

adrenal gland – releases **adrenaline**

Control of blood glucose levels

Blood glucose (sugar) concentration is monitored and controlled by the **pancreas**. Receptor cells are present, which detect glucose levels.

This is an example of **negative feedback** control, as the pancreas switches production between the hormones **insulin** and **glucagon** to control blood glucose levels.

Diabetes

Diabetes is a disease in which the body cannot either produce or respond to insulin, leading to uncontrolled blood glucose concentrations.

insulin released — pancreas — glucagon released

blood glucose too high

blood glucose too low

- glucose moves from the blood into cells
- excess glucose converted to glycogen in the liver and muscle cells for storage

blood glucose falls

normal level of blood glucose

blood glucose rises

- glycogen converted into glucose and released into the blood
- amino acids/fats are broken down

Type 1 diabetes	Type 2 diabetes
early onset	usually later onset, obesity is a risk factor
pancreas stops producing sufficient insulin	body doesn't respond to the insulin produced
commonly treated through insulin injections, also diet control and exercise	commonly treated through a carbohydrate-controlled diet and exercise, and drugs that help the cells respond to insulin

🔑 Key Terms

Make sure you can write a definition for these key terms.

ADH   adrenal gland   adrenaline   diabetes   endocrine system   glucagon   hormone
insulin   kidney tubule   negative feedback   pancreas   pituitary gland   urea   urine

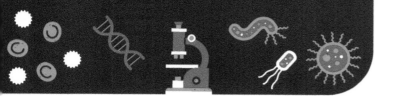

Maintaining water balance

Water leaves the body through the lungs during exhalation, and water, ions, and **urea** are lost from the skin in sweat. The body has no control over these losses.

Excess water, ions, and urea are removed by the kidneys in **urine**. Receptors in the brain detect the concentration of water in the blood and send messages to the kidney to control how much water is removed from the body.

· ·

Levels of water in the body must be balanced because cells do not function efficiently if they lose or gain too much water.

In the kidney:

- the blood is filtered
- all of the glucose is reabsorbed
- ions and water needed by the body are reabsorbed – this is known as selective reabsorption
- urea, excess ions and excess water are released as urine.

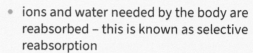

Role of ADH

The water level in the blood is controlled by the hormone **ADH**, which affects the amount of water absorbed by the **kidney tubules**.

This is a **negative feedback** cycle. Negative feedback systems work to maintain a steady state. Another example of negative feedback in the body is the control of body temperature.

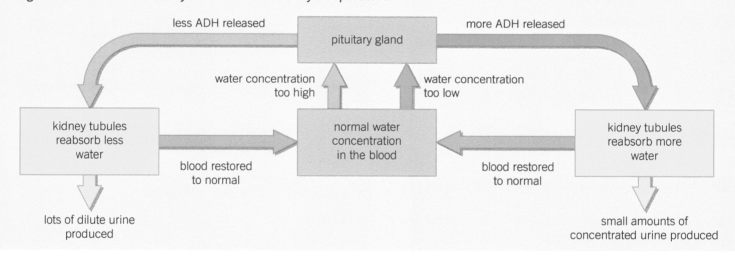

Waste products

The liver has three important roles in dealing with waste:
1. The digestion of proteins from food results in excess amino acids, which need to be excreted safely. These amino acids are deaminated in the liver to form ammonia. Ammonia is toxic, so it is immediately converted to urea for safe excretion.
2. Poisonous substances are detoxified and the breakdown products are excreted in the urine, via the kidneys.
3. Old blood cells are broken down and the iron is stored.

Retrieval

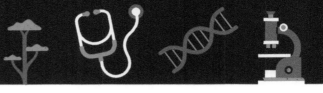

Learn the answers to the questions below then cover the answers column with
a piece of paper and write as many as you can. Check and repeat.

B13 questions

Answers

	B13 questions		Answers
1	What is the endocrine system?		system of glands that secrete hormones into the bloodstream
2	How do the effects of the endocrine system compare to those of the nervous system?		endocrine system effects are slower but act for longer over a larger area
3	Where is the pituitary gland located?	Put paper here	brain
4	Which organ monitors and controls blood glucose concentration?		pancreas
5	Which hormones interact to regulate blood glucose levels?		insulin and glucagon
6	What does insulin do?	Put paper here	causes glucose to move from the blood into the cells, and excess glucose to be stored as glycogen
7	What does glucagon do?		causes glycogen to be converted into glucose and released into the blood
8	What is the cause of Type 1 diabetes?	Put paper here	pancreas produces insufficient insulin
9	What is the cause of Type 2 diabetes?		body cells no longer respond to insulin
10	How is Type 1 diabetes treated?		careful diet, exercise, injecting insulin
11	How is Type 2 diabetes treated?	Put paper here	careful diet, exercise, and drugs that help cells respond to insulin
12	What is the function of the kidneys?		filter and reabsorb useful substances from the blood, and produce urine to excrete excess water, ions, and urea
13	How are excess amino acids excreted from the body?	Put paper here	deaminated to form ammonia in the liver, ammonia is converted to urea and excreted
14	Which hormone controls the water level in the body?		ADH
15	Where is ADH released?		from the pituitary gland
16	What happens if blood water levels are too low?		more ADH is released causing kidneys to absorb more water; concentrated urine produced
17	What happens if blood water levels are too high?		less ADH is released causing kidneys to absorb less water; dilute urine produced

Now use the questions below to check your knowledge from previous chapters.

B13

Previous questions | Answers

	Previous questions		Answers
1	Why are reflex actions described as rapid and automatic?		they do not involve the conscious part of the brain
2	What are the two parts of the central nervous system?	*Put paper here*	brain and spinal cord
3	Why are limiting factors important in the economics of growing plants in greenhouses?		greenhouses need to produce the maximum rate of photosynthesis whilst making profit
4	Give the limiting factors of photosynthesis.	*Put paper here*	temperature, carbon dioxide concentration, light intensity, and amount of chlorophyll
5	Write the balanced symbol equation for aerobic respiration.		$C_6H_{12}O_6 + 6O_2 \rightarrow 6CO_2 + 6H_2O$
6	Give the pathway of a nervous response.	*Put paper here*	stimulus $\rightarrow$ receptor $\rightarrow$ coordinator $\rightarrow$ effector $\rightarrow$ response
7	What is oxygen debt?	*Put paper here*	amount of oxygen the body needs after exercise to react with the accumulated lactic acid and remove it from cells

Working Scientifically

Practise your working scientifically skills using the worked example and practice questions below.

Identifying trends

Lines of best fit are often added to graphs to identify trends. Common trends are:

- A straight line of best fit sloping upwards: As the independent variable increases, the dependent variable increases.

- A straight line of best fit sloping upwards, passing through the origin: The independent variable is directly proportional to the dependent variable. Doubling the independent variable doubles the dependent variable.

- A straight line of best fit sloping downwards: As the independent variable increases, the dependent variable decreases.

If the line of best fit is curved, describe the trends shown in different places.

Worked example

Using the graph below, describe how temperature affects the rate of an enzyme-controlled reaction.

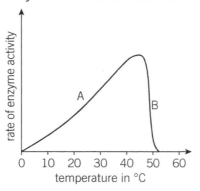

Between 0 and 45 °C, as the temperature increases the rate of enzyme activity increases.

The maximum rate of enzyme activity is at 45 °C.

Above 45 °C an increase in temperature causes the rate of enzyme activity to decrease rapidly.

At or above 52 °C the rate of enzyme activity drops to zero.

Practice

Describe the trends shown in the following graph.

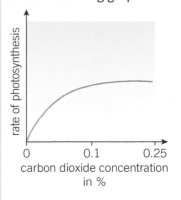

 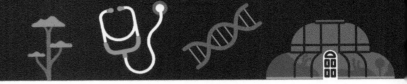

Exam-style questions

01 Controlling blood glucose levels in the human body is an example of homeostasis.

01.1 Define the term homeostasis. **[1 mark]**

_____

_____

01.2 The flow chart in **Figure 1** shows how the body responds when the blood glucose level becomes too high or too low.

Figure 1

```
pancreas          →    liver converts
produces A             B to C
   ↑                        ↓
blood sugar            blood sugar
increases              decreases
   ↑                        ↓
liver converts    ←    pancreas
C to B                 produces D
```

Name substances **A**, **B**, **C**, and **D**. **[4 marks]**

A _____

B _____

C _____

D _____

> **! Exam Tip**
>
> These words are all very similar so take extra care.
>
> Spelling could be the key to showing the examiner what you know, and making it clear that you know the difference between the substances.

01.3 A diabetic and a non-diabetic volunteer took part in a study of blood glucose levels. **Table 1** shows how their blood glucose levels varied over time. They both ate breakfast at 08:00.

Table 1

Time	Blood sugar levels in mg per litre of blood	
	Person A	Person B
07:00	80	75
08:00	75	70
09:00	135	340
10:00	100	280
11:00	85	235
12:00	75	200

Identify and explain which volunteer was diabetic and which volunteer was non-diabetic. **[3 marks]**

_____

_____

_____

01.4 Calculate the maximum rate of change of blood glucose concentration for Person **B** in mg per litre per minute. **[3 marks]**

_____ mg per litre per minute

01.5 Estimate the time at which Person **B**'s blood glucose concentration will return to the pre-meal level. **[2 marks]**

_____

_____

_____

02 The kidney plays an important role in the control of water levels through the production of urine.

02.1 Other than through urine, name **one** way water is lost from the body. **[1 mark]**

_____

_____

02.2 Identify the correct statement below to explain what happens when blood water levels are too low. **[1 mark]**

pituitary gland releases more ADH → kidney tubules reabsorb more water → concentrated urine produced ☐

pituitary gland releases more ADH → kidney tubules reabsorb less water → dilute urine produced ☐

pituitary gland releases less ADH → kidney tubules reabsorb more water → dilute urine produced ☐

pituitary gland releases less ADH → kidney tubules reabsorb less water → concentrated urine produced ☐

02.3 Explain how the kidney and liver work together to safely remove toxins from the body. **[4 marks]**

_____

_____

_____

_____

_____

03 Blood glucose levels in the body are constantly controlled.

03.1 Explain why blood glucose levels need to be maintained at a constant level. **[3 marks]**

03.2 People with diabetes have difficulty controlling their blood glucose levels. There are two main types of diabetes – Type 1 and Type 2. Describe the differences between Type 1 and Type 2 diabetes.

[4 marks]

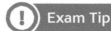 **Exam Tip**

This question is just about the differences – don't waste time writing about similarities.

03.3 Compare the available treatments for Type 1 and Type 2 diabetes. **[4 marks]**

03.4 Suggest **two** actions that a government could take to reduce the number of new cases of diabetes. **[2 marks]**

04 Hormones play an important role in homeostasis.

04.1 Identify the hormone that is likely to increase after consuming a chocolate bar. Choose **one** answer. **[1 mark]**

adrenaline   insulin   glucagon   thyroxine

 Exam Tip

Start by crossing out any you know are wrong.

04.2 Explain your answer to **04.1**. **[4 marks]**

04.3 Many systems in homeostasis rely on negative feedback. Describe how a negative feedback system works. **[3 marks]**

05 Water and ion levels are two conditions that are kept constant in the body.

05.1 Name **one** other internal condition that must be carefully controlled. **[1 mark]**

05.2 Describe the function of the kidney in homeostasis. **[4 marks]**

05.3 The kidney uses a negative feedback system involving the hormone ADH to control water levels in the body. Describe how a negative feedback system works. **[3 marks]**

 Exam Tip

This question is not asking you to describe how ADH controls body water levels. You are being asked to describe the features of a negative feedback system that are present in all systems.

06 **Figure 2** shows how the blood glucose concentration varies in a healthy person and in a person with Type 1 diabetes who treats themselves with insulin injections.

Figure 2

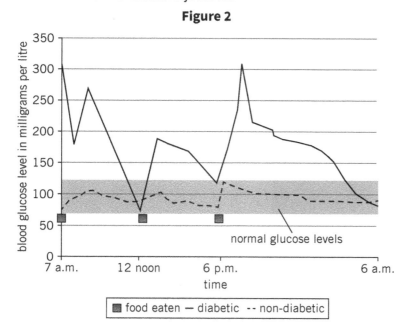

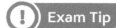

06.1 Describe why a person with Type 1 diabetes cannot control their blood glucose concentration. **[1 mark]**

06.2 Compare the effect of eating a meal on a healthy person with the effect on a person who has Type 1 diabetes. **[2 marks]**

Exam Tip

Look at the differences between the two lines in **Figure 2**.

06.3 Using information from **Figure 2**, suggest **one** time at which the person with Type 1 diabetes injected insulin. **[1 mark]**

06.4 Calculate the percentage change in blood glucose concentration immediately following the midday meal for a person with Type 1 diabetes. **[2 marks]**

06.5 Discuss the potential for a cure for Type 1 diabetes. **[5 marks]**

07 Blood glucose levels are maintained in a healthy person by the action of insulin and glucagon.

07.1 Name the organ that produces these hormones. **[1 mark]**

07.2 Explain how blood glucose levels are maintained in a healthy person by the action of insulin and glucagon. **[6 marks]**

Exam Tip

Use data in your answer. You'll have to do some calculations to provide evidence for your comparison.

07.3 In 2015, approximately 3.5 million people in the UK were living with diabetes from a total population of 65 million. 9.4% of the US population has diabetes. Compare the rates of diabetes in the UK and the US. **[3 marks]**

08 The body responds to changes in its internal and external environment using the endocrine and nervous systems.

08.1 Write down the name given to a change that occurs in a person's environment. **[1 mark]**

08.2 When it is very hot the body loses lots of water. Name the hormone that is released in response to low water levels in the blood. **[1 mark]**

Exam Tip

Use named hormones as examples in your answer.

08.3 Compare the actions of hormones in the endocrine system to nerves in the nervous system. **[6 marks]**

09 The kidney is responsible for removing some waste materials from the blood.

09.1 Name **one** waste product it removes. **[1 mark]**

09.2 **Table 2** shows the concentrations of plasma protein and glucose present in the blood entering the kidney, and in the urine it produces.

Table 2

Substance	Blood concentration in mg/ml	Urine concentration in mg/ml
plasma protein	700	0
glucose	100	0

Exam Tip

You need to use numbers and examples from the table in your answer.

Explain the differences between the blood and urine concentrations of protein and glucose. **[4 marks]**

09.3 The water content of urine produced throughout the day can vary. On a hot day, if a person does not drink a lot of water their urine contains very little water. Explain how the kidney controls the water content of the urine it produces on a hot day. **[4 marks]**

09.4 Diabetes can lead to kidney failure. Severe cases of kidney failure can lead to death. Explain **one** reason why severe kidney failure can lead to death. **[2 marks]**

! **Exam Tip**

09.3 is specific to hot days, so a general answer on the control of water content in the urine will not get full marks.

10 Chronic kidney disease (CKD) reduces kidney function, leading to a build-up of poisonous waste products in the body. Kidney dialysis is used for those living with CKD to reproduce kidney function. **Figure 3** shows the dialysis process.

Figure 3

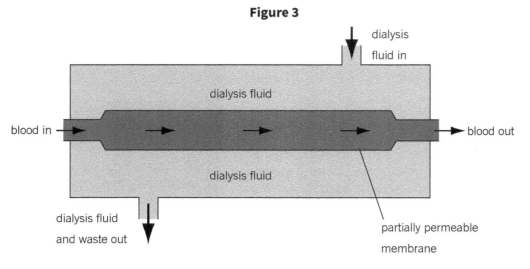

The main steps in kidney dialysis are described below:

1 The patient's blood is taken from vessels in the arm and pumped into the dialysis machine.

2 Within the machine, the patient's blood is passed close to dialysis fluid. The blood and dialysis fluid are separated by a partially permeable membrane.

3 The patient's blood is then returned to their body.

Explain why dialysis fluid contains:

- a glucose concentration similar to the normal level in the blood
- a concentration of ions similar to that found in normal blood plasma
- no urea. **[6 marks]**

11 If you touch a hot saucepan, your body responds rapidly using a reflex response.

11.1 Identify the correct order of neurones in a reflex arc. Choose **one** answer. **[1 mark]**

stimulus → sensory neurone → relay neurone → motor neurone → effector

stimulus → motor neurone → relay neurone → sensory neurone → effector

stimulus → sensory neurone → motor neurone → relay neurone → effector

stimulus → relay neurone → sensory neurone → motor neurone → effector

11.2 The average speed at which an impulse travels through this pathway is 65.5 m/s. The length of the pathway from the receptor cell in a person's finger to the muscle in the arm is 1.4 m. Calculate the time it takes for the impulse to travel along this reflex arc. **[2 marks]**

11.3 Explain **two** ways a sensory neurone is adapted to its function. **[2 marks]**

11.4 Coordination in the body can be brought about by nervous or hormonal responses. Discuss the similarities and differences between nervous and hormonal coordination in the body. **[4 marks]**

> **! Exam Tip**
>
> There are no equations that include this specifically for biology but you are expected to have a good general knowledge of the equations you need for maths.

12 There is an old English saying: 'the child who picks a dandelion will wet their bed before the day is out'. Scientists have discovered that there is some truth in this belief. Dandelion leaves contain a natural diuretic that increases urine production in the kidney. Suggest why eating dandelion leaves results in more urine being produced by the body. **[5 marks]**

13 Sucrose is an example of a carbohydrate molecule. It is made when two simple sugars, glucose and fructose, bind together.

13.1 Explain why sucrose is classified as a carbohydrate molecule. **[1 mark]**

13.2 Enzymes are used to make some soft-centred chocolates. An enzyme called invertase will catalyse the breakdown of sucrose into glucose and fructose. This causes chocolate to become softer and sweeter to the taste. Explain why invertase is an example of a catalyst. **[2 marks]**

> **! Exam Tip**
>
> Don't worry if you've never heard of this enzyme before, just apply what you know about the action of other enzymes to this example.

13.3 Use the lock and key model to explain why invertase is only able to catalyse the breakdown of sucrose. **[3 marks]**

13.4 Suggest and explain **one** possible health benefit of adding invertase to chocolate. **[2 marks]**

Knowledge

Types of animal behaviour

Behaviour is an action made in response to a stimulus that modifies the relationship between the organism and the environment.

Some types of behaviour are **innate** whereas others are learnt.

Innate behaviour

Innate behaviour is not learnt. These behaviours result from specific nerve pathways formed as an embryo develops; an example is the ability of a spider to build a web.

Learned behaviours

Learned behaviours include:
- **imprinting** – an animal attaches itself emotionally to a large organism (normally the parent) at a very early stage in life; this enables an animal to recognise other animals of the same species
- **habituation** – this occurs when a stimulus is repeated many times and nothing occurs; eventually the animal stops responding to this stimulus
- **classic conditioning** – this takes place when an animal learns to associate an existing unconditioned reflex with a new stimulus; demonstrated through the 'Pavlov's dogs' experiment
- **operant conditioning** (trial and error) – an animal repeats a behaviour several times; if something good occurs each time, it repeats the behaviour; if something bad occurs, it stops.

Using operant conditioning

Humans use operant conditioning when training animals. Desirable behaviour is rewarded with treats/attention, whilst undesirable behaviour is ignored.

This technique is used when training sniffer dogs to locate drugs and explosives, and in training police horses to remain calm when managing crowds.

Behaviours for sexual reproduction

Sexual reproduction requires an animal to find and select a mate. To give their offspring the best chance of survival, animals (normally females) need to select the best quality mate to pass their genetic material on to the next generation.

Courtship behaviours

Courtship behaviours have evolved to advertise the quality of a male as a potential mate. These include:
- male fighting
- singing
- displaying dramatic feathers or markings
- bringing food gifts
- building nests.

Mating behaviours

Animals have different mating strategies, including:
- a mate for life (rare), e.g., swan
- having several mates over a life time, e.g., lions
- having a mate for a breeding season, e.g., garden birds
- having several mates over one breeding season, e.g., wild dogs.

For example, some ducks use courtship display to select their mate for the breeding season.

Tail-shaking   Bill-shaking   Grunt-whistling   Head-flicking

Nod-swimming   Raising head/tail

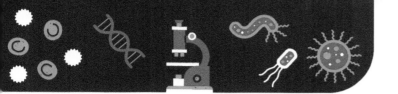

Methods of communication

Animals use a variety of methods to communicate, including sound signals, chemical signals, and visual signals.

Sound signals

To communicate using sound, animals need to make, hear, and interpret sounds. For example, humans shape sounds into speech, and crickets rub body parts.

Different animals can hear sounds in different frequency ranges. For example, bats use echolocation using ultrasonic sounds.

Sounds are used to communicate complex emotions, mark territories, find mates, and warn off rivals.

Visual signals

Visual cues can indicate an animal's mood, whether they are hungry, sleepy, playful, or aggressive. They can often be read by more than one species.

Visual signals are often linked to selecting a mate, reproduction, and protecting offspring.

They can also warn of danger, such as the black and yellow colouring of a bee.

Chemical signals

These include scents you are aware of and chemicals (pheromones) that you cannot consciously smell but affect your behaviour.

Chemical signals are used:

- to identify members of the same species and individuals within the species
- to indicate fertility
- to show dominance in a group
- in defence, by releasing unpleasant smelling/tasting substances.

Parental care

Some animals have developed special behaviours for raising their young. This can be a successful evolutionary strategy as it increases the chance of survival of the offspring, and it increases the chance of parental genes being passed on to the next generation.

Disadvantages

In some cases parental care may involve risks to the parents.

It uses up time and resources and can make the parents vulnerable to starvation and predators.

Examples of parental care

Examples include:

- mouthbrooding
- egg-laying
- incubation.

Mammals have very high levels of parental care – offspring develop fully in the womb, are born in very small numbers, and are reared on milk, alongside being taught how to behave and fend for themselves.

 **Key Terms**

Make sure you can write a definition for these key terms.

behaviour	classic conditioning	courtship behaviour	habituation
	imprinting	innate	operant conditioning

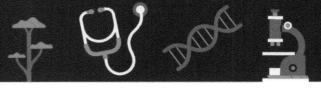

Learn the answers to the questions below, then cover the answers column with a piece of paper and write as many as you can. Check and repeat.

B14 questions

Answers

	Question	Answer
1	What is behaviour?	an action made in response to a stimulus that modifies the relationship between the organism and the environment
2	What is innate behaviour?	instinctive behaviour that is not learnt but present from birth
3	What are the different types of learnt behaviour?	imprinting, habituation, classic conditioning, and operant conditioning
4	What is imprinting?	when an animal attaches itself emotionally to a large organism (normally the parent) at a very early stage in life
5	What is habituation?	when an animal stops responding to a particular stimulus
6	What is classic conditioning?	when an animal learns to associate an existing unconditioned reflex with a new stimulus
7	What is operant conditioning?	learning through trial and error: if something good happens, the behaviour is repeated
8	Give two examples of ways humans use conditioned captive animals.	sniffer dogs and police horses
9	What are courtship behaviours?	behaviours that advertise the quality of a male as a potential mate
10	Give some examples of courtship behaviours.	male fighting, singing, displaying dramatic markings, bringing food gifts, building nests
11	Give some examples of mating strategies.	having a mate for life, or for one breeding season; having several mates over a life time, or over one breeding season
12	Why is parental care important?	it significantly increases the survival chances of the offspring and the chance of parental genes being passed on to the next generation
13	Give some examples of parental care.	mouthbrooding, egg-laying and incubation, giving birth to live young, rearing on milk
14	What are the risks to parents of parental care?	can make them vulnerable to predators and starvation
15	How do animals communicate?	through sound, visual, and chemical signals
16	Give some uses of sound signals.	navigation, communicate complex emotions, mark territories, find mates, warn off rivals
17	Give some uses of visual signals.	to show an animal's mood, to select a mate, to warn of danger
18	Give some uses of chemical signals.	to identify members of the same species, to indicate fertility, to communicate dominance

Put paper here

Now use the questions below to check your knowledge from previous chapters.

Previous questions — Answers

	Previous questions	Answers
1	Why are enzymes described as specific?	each enzyme only catalyses a specific reaction, because the active site only fits together with certain substrates (like a lock and key)
2	How is the palisade mesophyll adapted for its function?	tightly packed cells with lots of chloroplasts to absorb as much light as possible for photosynthesis
3	What is the function of a root hair cell?	absorbs minerals and water from the soil
4	What is a stimulus?	a change in the internal or external environment
5	What is the function of the phloem?	transport dissolved sugars from the leaves to the rest of the plant
6	Why is homeostasis important?	maintains optimal conditions for cell and organ function, and enzyme activity
7	What is the purpose of transpiration?	• provides water to keep cells turgid • provides water to cells for photosynthesis • transports mineral ions to leaves
8	Describe the effect of pH on enzyme activity.	different enzymes have a different optimum pH at which their activity is greatest – at a pH much lower or higher than this, enzyme activity decreases and stops

Put paper here Put paper here Put paper here Put paper here

Working Scientifically

Practise your working scientifically skills using the worked example and practice questions below.

Evaluating an investigation – confidence in data

When commenting on the confidence you have in a conclusion, you should consider some or all of the following aspects:

- Repeatability – data is repeatable when, using the same method and equipment, results are generated that are very close to each other (have a small spread). Repeatable results increase the confidence in a conclusion.
- Data with a large spread often indicates the presence of errors – either random or systematic – within results. The greater the number of suspected errors, the lower the confidence in a conclusion.
  - Random errors are caused by unexpected factors beyond your control; for example, the Sun going behind a cloud during a photosynthesis experiment.
  - Systematic errors add a constant margin of error to all results; for example, if a balance reads 0.2 g with no mass upon it, all measured values will be 0.2 g higher than the true value.
- Reproducibility – data is said to be reproducible when similar results are generated by a different person, method, or equipment. Reproducible data increases the confidence in a conclusion.
- Validity – data is valid when all variables, other than the independent and dependent variables, have been controlled effectively. Where data is believed to be invalid, a conclusion should not be formed.

Practice

Look again at the data collected in a Required Practical. How confident are you in the conclusion you formed in your investigation?

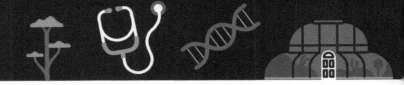

Exam-style questions

01 Behaviour can be innate or learnt.

01.1 Describe the difference between innate and learnt behaviour.

[2 marks]

_____

_____

_____

_____

01.2 Give **one** example of innate behaviour in animals. **[1 mark]**

_____

_____

01.3 Match the example to the type of learnt behaviour it illustrates.

[2 marks]

ducklings following their mother		classic conditioning
dogs salivating when a bell is rung		operant conditioning
horse not running away when people approach		imprinting

> **! Exam Tip**
>
> In match the box style exam questions make sure you use a single line to join one box on the left with one box on the right.

02 A scientist carried out an investigation into habituation response in giant African land snails.

The scientist followed the method below:

1 Collect one snail and place it on a clean, firm surface.

2 Wait for a few minutes until the snail has fully emerged from its shell and is comfortable in its new surroundings.

3 Dampen a cotton wool bud with water.

4 Touch the snail between the eye stalks with the dampened cotton wool bud and immediately start the stopwatch. Observe the snail retract into its shell.

5 Measure the length of time between the touch and the snail fully re-emerging from its shell.

6 Repeat steps 2–5 ten times.

7 Repeat the entire investigation with another snail.

02.1 State **one** ethical consideration that should be followed in this investigation. **[1 mark]**

_____

_____

02.2 State **one** factor that should be controlled in the investigation.

[1 mark]

_____

_____

02.3 Suggest **one** reason why this method is unlikely to generate reproducible data. **[1 mark]**

_____

_____

02.4 The scientist's results for the first snail are shown in **Table 1**:

Table 1

Repeat number	1	2	3	4	5	6	7	8	9	10
Time to emerge in s	125	110	102	88	80	69	55	38	21	8

Describe the pattern shown by the results. **[1 mark]**

_____

_____

02.5 Explain how you would know when habituation has occurred.

[1 mark]

_____

_____

02.6 Suggest a reason why snails may become habituated to being touched on the head in the wild. **[1 mark]**

_____

_____

03 When scientists raise rare birds, they use puppets to feed the birds. This allows them to stay hidden from the chicks.

Figure 1

03.1 Explain the importance of parental care. **[2 marks]**

03.2 Suggest and explain why scientists use puppets when rearing rare birds. **[4 marks]**

04 Animals display several different types of behaviour.

04.1 Identify which of the following is an example of innate behaviour.
Choose **one** answer.   **[1 mark]**

A honey bee doing 'the waggle dance'

A bird not eating a particular berry that made them sick

Learning not to react to a particular stimulus

A dog offering its paw for a treat

04.2 Identify what causes an innate behaviour to develop.
Choose **one** answer.   **[1 mark]**

Repeated stimulus in an animal's environment

The genes an organism inherits from its parents

A combination of the genes an organism inherits with
the organism's environment

A negative response to a particular behaviour

04.3 Using examples, describe **three** ways animals communicate.
                                                        [6 marks]

05 This question is about two investigations into animal behaviour.

Thorndike placed a cat inside a "puzzle box" – the animal could
only escape from the box and gain a food treat by pressing a lever.
He measured how quickly the cat gained its release from the box
on repeated trials. He observed that in early trials the animal
would move around randomly, stumbling on the correct response
by chance. However, with repeated trials the cat would eventually
locate and press the lever within a few seconds of being placed in
the box, allowing them to escape and achieve their food reward.

Pavlov carried out experiments on dogs. In his most famous
experiment, the dogs were exposed to a bell being rung whilst they
waited for food. This was repeated for several days. The food was
then removed and a bell rung without any additional stimulus.
Pavlov found that the dogs salivated whenever a bell was rung.

Explain how the behaviour shown by the cats in Thorndike's
experiment differs from the behaviour shown by dogs in Pavlov's
experiment.   **[6 marks]**

> **! Exam Tip**
>
> Don't let the large block
> of text intimidate you. Use
> highlighters to pull out key
> bits of information and break
> up the text.

06 The peacock in **Figure 2** is displaying courtship behaviour.

Figure 2

06.1 Describe the purpose of courtship behaviour. **[1 mark]**

06.2 State the form of communication being shown in **Figure 2** by the peacock. **[1 mark]**

06.3 Describe **one** other form of courtship behaviour **[1 mark]**

06.4 Explain why courtship behaviour is important. **[2 marks]**

07 Different species of animal give different levels of parental care.

07.1 Select the vertebrate group from the list below that provides the highest level of parental care. **[1 mark]**

fish   mammals   reptiles   birds

07.2 Some animals, blowflies for example, provide no parental care. They lay large numbers of eggs on dead bodies. Discuss the benefits and limitations of this form of reproduction. **[4 marks]**

07.3 Different species of animals have different mating strategies. Using examples, describe **two** mating strategies. **[4 marks]**

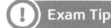

> **(!) Exam Tip**
>
> This is a discuss question so to achieve a high mark your answer needs to refer to both the advantages and disadvantages of this technique.

08 Humans use operant conditioning when teaching animals to perform specific tasks. One example is the use of police sniffer dogs.

08.1 Describe **one** other example of animals being trained to benefit humans. **[1 mark]**

08.2 Explain how operant conditioning could be used to train police dogs to locate drugs. **[4 marks]**

09 Duckweed is commonly found on the surface of ponds.

Table 2 shows the concentrations of some minerals in the duckweed cells and in the surrounding pond water.

Table 2

	Ion concentration in M×10^{-3}		
Sample	Calcium	Sulfate	Potassium
plant cells	12.0	12.0	45.0
pond water	0.9	0.3	0.5

09.1 Identify and explain the process by which the duckweed would take the minerals into its cells. **[3 marks]**

09.2 Duckweed has a number of features that make it highly adapted for living in a pond. One of these features is air pockets inside the leaf called aerenchyma. Suggest how these, in combination with the roots, help the plant to float. **[2 marks]**

09.3 Unlike most plants, the stomata in duckweed are found on the upper surface of the leaves. Suggest why this is an important adaptation. **[2 marks]**

09.4 Explain why controlling transpiration is not very important to duckweed. **[2 marks]**

Knowledge

B15 Preventing and treating disease

Pathogens

Microorganisms that cause disease are called **pathogens**.

There are four types of pathogen – viruses, bacteria, fungi, and protists.

Viruses live and reproduce rapidly inside an organism's cells. This can damage or destroy the cells.

Bacteria reproduce rapidly inside organisms and may produce **toxins** that damage tissues and cause illness.

White blood cells

If a pathogen enters the body, the immune system tries to destroy the pathogen. The function of **white blood cells** is to fight pathogens.

White blood cells fight pathogens in three ways:

- Produce **antitoxins** that bind to the toxins produced by some pathogens (usually bacteria). This neutralises the toxins.
- Produce **antibodies** that target and help to destroy specific pathogens by binding to **antigens** (proteins) on the surface of the pathogen. This leads to immunity from the pathogen.

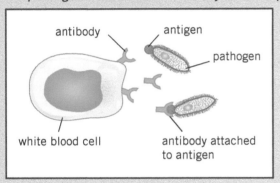

- By phagocytosis.

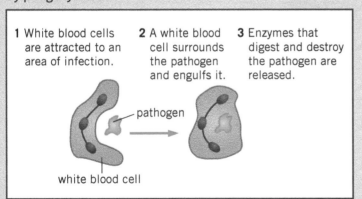

1 White blood cells are attracted to an area of infection.

2 A white blood cell surrounds the pathogen and engulfs it.

3 Enzymes that digest and destroy the pathogen are released.

Vaccination

Vaccination involves injecting small quantities of dead or inactive forms of a pathogen into the body.

This stimulates white blood cells to produce the specific antibodies that destroy the pathogen.

If the same pathogen re-enters the body, the correct antibodies can be produced quickly to prevent infection. This is known as **immunity**.

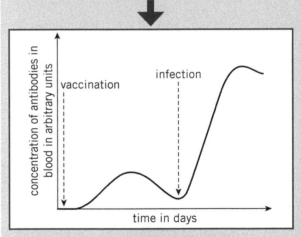

The MMR **vaccine** is used to protect children against measles, mumps, and rubella.

Key Terms **Make sure you can write a definition for these key terms.**

antibiotic	antibiotic resistance	antibody	antigen	antitoxin	bacteria
immunity	pathogen	toxin	vaccination	vaccine	virus	white blood cell

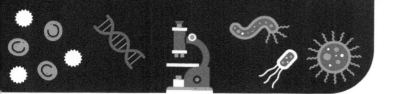
Treating diseases

Antibiotics

- **Antibiotics**, such as penicillin, are medicines that can kill *bacteria* in the body.
- Specific bacteria need to be treated by specific antibiotics.
- Antibiotics have greatly reduced deaths from infectious bacterial diseases, but antibiotic-resistant strains of bacteria are emerging.

Treating viral diseases

- Antibiotics *do not* affect viruses.
- Drugs that kill viruses often damage the body's tissues.
- Painkillers treat the symptoms of viral diseases but do not kill pathogens.

Resistant bacteria

Bacteria can evolve rapidly because they reproduce very quickly.

This has led to many strains of bacteria developing **antibiotic resistance**, through mutations. These new strains, such as MRSA, spread rapidly as people are not immune and there is no effective treatment.

Emergence of antibiotic resistance

The development of new antibiotics is expensive and slow, so is unlikely to keep up with the emergence of new antibiotic-resistant bacteria strains:

To reduce the rise of antibiotic-resistant strains

- doctors should only prescribe antibiotics for serious bacterial infections
- patients should complete their courses of antibiotics so all bacteria are killed and none survive to form resistant strains
- the use of antibiotics in farming and agriculture should be restricted.

Herd immunity

If a large proportion of a population is vaccinated against a disease, the disease is less likely to spread, even if there are some unvaccinated individuals.

 Revision Tip

It's a common misconception that antibiotic resistance arises when people become resistant to a drug. In reality, it is the bacteria that evolve resistance.

Key

■ bacteria not resistant to antibiotic

▭ bacteria with mutation giving antibiotic resistance

antibiotic used to treat disease for the first time

resistant bacteria grow and reproduce

non-resistant bacteria stop growing and reproducing or are killed

antibiotic continues to be used

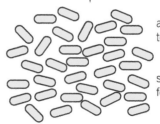

all bacteria now resistant to the antibiotic

selection has occurred for antibiotic resistance

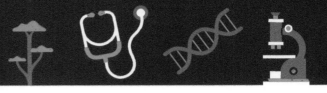

Retrieval

Learn the answers to the questions below then cover the answers column with a piece of paper and write as many as you can. Check and repeat.

B15 questions

Answers

1	What is a pathogen?	microorganism that causes disease
2	Give some examples of pathogens.	bacteria, viruses, protists, and fungi
3	How do bacteria cause disease?	reproduce rapidly inside organisms and may produce toxins
4	How do viruses cause disease?	reproduce rapidly inside an organism's cells damaging or destroying the cells
5	What three functions do white blood cells have?	phagocytosis, producing antibodies, producing antitoxins
6	What happens during phagocytosis?	white blood cell is attracted to the area of infection, engulfs a pathogen, and releases enzymes to digest the pathogen
7	What are antigens?	proteins on the surface of a pathogen
8	Why are antibodies a specific defence?	antibodies have to be the right shape for a pathogen's unique antigens, so they target a specific pathogen
9	What is the function of an antitoxin?	neutralise toxins produced by pathogens by binding to them
10	What does a vaccine contain?	small quantities of a dead or inactive form of a pathogen
11	How does vaccination protect against a specific pathogen?	vaccination stimulates the body to produce antibodies against a specific pathogen – if the same pathogen re-enters the body, white blood cells rapidly produce the correct antibodies
12	What is herd immunity?	when most of a population is vaccinated against a disease, meaning it is less likely to spread
13	What is an antibiotic?	a drug that kills bacteria but not viruses
14	Why can bacteria evolve rapidly?	they reproduce at a fast rate
15	How do antibiotic-resistant strains of bacteria develop?	some bacteria have mutations that make them resistant to antibiotics; when antibiotics are used, these bacteria survive while non-resistant bacteria are killed; eventually, the whole population of bacteria is resistant to the antibiotic

Put paper here

Now use the questions below to check your knowledge from previous chapters.

Previous questions / Answers

	Previous questions	Answers
1	What is an organ?	group of tissues working together to perform a specific function
2	Give three adaptations of the xylem.	• made of dead cells • no end wall between cells • walls strengthened by a chemical called lignin to withstand the pressure of the water
3	What happens if blood water levels are too low?	more ADH is released causing kidneys to absorb more water; concentrated urine produced
4	Give two examples of ways humans use conditioned captive animals.	sniffer dogs and police horses
5	What is the function of the liver in digestion?	produces bile, which neutralises hydrochloric acid from the stomach and emulsifies fat to form small droplets with a large surface area
6	What is the function of guard cells?	control the opening and closing of stomata
7	What happens if body temperature is too low?	blood vessels constrict (vasoconstriction), sweating stops, and shivering takes place

Put paper here

Put paper here

Put paper here

Required Practical Skills

Practise answering questions on the required practicals using the example below. You need to be able to apply your skills and knowledge to other practicals too.

Culturing microorganisms

This practical tests your ability to observe biological changes and responses to environmental factors, in particular the effect of antiseptics and antibiotics on bacterial growth.

You should be familiar with measuring, comparing, and explaining zones of inhibition of bacterial growth. You also need to be able to describe and explain aseptic technique for culturing microorganisms.

Worked example

A student wanted to test how an antiseptic inhibited the growth of bacteria. They soaked three small discs in the antiseptic and placed them on a lawn of bacteria grown on an agar plate. Two days later they measured the diameter of the clear zones around the discs.

The three discs had circular clear zones of 17, 19, and 20 mm in diameter. Calculate the average area of the clear zone for the antiseptic.

Answer:

$$\text{average diameter} = \frac{(17 + 19 + 20)}{3} = 18.67\,\text{mm}$$

$$\text{area of circle} = \pi r^2$$

$$r = \frac{18.67}{2} = 9.3$$

$$\text{area of clear zone} = \pi \times 9.3^2 = 274\,\text{mm}^2$$

Practice

1 Suggest why agar plates must not be airtight when incubating.

2 Describe and explain a modification to this experiment that would make the results more valid.

3 Suggest why the discs should be spread evenly around the plate and not positioned next to each other.

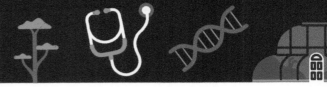

Practice

Exam-style questions

01 Many children are vaccinated against tetanus.

Tetanus is a serious disease caused by a bacterial toxin that affects the nervous system.

01.1 Name the component in the vaccine that will make a child immune to tetanus. **[1 mark]**

_____

01.2 A few weeks after vaccination, a child becomes infected with the bacteria that cause tetanus.

Figure 1 shows the number of tetanus antibodies present in the child's blood.

Use your knowledge of vaccination to complete the graph to show what you think will happen to the number of tetanus antibodies present in the child's blood. **[2 marks]**

Figure 1

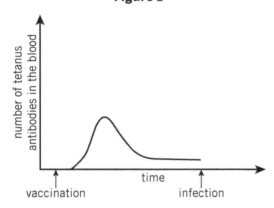

! Exam Tip

Sometimes the scale of the graph can give you a clue.

01.3 Alongside tetanus, mumps is another disease for which vaccination is available.

Explain the advantages of vaccinating a large proportion of the population against mumps. **[2 marks]**

_____

_____

_____

! Exam Tip

Don't waste time writing down anything that isn't an advantage.

01.4 Another vaccination offers protection against the bacteria that cause some strains of meningitis.

Explain why a person who has only received vaccinations against tetanus and mumps would not have protection against meningitis. **[3 marks]**

_____

_____

_____

_____

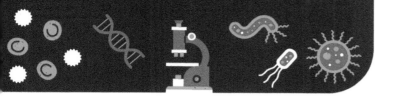

02 *Streptococcus pyogenes* is a bacterium that can cause an infection of the upper respiratory tract. This is an example of a communicable disease.

02.1 Scientists tested the ability of two antiseptics to kill *S. pyogenes* bacteria. They spread the bacteria on two agar plates. They then placed a small disc of filter paper, which had been soaked in antiseptic, on the centre of each dish.

Both agar plates were incubated for 24 hours.

Give **two** other variables the scientists would need to control during the test. **[2 marks]**

1 _____

2 _____

Figure 2 shows the results of their investigation after 24 hours of incubation.

Figure 2

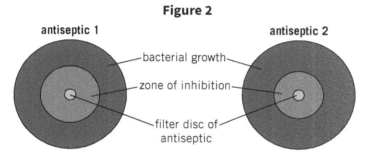

02.2 Give **two** conclusions the scientists can draw from their investigation. **[2 marks]**

1 _____

_____

2 _____

_____

02.3 Calculate the area of the zone of inhibition for antiseptic **2**. Give your answer to three significant figures. **[3 marks]**

 Exam Tip

You have to make two different measurements for this question.

Area _____ mm^2

02.4 Suggest **one** reason why the scientists may not be able to recommend the use of antiseptic **1** in the home. **[1 mark]**

_____

_____

03 A student is investigating the effects of a range of household chemicals on the growth of bacteria. **[2 marks]**

03.1 Describe **two** safety precautions that they should take. **[2 marks]**

03.2 Before they could test the different chemicals, the student needed to prepare an agar plate containing an uncontaminated culture of harmless bacteria. Describe the main steps the student should have followed to prepare this plate. **[4 marks]**

(!) **Exam Tip**

Aseptic technique is a key skill in biology.

03.3 The student then soaked a small disc of filter paper in each chemical and placed the discs on the agar plate. The student also added one disc of filter paper that had been soaked in distilled water. The agar plate was then left for one week. The student's results are shown in **Figure 3**.

Figure 3

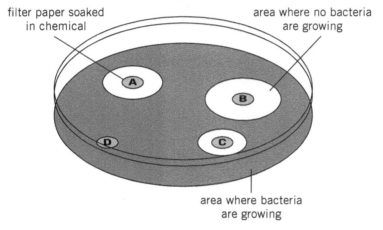

filter paper soaked in chemical

area where no bacteria are growing

area where bacteria are growing

Identify which of the discs, **A–D**, was soaked in distilled water. Give a reason for your answer. **[2 marks]**

03.4 Calculate how much more effective chemical **B** was than chemical **C**. The diameter of **B** = 10.4 mm, and the diameter of **C** = 6.2 mm. **[3 marks]**

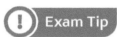
(!) **Exam Tip**

The first thing you need to do is work out the area.

04 Since the discovery of penicillin as an antibiotic drug, many other antibiotics have been created.

04.1 Explain why an antibiotic drug would not be prescribed to treat a measles infection. **[2 marks]**

04.2 Penicillin and erythromycin are two types of antibiotic drugs. Explain why doctors have a range of antibiotic drugs available to prescribe. **[2 marks]**

(!) **Exam Tip**

The social history of science is just as important as the results.

04.3 Erythromycin is taken orally in tablet form. It is possible to cover the tablet in a coating that affects the rate at which the drug is absorbed into the bloodstream. **Figure 4** shows the level of erythromycin in the bloodstream over time for both forms of the tablet – coated and uncoated. Erythromycin is taken every 12 hours.

Figure 4

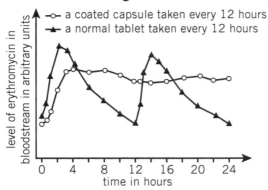

Use **Figure 4** to compare the effects of the two types of tablet on a patient suffering from a bacterial infection. **[6 marks]**

Exam Tip

For this question, it's important you describe both lines carefully, use data from the graph, and talk about any changes that you can see over time.

05 Some bacteria have evolved a resistance to antibiotics. One type of antibiotic-resistant bacteria is called MRSA. MRSA infections cause dizziness, nausea, high body temperature, and skin rashes. They can be fatal.

05.1 Explain how MRSA bacteria have evolved a resistance to antibiotics. **[4 marks]**

Exam Tip

Do not start your answer "MRSA bacteria have evolved a resistance to antibiotics because…". That is just repeating the question and will gain you no marks.

05.2 **Figure 5** shows the number of fatal cases of MRSA between 1995 and 2005 in the UK.

Figure 5

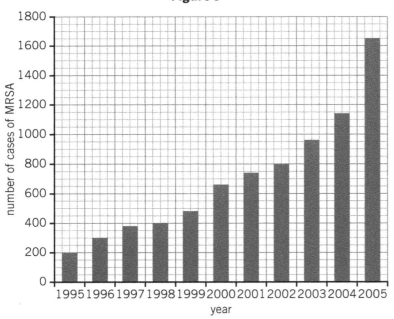

Calculate the percentage change in the number of fatal cases of MRSA between 1995 and 2005. **[2 marks]**

Exam Tip

Draw lines across from the bars at 1995 and 2005 to help you read off the values on the y-axis.

06 Measles used to be a very common disease in children. It spreads quickly through groups of people through droplet infection.

06.1 Explain why measles cannot be treated using antibiotics. **[1 mark]**

06.2 People who have been infected with measles may be advised to take a painkiller such as aspirin. Explain why aspirin may be beneficial for a person with measles, even though it does not cure the disease. **[2 marks]**

06.3 The best way to prevent the spread of measles is through a national vaccination programme. Describe how the measles vaccine works. **[4 marks]**

06.4 In 2017–2018, 91.2% of children in the UK were vaccinated against measles. This was the lowest recorded vaccination level since 2010–2011. Suggest how this will affect the number of people who are infected with measles. **[2 marks]**

> **! Exam Tip**
>
> This question isn't asking about *why* the levels of vaccination have dropped, but what problems this has caused.

07 Diphtheria is a highly contagious condition that affects the nose, throat, and skin. It is transmitted through the air, or by sharing items such as cups or cutlery with an infected person. **Figure 6** shows the number of diphtheria cases in England and Wales, and the number of deaths due to the illness, between 1914 and 2014.

Figure 6

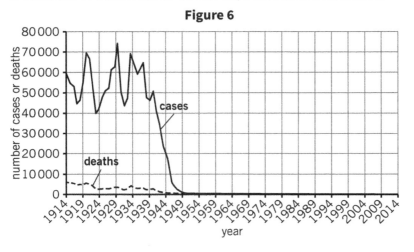

07.1 Identify the highest annual number of deaths due to diphtheria. **[1 mark]**

> **! Exam Tip**
>
> Draw lines on the graph to help you work out the answer to **07.1**.

07.2 Suggest **two** reasons why the year with the highest number of deaths due to diphtheria does not correspond to the year with the highest number of cases of diphtheria. **[2 marks]**

> **! Exam Tip**
>
> Don't just think about the number of cases, but also what happens when people get ill.

07.3 Calculate the percentage change in the number of cases of diphtheria between 1914 and 1944. **[2 marks]**

> **! Exam Tip**
>
> Use data from the graph.

07.4 Using **Figure 6**, suggest and explain in which year the diphtheria vaccine was introduced in England and Wales. **[3 marks]**

07.5 Due to the effective childhood vaccination programme, diphtheria is now an extremely rare disease in England and Wales. However, there were 14 confirmed cases of diphtheria in 2014. Suggest why diphtheria has not been eliminated entirely as a disease from England and Wales. **[3 marks]**

> **! Exam Tip**
>
> This can be a very emotive issue – stick to the facts in a science exam.

08 A range of chemicals can be used to kill bacteria.

08.1 Draw **one** line between each chemical and its use. **[2 marks]**

Chemical	Use
antibiotic	kill bacteria on the skin
antiseptic	kill bacteria on surfaces in the home
disinfectant	kill bacteria inside the body

> **!** **Exam Tip**
>
> Draw one line from each box. More than one will lose you the mark.

08.2 A group of students tested the effectiveness of four different disinfectants on bacteria. They placed filter paper discs soaked in disinfectant onto an agar plate containing bacteria. The plate was then incubated for five days.

The results are shown in **Table 1**.

Table 1

Disinfectant	Area of clear zone on agar plate in mm²
A	2.5
B	3.6
C	2.8
D	1.8

Describe what is meant by the clear zone. **[1 mark]**

08.3 Identify which is the most effective disinfectant. **[1 mark]**

08.4 Explain how the results show that all of the solutions tested acted as a disinfectant. **[2 marks]**

> **!** **Exam Tip**
>
> Use data from **Table 1** in your answer.

09 **Figure 7** shows the number of people who contracted measles in the UK between 1996 and 2008.

Figure 7

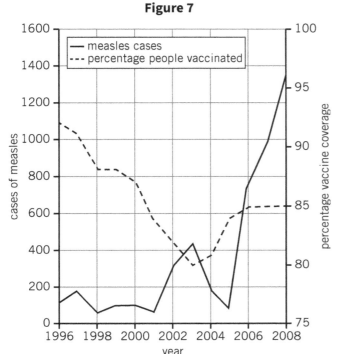

To protect people from contracting measles, children in the UK are offered the measles vaccination.

09.1 Explain how the measles vaccination prevents children from contracting measles. **[6 marks]**

09.2 Using **Figure 7**, evaluate the effectiveness of the vaccine. **[4 marks]**

09.3 A student concluded that herd immunity for measles is achieved with a vaccination rate of 85%. Justify the extent to which you agree, or disagree, with this conclusion. **[4 marks]**

10 A chef prepares a dessert. They cut up some strawberries, put them in a bowl, and add sugar. The bowl is then left at room temperature (**Figure 8**). A few hours later, the fruit is surrounded by syrup. Syrup is a concentrated sugar solution.

Figure 8

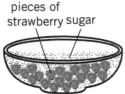

pieces of strawberry sugar

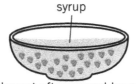

syrup

dessert when prepared   dessert after several hours

10.1 Explain why the syrup formed around the strawberries. **[2 marks]**

10.2 Explain how the volume of syrup would have been different if the chef had left the bowl of strawberries and sugar in the fridge. **[3 marks]**

10.3 The chef investigates how the size of the strawberry pieces affects the time taken to produce 10 cm³ of syrup. The results are in **Table 2**.

Table 2

Surface area of strawberry pieces in cm²	Time taken in min
8	240
10	190
16	120
18	105
20	95

Plot the data from **Table 2** onto **Figure 9**. **[2 marks]**

Figure 9

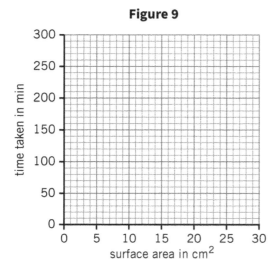

> **Exam Tip**
>
> You'll need to refer to specific years and talk about both lines on the graph.

> **Exam Tip**
>
> Look at the size of the strawberries in **Figure 8**.

> **Exam Tip**
>
> **10.2** links to chemistry. Think about how quickly things happen at different temperatures.

10.4 Draw a line of best fit on **Figure 9**. **[1 mark]**

10.5 Identify and explain the trend shown by the graph. **[3 marks]**

11 A student is given samples of two different types of plant fluid. One was collected from a phloem vessel and one from a xylem vessel.

11.1 Describe the structure of the phloem vessel. **[2 marks]**

11.2 The student is asked to work out which plant vessel each sample has been taken from. To do this the student measures the pH, and the sugar and nitrate ion concentration, of each fluid. The results are shown in **Table 3**.

Table 3

	Sample A	Sample B
pH	7.2	5.8
Sugar concentration in mg/cm³	115	0.8
Nitrate ion concentration in mg/cm³	250	490

Use **Table 3** and your own knowledge to identify which sample was taken from the phloem vessel. Give reasons for your answer. **[2 marks]**

> (!) **Exam Tip**
>
> You must give examples from the table in your answer.

11.3 Calculate how many times greater the concentration of nitrate ions is in sample **B** compared to sample **A**. Give your answer to two significant figures. **[2 marks]**

11.4 Maple syrup has a sugar concentration of 1.38 g/cm³. Calculate how much more concentrated the sugar content of maple syrup is compared to sample **A**. **[3 marks]**

12 A student measured how fast their heart was beating. They counted 17 beats in 15 seconds.

12.1 Calculate the student's resting heart rate in beats per minute. **[1 mark]**

12.2 The natural resting rate of the heart is maintained by a group of cells which act as a pacemaker. Identify where these cells are found. **[1 mark]**

left atrium   right atrium   left ventricle   right ventricle

12.3 Describe how an artificial pacemaker works. **[3 marks]**

B16 Reproduction and cell division

Chromosomes

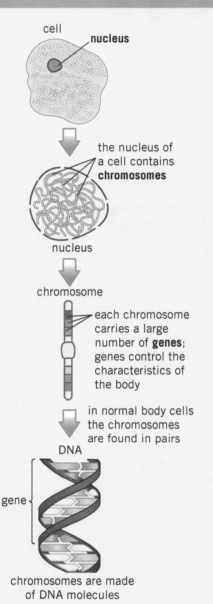

cell
nucleus

the nucleus of
a cell contains
chromosomes

nucleus

chromosome

each chromosome
carries a large
number of **genes**;
genes control the
characteristics of
the body

in normal body cells
the chromosomes
are found in pairs

DNA

gene

chromosomes are made
of DNA molecules

Types of reproduction

Key facts		Sexual reproduction	Asexual reproduction
	No. of parents	two parents	one parent
	Cell division	cell division through **meiosis**	cell division through **mitosis**
	Formulation	joining (fusion) of male and female sex cells (**gametes**) – sperm and egg in animals, pollen and ovule in plants	no fusion of gametes
	Offspring	produces non-identical offspring that are genetically different to parents	produces offspring that are genetically identical to parent (**clones**)
	Genetic variation	results in wide variation within offspring and species	no mixing of genetic information

Mitosis

Body cells divide to form two identical **daughter cells** by mitosis.

Mitosis is important for the growth and repair of cells, for example, the replacement of skin cells.

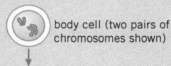

body cell (two pairs of chromosomes shown)

a copy of each chromosome is made

cell divides once to form two genetically identical daughter cells

📷 Revision Tip

Mitosis has a 't' in it, so that should help you remember that it makes *two* daughter cells.

Meiosis

Meiosis is a type of cell division that makes gametes in the reproductive organs. In this type of cell division the cell divides twice.

Meiosis halves the number of chromosomes in gametes, and fertilisation (joining of two gametes) restores the full number of chromosomes.

The fertilised cell divides by mitosis, producing more cells. As the embryo develops, the cells differentiate.

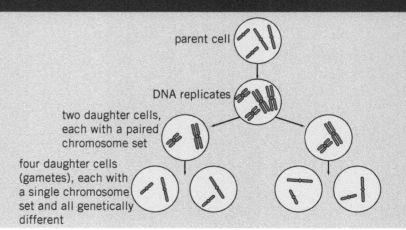

parent cell

DNA replicates

two daughter cells, each with a paired chromosome set

four daughter cells (gametes), each with a single chromosome set and all genetically different

Stem cells in medicine

A stem cell is an undifferentiated cell that can develop into one or more types of specialised cell.

There are two types of stem cell in mammals: **adult stem cells** and **embryonic stem cells**.

Stem cells can be **cloned** to produce large numbers of identical cells. These may be able to help conditions such as paralysis.

Type of stem cell	Where are they found?	What can they differentiate into?	Advantages	Disadvantages
adult stem cells	specific parts of the body in adults and children – for example, bone marrow	can only differentiate to form certain types of cells – for example, stem cells in bone marrow can only differentiate into types of blood cell	• fewer ethical issues – adults can consent to have their stem cells removed and used • an established technique for treating diseases such as leukaemia • relatively safe to use as a treatment and donors recover quickly	• requires a donor, potentially meaning a long wait time to find someone suitable • can only differentiate into certain types of specialised cells, so can be used to treat fewer diseases
embryonic stem cells	early human embryos (often taken from spare embryos from fertility clinics)	can differentiate into any type of specialised cell in the body – for example, a nerve cell or a muscle cell	• can treat a wide range of diseases as can form any specialised cell • may be possible to grow whole replacement organs • usually no donor needed as they are obtained from spare embryos from fertility clinics	• ethical issues as the embryo is destroyed and each embryo is a potential human life • risk of transferring viral infections to the patient • newer treatment so relatively under researched – not yet clear if they can cure as many diseases as thought

Therapeutic cloning

In **therapeutic cloning**:

- cells from a patient's body are used to create a cloned early embryo of themselves
- stem cells from this embryo can be used for medical treatments and growing new organs
- these stem cells have the same genes as the patient, so are less likely to be rejected when transplanted.

Cancer

Cancer is the result of changes in cells that lead to uncontrolled growth. The rapid division of abnormal cells can form a **tumour**.

Malignant tumours are cancerous tumours that invade healthy tissues. They may spread to other parts of the body in the blood, forming secondary tumours.

Benign tumours are non-cancerous; they do not spread in the body.

Tumours can be caused by chemical carcinogens (such as those in tobacco smoke and asbestos) and ionising radiation (such as UV and X rays).

 Key Terms

Make sure you can write a definition for these key terms.

adult stem cell	asexual reproduction	benign tumour	cancer	chromosome	clone
daughter cell	embryonic stem cell	gamete	gene	malignant tumour	meiosis
mitosis	nucleus	sexual reproduction	therapeutic cloning	tumour	

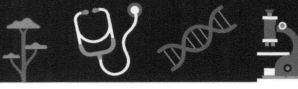

Learn the answers to the questions below then cover the answers column with a piece of paper and write as many as you can. Check and repeat.

B16 questions | Answers

#	Question	Answer
1	What is sexual reproduction?	joining (fusion) of male and female gametes
2	What type of cell division is involved in sexual reproduction?	meiosis
3	What type of cell division is involved in asexual reproduction?	mitosis
4	What is cell division by mitosis?	body cells divide to form two identical daughter cells
5	What is the purpose of mitosis?	growth and repair of cells, and asexual reproduction
6	What happens during mitosis?	one set of chromosomes is pulled to each end of the cell and the nucleus divides
7	What is meiosis?	cell division that produces four daughter cells (gametes), each with a single set of chromosomes
8	What is a stem cell?	undifferentiated cell that can differentiate into one or more specialised cell types
9	What are adult stem cells?	stem cells from adults that can only differentiate into certain specialised cells
10	Where are adult stem cells found?	bone marrow
11	What are embryonic stem cells?	stem cells from embryos that can differentiate into any specialised cell
12	Where are embryonic stem cells found?	early human embryos (usually from spare embryos from fertility clinics)
13	What is therapeutic cloning?	patient's cells are used to create an early embryo clone of themselves – stem cells from the embryo can then be used to treat the patient's medical conditions
14	Give one advantage of using therapeutic cloning.	stem cells from the embryo are not rejected when transplanted because they have the same genes as the patient
15	Give one advantage of using adult stem cells.	fewer ethical issues as obtained from adults who can consent to their use
16	Give two disadvantages of using adult stem cells.	• can take a long time for a suitable donor to be found • can only differentiate into some specialised cell types, so treat fewer diseases
17	Give two advantages of using embryonic stem cells.	• can differentiate into any specialised cell, so can be used to treat many diseases • easier to obtain as they are found in spare embryos from fertility clinics
18	Give two disadvantages of using embryonic stem cells.	• ethical issues surrounding their use, as every embryo is a potential life • potential risks involved with treatments, such as transfer of viral infections

Put paper here

Now use the questions below to check your knowledge from previous chapters.

Previous questions | Answers

Put paper here

1	Where is DNA found in animal and plant cells?	in the nucleus
2	Name two types of eukaryotic cell.	animal and plant
3	What is the function of the cell membrane?	controls movement of substances into and out of the cell
4	What is a pathogen?	microorganism that causes disease
5	What does a vaccine contain?	small quantities of a dead or inactive form of a pathogen
6	What is the function of ribosomes?	enable production of proteins (protein synthesis)
7	Which hormones interact to regulate blood glucose levels?	insulin and glucagon
8	What is diffusion?	net movement of particles from an area of high concentration to an area of low concentration along a concentration gradient – this is a passive process (does not require energy from respiration)
9	What is osmosis?	diffusion of water from a dilute solution to a concentrated solution through a partially permeable membrane

Maths Skills

Practise your maths skills using the worked example and practice questions below.

Converting units	Worked example	Practice
The size of a cell or organelle is most often shown in millimetres (mm), micrometres (μm), or nanometres (nm). You may be asked to convert between mm, μm, and nm. If you are converting from a smaller unit to a larger unit, your number should get smaller. If you are converting a larger unit to a smaller unit, the number should get bigger.	• to convert mm to μm: multiply the mm reading by 1000 • to convert μm to nm: multiply the μm reading by 1000 • to convert nm into μm: divide the nm reading by 1000 • to convert μm into mm: divide the μm reading by 1000	Convert the following cell and organelle sizes to complete the table.

Worked example table

Cell	Size in mm ÷1000	Size in μm	Size in nm ×1000
red blood cell	0.007	7	7000
leaf cell	0.06	60	60 000
egg cell	0.1	100	10

Practice table

Cell	Size in mm	Size in μm	Size in nm
ant	3		
human hair		100	
palisade leaf cell		70	
plant cell ribosome			20
HIV virus			100
egg cell mitochondria	0.002		

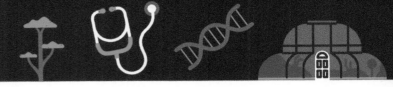
01 **Figure 1** shows some plant cells undergoing mitosis.

Figure 1

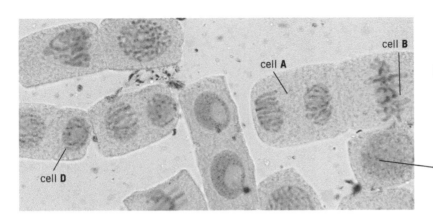

> **! Exam Tip**
>
> In mitosis you get two identical daughter cells.

01.1 Describe what is happening in cell **C**. **[3 marks]**

_____

_____

_____

_____

> **! Exam Tip**
>
> Think about what needs to happen to the DNA before it can divide.

01.2 Identify which sequence of cells from **Figure 1** best represents the process of mitosis.

Tick **one** box. **[1 mark]**

cell **D** → cell **A** → cell **B** → cell **C** ☐

cell **C** → cell **B** → cell **A** → cell **D** ☐

cell **A** → cell **B** → cell **C** → cell **D** ☐

cell **C** → cell **D** → cell **B** → cell **A** ☐

01.3 Cells **A–D** do not show the final stage of mitosis.

Describe what would happen at the next stage in this process.

[2 marks]

_____

_____

_____

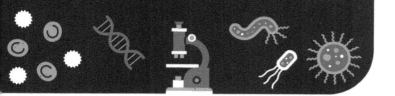

01.4 When looking at cells under a microscope, the length of different stages of the cell cycle can be estimated using the formula:

$$\text{length of stage} = \frac{\text{number of cells at that stage} \times \text{total length of time in the cell cycle}}{\text{total number of cells}}$$

The average time taken for the plant cells in **Figure 1** to complete the cell cycle is 24 hours.

One stage in the mitosis cycle is called metaphase; this is where chromosomes line up at the centre of the cell.

Using the information in **Figure 1**, calculate the time taken for the metaphase stage. **[3 marks]**

> **!** **Exam Tip**
>
> You may not have seen this equation before, but don't worry! You need to get used to using new and unfamiliar equations so you're ready for the exam.
>
> Just plug in the numbers and away you go!

_____ hours

02 People with Type 1 diabetes do not produce enough insulin. This is because the insulin-producing cells in the pancreas are destroyed by the body's immune system.

Patients with this form of diabetes have to inject themselves regularly with insulin.

Scientists hope that stem cells could be used to treat this condition one day.

02.1 Describe what is meant by a stem cell. **[1 mark]**

_____

_____

02.2 Suggest the role that stem cells could play in a diabetic person's body. **[1 mark]**

_____

_____

> **!** **Exam Tip**
>
> Think about the cells that don't work properly in a diabetic.

02.3 A group of scientists carried out a study into the use of adult stem cells to treat Type 1 diabetes.

Describe the main difference between these stem cells and embryonic stem cells. **[2 marks]**

_____

_____

_____

02.4 Suggest **one** reason why it is preferential to use stem cells from the actual patient instead of using cells from a donor. **[1 mark]**

_____

_____

02.5 The study used 23 patients. The patients taking part in the trial were tracked over a 30-month period. At the end of the investigation, 12 patients did not have to inject themselves with insulin anymore.

Calculate the percentage of patients for which the treatment was successful. **[1 mark]**

Exam Tip

A common mistake when working out percentages is forgetting to multiply the answer by 100 at the end.

_____ %

02.6 Suggest and explain whether this technique is a successful treatment for Type 1 diabetes. **[1 mark]**

_____

_____

_____

03 All cells in the human body contain genetic information.

03.1 Describe how the genetic material is organised in the nucleus of a human cell. **[3 marks]**

03.2 As a baby grows, its cells change in a number of ways. Explain why mitosis and cell differentiation are important in the growth and development of a baby from a fertilised egg. **[4 marks]**

Exam Tip

This is a four-mark question, so try to write two points for each section.

03.3 Describe the main steps in mitosis. **[4 marks]**

04 Scientists hope that in the future it will be possible to use stem cells to help treat patients with a number of conditions, such as diabetes.

04.1 Explain why stem cells may be able to offer treatments for conditions such as diabetes that currently have no cure. **[3 marks]**

04.2 Name where in the human body stem cells can be found that can differentiate into different types of blood cell. **[1 mark]**

04.3 There are mixed opinions about the potential use of embryonic stem cells for the treatment of human diseases. Many people feel there are good reasons for carrying out this research, but others are opposed to these studies. Evaluate the ethical arguments surrounding the use of embryonic stem cells in medical research. **[6 marks]**

Exam Tip

For an evaluate question, you need four key points:

1 the good things
2 the bad things
3 your opinion
4 the because (why you have that opinion).

If you don't include all of these, you won't get top marks.

05 Most species of tomato have 24 chromosomes present in the nucleus of their cells.

05.1 Write down how many chromosomes would be present in an adult tomato cell. **[1 mark]**

05.2 Write down how many chromosomes would be present in a tomato pollen cell. **[1 mark]**

05.3 Tomato plants reproduce sexually. Identify from the list below the **two** features that are present in sexual reproduction. **[2 marks]**

no mixing of genetic information
two parents are required
gametes fuse together
clones are produced

05.4 Describe the main steps in the production of a tomato pollen cell. **[4 marks]**

06 There are two types of cell division that occur in humans: meiosis and mitosis.

06.1 Write down where meiosis occurs in a female. **[1 mark]**

06.2 Write down where meiosis occurs in a male. **[1 mark]**

06.3 Compare the processes of mitosis and meiosis. **[4 marks]**

06.4 Explain why meiosis results in genetic variation. **[3 marks]**

06.5 Explain why the development of a fetus involves both mitosis and meiosis. **[4 marks]**

07 Scientists study large volumes of data to look for factors that increase the risk of disease.

07.1 Unprotected exposure to sunlight is a risk factor for developing skin cancer. Explain what is meant by the term cancer. **[2 marks]**

07.2 Explain how sun exposure increases a person's risk of developing skin cancer. **[2 marks]**

07.3 Smoking is a risk factor for the development of tumours. Most tumours caused by smoking are malignant. Explain the difference between a benign tumour and a malignant tumour. **[3 marks]**

08 Scientists can now grow a number of different types of stem cells from embryonic stem cells. Many of the stem cells are taken from spare embryos created during fertility treatments, such as *in vitro* fertilisation (IVF).

08.1 Identify which type of microscope a scientist would use to check that an egg cell had been fertilised and developed into a healthy embryo. Give reasons for your answer. **[2 marks]**

> **Exam Tip**
>
> Which type of microscope can view living cells?

08.2 Suggest **one** ethical concern some people may have with using embryonic stem cells. **[1 mark]**

08.3 A human egg cell is approximately 0.1 mm in diameter. A human sperm cell is approximately 2.5 µm. Calculate the difference in order of magnitude between a sperm cell and an egg cell. **[2 marks]**

09 **Figure 2** shows some cells taken from the root tips of an onion viewed under a microscope.

Figure 2

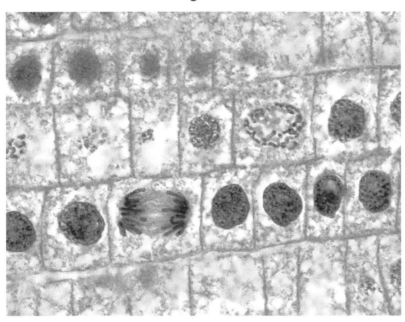

09.1 Describe how you can tell that these cells are undergoing mitosis. **[1 mark]**

> **Exam Tip**
>
> Link your answer to what you can see in the image.

09.2 Suggest why the cells are undergoing mitosis. **[1 mark]**

09.3 Root hair cells are an example of a specialised cell. Write down **two** ways in which they are adapted for taking water into a plant. **[1 mark]**

10 Two types of cell division occur in the body, meiosis and mitosis.

10.1 State the type of division that occurs in the testes. **[1 mark]**

10.2 State the type of cell division that occurs when the body needs to heal a cut. **[1 mark]**

10.3 Describe the process of meiosis. **[3 marks]**

11   An athlete volunteers to take part in a study of how the body responds to changes in its internal environment. On one day of the study, the athlete monitors their blood glucose levels hourly and the results are shown in **Figure 3**.

Figure 3

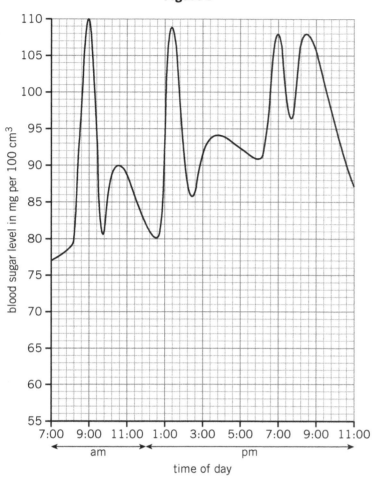

11.1   Give the name of the term that means 'to maintain a constant internal environment'. **[1 mark]**

11.2   Suggest and explain when the athlete ate lunch. **[2 marks]**

11.3   Explain the changes that took place in the athlete's body after eating lunch. **[4 marks]**

! Exam Tip

Use data from the graph to support your answer.

11.4   Calculate the percentage change in the athlete's blood sugar level between 7:00 am and 9:00 am. **[3 marks]**

! Exam Tip

Draw lines on the graph to help you work out the values you need to use.

11.5   A second volunteer in the test has Type 1 diabetes. Suggest how the graph would have looked different for this second volunteer, in comparison to the athlete's data. **[3 marks]**

12   Dementia is a condition that causes a decline in brain function. Symptoms include memory loss, difficulties with movement, and speech problems. Stem cells are being investigated as a possible cure for dementia. Discuss the arguments for and against using stem cell research to find a cure for dementia. **[6 marks]**

B17 Variation and inheritance

DNA and the genome

Genetic material in the nucleus of a cell is composed of **DNA**. It is a chemical code that contains all the information needed to make an organism (its **genome**).

DNA is made up of two strands, which are twisted to form a **double helix**.

DNA is contained in long structures called **chromosomes**.

A **gene** is a small section of DNA on a chromosome that codes for a specific sequence of amino acids, to produce a specific protein.

Variation in populations

Differences in the characteristics of individuals in a population are called **variation**.

Variation may be due to differences in:

- the genes they have inherited, for example, eye colour (genetic causes)
- the environment in which they have developed, for example, language (environmental causes)
- a combination of genes and the environment.

A characteristic that can take any value within a range, such as height, shows **continuous variation**.

A characteristic that can only result in a specific value, such as blood group, shows **discontinuous variation**.

Structure of DNA

DNA is a polymer made from four different compounds, called bases.

A sequence of three bases codes for a particular amino acid.

The order of the bases determines the order in which amino acids are assembled to produce a specific protein.

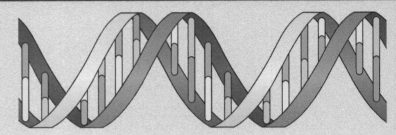

Genetic inheritance

You need to be able to explain these terms about genetic inheritance:

allele	different forms of the same gene
dominant	allele that only needs one copy to be expressed (it is always expressed)
recessive	allele that needs two copies present to be expressed
homozygous	when an individual carries two copies of the same allele for a trait
heterozygous	when an individual carries two different alleles for a trait
genotype	combination of alleles an individual has
phenotype	physical expression of the genotype – the characteristic shown

Key Terms

Make sure you can write a definition for these key terms.

allele   chromosome   continuous variation   discontinuous variation   dominant   DNA
double helix   gene   genetic cross   genome   genotype   heterozygous   homozygous
phenotype   Punnett square   recessive   variation

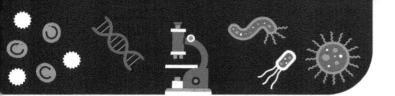

Understanding of genetics

Gregor Mendel developed our understanding of genetics by carrying out breeding experiments with plants in the mid-nineteenth century.

For example, he showed that crossing a plant that produces yellow peas and a plant that produces green peas always bred offspring with green peas. But when crossing these offspring, some offspring of later generations might have yellow peas again.

Through experiments like these, Mendel observed that the inheritance of each characteristic is determined by units – later called genes – that are passed on unchanged to offspring, and that these genes can be dominant or recessive.

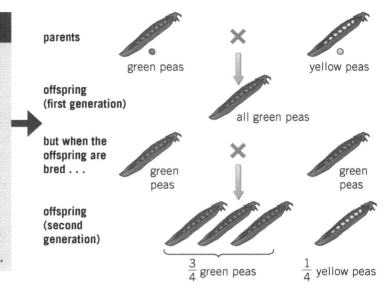

The significance of Mendel's work was not recognised until after his death, because:

- most scientists believed in blended inheritance (e.g., a white flower and a red flower producing a pink flower)
- he published his work in an obscure journal so not many people saw it
- he was a monk as well as a scientist.

Genetic crosses

A **genetic cross** is when you consider the offspring that might result from two known parents. **Punnett squares** can be used to predict the outcomes of a genetic cross, for both the genotypes and phenotypes the offspring might have.

For example, the cross bb (brown fur) × BB (black fur) in mice:

		Mother	
		B	**B**
Father	**b**	Bb	Bb
	b	Bb	Bb

offspring genotype: 100% Bb

offspring phenotype: all black fur (B is dominant)

Sex determination

Normal human body cells contain 23 pairs of chromosomes. One of these pairs determines the sex of the offspring.

In human females the sex chromosomes are the same (XX, homozygous) and in males they are different (XY, heterozygous).

A Punnett square can be used to determine the probability of offspring being male or female. The probability is always 50% in humans as there are two XX outcomes and two XY outcomes.

		Mother	
		X	**X**
Father	**X**	XX	XX
	Y	XY	XY

Inherited disorders

Some disorders are due to the inheritance of certain alleles:

- Polydactyly (extra fingers or toes) is caused by a dominant allele.
- Cystic fibrosis (a disorder of cell membranes) and sickle cell anaemia (misshapen red blood cells) are caused by a recessive allele.

Some disorders are caused by inheriting a different number of chromosomes. This includes Down's syndrome, which results from the presence of an extra chromosome.

Retrieval

Learn the answers to the questions below then cover the answers column with a piece of paper and write as many as you can. Check and repeat.

	B17 questions	Answers
1	What can cause variation?	genetic causes, environmental causes, and a combination of genes and the environment
2	What is the genetic material in cells called?	DNA
3	What is DNA?	chemical code that contains all the information needed to make an organism
4	What is the structure of DNA?	two long strands containing four bases, which are twisted to form a double helix
5	What is a chromosome?	a long strand of DNA
6	What is a gene?	small section of DNA that codes for a particular amino acid sequence, to make a specific protein
7	How many bases code for an amino acid?	three
8	What are alleles?	different forms of the same gene
9	What is a recessive allele?	allele that needs to be present twice to be expressed
10	What is a dominant allele?	allele that is always expressed, even if only one copy is present
11	Define the term homozygous.	two of the same alleles present in an organism
12	Define the term heterozygous.	two different alleles present in an organism
13	Where in the cell are proteins made?	on the ribosomes
14	What type of allele causes polydactyly?	dominant allele
15	What type of allele causes cystic fibrosis?	recessive allele
16	How many chromosomes do normal human body cells have?	23 pairs
17	What did Mendel discover through breeding experiments with plants?	inheritance of characteristics is determined by units (genes) passed on unchanged to offspring
18	What are the male and female sex chromosomes in humans?	XX – female, XY – male

Put paper here

Now use the questions below to check your knowledge from previous chapters.

B17

Previous questions	Answers
1 What happens to muscles during long periods of activity?	muscles become fatigued and stop contracting efficiently
2 Where are adult stem cells found?	bone marrow
3 What are embryonic stem cells?	stem cells from embryos that can differentiate into any specialised cell
4 What is the function of an antitoxin?	neutralise toxins produced by pathogens by binding to them
5 What is the difference between aerobic and anaerobic respiration?	aerobic respiration uses oxygen, anaerobic respiration does not
6 Why do different digestive enzymes have different optimum pHs?	different parts of the digestive system have very different pHs – the stomach is strongly acidic, and the pH in the small intestine is close to neutral

Put paper here *Put paper here*

Maths Skills

Practise your maths skills using the worked example and practice questions below.

Probability	Worked example	Practice
Probability is a number that tells you how likely something is to happen.	The Punnett square shows the inheritance of sex chromosomes in a genetic cross between two parents.	1 The Punnett square shows the inheritance of eye colour in a genetic cross. BB and Bb represent brown eyes. bb represents blue eyes.

Probability is a number that tells you how likely something is to happen.

It is important that you understand probability as this is key to genetic inheritance.

For example, you could be asked to use a Punnett square to work out the probability of a child inheriting a genetic disease from its parents.

A value for probability can be expressed in the form of a fraction, decimal, or percentage.

Probability can be calculated using the formula:

$$\text{probability} = \frac{\text{number of ways the outcome can happen}}{\text{total number of outcomes}}$$

Worked example

The Punnett square shows the inheritance of sex chromosomes in a genetic cross between two parents.

	X	Y
X	XX	XY
X	XX	XY

male = XY
female = XX

What is the probability that the offspring from the genetic cross will be female?

- number of ways the outcome can happen = 2
- total number of outcomes = 4

$$\text{probability} = \frac{2}{4} = 0.5$$

This probability can also be expressed as a fraction $\left(\frac{1}{2}\right)$ or a percentage (50%).

Practice

1 The Punnett square shows the inheritance of eye colour in a genetic cross. BB and Bb represent brown eyes. bb represents blue eyes.

What is the probability that the offspring of the cross would have blue eyes?

	B	b
B	BB	Bb
b	Bb	bb

2 The Punnett square shows whether the offspring of a genetic cross between plants will be tall or short. TT and Tt represent tall plants, and tt represents short plants.

What is the probability that the offspring of the cross would be tall?

	T	t
T	TT	Tt
t	Tt	tt

 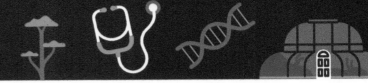

Practice

Exam-style questions

01.1 Complete the following sentences about genetic inheritance by circling the correct words. **[5 marks]**

Each human gamete contains **23 / 46 / 92** chromosomes. When a sperm and an egg fuse, a new cell called a zygote is formed. This new cell contains **23 / 46 / 92** chromosomes.

Two forms of each gene are inherited – these are called **alleles / dominant / recessive**.

One form of the gene is **allele / dominant / recessive** – this form is always expressed if present.

The other form of the gene is **allele / dominant / recessive** – a person must inherit this form of the gene from both parents if it is to be expressed.

> **! Exam Tip**
>
> Take each sentence in turn. Don't let the large block of text overwhelm you.

01.2 Eye colour is controlled by a gene. Two forms of the gene exist:

- brown eyes – dominant – **B**
- blue eyes – recessive – **b**

Classify each of the possible genotypes by matching the allele combination to its correct description. **[2 marks]**

Allele combination		Description
BB		homozygous recessive
Bb		homozygous dominant
bb		heterozygous

> **! Exam Tip**
>
> There are lots of key words in this topic – make sure you're clear on all the different definitions.

01.3 Write down the phenotype for each of the allele combinations. **[3 marks]**

BB: _____

Bb: _____

bb: _____

01.4 A couple is expecting a baby. The father has blue eyes and the mother has brown eyes. Select the correct statement about their new baby's eye colour.

Tick **one** box. **[1 mark]**

The baby will definitely have brown eyes. ☐

The baby may be born with brown eyes or may be born with blue eyes. ☐

The baby will definitely have blue eyes. ☐

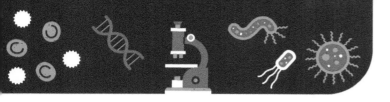

01.5 Give a reason for your answer to **01.4**. [1 mark]

_____

_____

02 **Figure 1** shows the sex chromosomes from two different people, **A** and **B**.

Figure 1

A   B

Exam Tip

The sizes of the X and Y chromosome are very different.

02.1 Identify which image represents the chromosomes from a female. Give reasons for your answer. [2 marks]

_____

_____

02.2 Carry out a genetic cross to show how sex is inherited. Use your diagram to show the likelihood of a couple having a baby girl. [4 marks]

Exam Tip

Space your diagram out clearly – you get marks for showing working here.

Likelihood of having a baby girl: _____

02.3 A couple has three children. Calculate the probability that all three children are girls. [3 marks]

Exam Tip

Show all of your working for this question. If you get the wrong final answer, you can still pick up some marks for the working.

Probability: _____

02.4 A scientist studies two population groups:

• inhabitants of Manchester (population 500 000)

• inhabitants of Bath (population 90 000)

Explain which population is more likely to have a 1:1 ratio of males to females. [3 marks]

_____

_____

_____

03 Many people in the population have dimples. This is because having dimples is caused by a dominant allele **D**. The allele for no dimples is **d**.

03.1 Write down what is meant by a dominant allele. **[1 mark]**

03.2 Which of the following allele combinations would lead to a child having dimples? Select as many combinations as required. **[1 mark]**

DD   **Dd**   **dd**

> ! **Exam Tip**
>
> There is a clue in the wording of the question. 'Select as many combinations as required' tells you it's probably more than one!

03.3 A couple decided to start a family. The alleles of the mother and father are shown in **Figure 2**. Complete the Punnett square to predict the possible allele combinations that the baby could have. **[2 marks]**

Figure 2

Mother's alleles	Father's alleles	
	D	d
D		
D		

> ! **Exam Tip**
>
> Approach Punnett squares logically – do either the rows first or the columns first.

03.4 Calculate and explain the probability of their child having dimples. **[2 marks]**

03.5 If the parents have a second child, explain why the two children are likely to look similar but not the same. **[4 marks]**

04 Polydactyly is an inherited condition caused by a dominant allele. A couple is having a child; the father has polydactyly and is heterozygous for this disorder. The mother does not have polydactyly.

04.1 Polydactyly can be observed in a newborn baby. Write down the characteristic that would be observed for a baby who has inherited polydactyly. **[1 mark]**

04.2 Explain how polydactyly is inherited. **[1 mark]**

04.3 Write down the allele combinations of the father and mother. **[2 marks]**

> ! **Exam Tip**
>
> Polydactyly is generally corrected by surgery during infancy, so the phenotype is not seen very often.

04.4 Over time, the mother and father have four more children. Draw a genetic cross diagram to show the possible alleles of the offspring. **[2 marks]**

04.5 Write down the expected ratio of children with polydactyly to children without polydactyly. **[1 mark]**

04.6 Explain why the actual ratio of children with or without polydactyly is not necessarily the same as the ratio shown in **04.5**. **[3 marks]**

04.7 In the USA, 1 in 3500 babies are born with cystic fibrosis. In comparison, 1 in 500 babies are born with polydactyly. Suggest and explain **two** reasons for this trend. **[6 marks]**

> ! **Exam Tip**
>
> Think about the different options people have before having a child.

05 Cystic fibrosis (CF) is an inherited disorder .

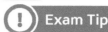

05.1 Write down **two** symptoms of CF. **[2 marks]**

05.2 Explain why a carrier (heterozygote) of CF will not suffer from the disorder. **[3 marks]**

05.3 Draw a genetic diagram to show the possible genotypes of the offspring of two carriers of CF. **[2 marks]**

05.4 Using your diagram from **05.3**, calculate the percentage probability that a child born from two carriers of CF will inherit the disorder. **[2 marks]**

05.5 Using the information below, and your answer to **05.4**, calculate the number of expected births with the genetic disorder CF in a certain year.

- 1 in 25 people in the population are carriers of the CF allele
- expected number of births is 700 000

[5 marks]

06 A group of students investigated the variation in height that existed amongst students in their school.

Their results are shown in **Table 1**.

Table 1

Height in cm	$100 \leq h < 120$	$120 \leq h < 140$	$140 \leq h < 160$	$160 \leq h < 180$	$180 \leq h < 200$
Number of students	12	18	36	22	6
Midpoint					

06.1 Plot an appropriate graph of this data using the graph paper in **Figure 3**. **[3 marks]**

Figure 3

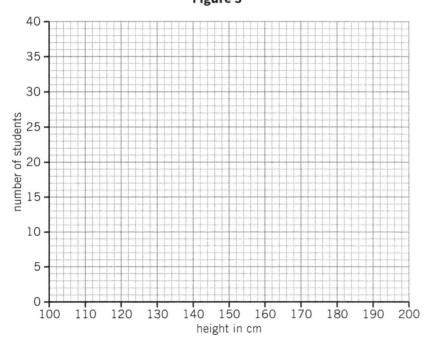

06.2 Explain the cause of the variation shown in the graph. **[2 marks]**

06.3 The mean height of a person in the population is 168 cm. Calculate the mean height of the students in the school. **[4 marks]**

06.4 The students concluded that the distribution of heights in their school reflects that of the whole population. Discuss the extent to which you agree, or disagree, with their conclusion. **[2 marks]**

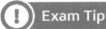
07 The genetic material found in the nucleus of human cells is composed of the chemical DNA.

07.1 Describe the main features in the structure of DNA. **[3 marks]**

07.2 Genes are small sections of DNA. Each gene contains a code. Describe what a gene codes for. **[2 marks]**

07.3 State how many amino acids would be coded for a sequence of 12 bases. **[1 mark]**

08 A group of scientists pooled their research data on differences caused by genetic and environmental factors. Three groups were studied:

- identical twins who were brought up together
- identical twins who were brought up separately
- non-identical twins who were brought up together

The data was summarised into the differences between the pairs studied, as shown in **Table 2**.

Table 2

	Mean difference in height in cm	Mean difference in mass in kg	Mean difference in IQ
Identical twins, brought up together	1.4	1.1	4.9
Identical twins, brought up separately	1.6	3.5	8.2
Non-identical twins, brought up together	5.8	3.6	4.8

Each of the characteristics included in the study is affected by both a person's genes and their environment.

08.1 Identify the extent to which each factor is influenced by a person's genes or their environment. Justify your answers using data from **Table 2**. **[6 marks]**

08.2 Suggest **two** possible extensions to the study that would increase the validity of any conclusions made. **[2 marks]**

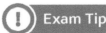

09 In the mid-nineteenth century, a series of experiments on pea plants developed our understanding of genetics.

09.1 Name the scientist who carried out these experiments. **[1 mark]**

09.2 One of the experiments investigated crossing green pea plants with yellow pea plants. Alleles for green-coloured peas (G) are dominant. Alleles for yellow-coloured peas (g) are recessive.

Use the Punnett square diagram (**Figure 4**) to calculate the likelihood of two heterozygous green pea plants producing offspring with yellow peas. **[2 marks]**

Figure 4

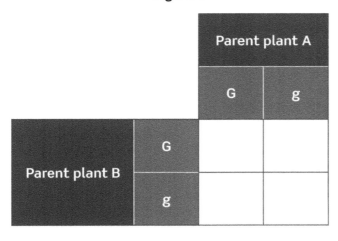

> **! Exam Tip**
>
> Complete Punnett squares one or two columns at a time. One place to start is with parent plant A allele G, then parent plant A allele g, and so on. This way you're less likely to get confused and repeat one allele or miss one allele out.

09.3 Use the most appropriate bold words to complete the sentences about the pea plant experiments. **[4 marks]**

The scientist noticed that characteristics are inherited in a clear, **random** / **predictable** pattern. He explained his experiments by suggesting that organisms contain different units of **inherited** / **environmental** material which can be passed on to offspring. The units never mix, and some characteristics are **dominant** / **recessive** over others. These units of inheritance are now called **genes** / **cells**.

> **! Exam Tip**
>
> Take this one sentence at a time. It you can't decide between random or predictable at the start, don't let this prevent you from trying the second sentence.

09.4 Suggest **one** reason why the work was not accepted by the scientific community at the time. **[1 mark]**

10 Sickle cell anaemia is an inherited disorder that causes red blood cells to develop abnormally **(Figure 5)**.

Figure 5

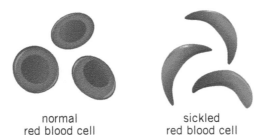

normal
red blood cell

sickled
red blood cell

Sickle-shaped red blood cells cannot carry out their function properly.

10.1 Red blood cells are full of the protein haemoglobin. In a person with sickle cell anaemia haemoglobin does not function properly. Describe the function of haemoglobin. **[1 mark]**

10.2 Suggest **one** symptom of sickle cell anaemia. **[1 mark]**

10.3 Sickle cell anaemia is caused by a recessive allele. A mutation in the DNA led to a change in the order of one set of DNA bases. Explain how this DNA mutation can result in the production of a faulty version of haemoglobin. **[5 marks]**

> **! Exam Tip**
>
> Relate this to the function of red blood cells.

11 **Figure 6** shows the family tree of five people (**1–5**).

Figure 6

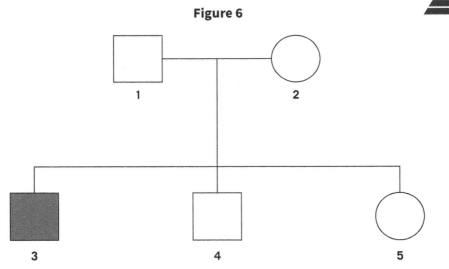

3   4   5

Key

☐ male

◯ female

shaded – red hair

unshaded – brown hair

11.1 Write down the phenotype of person **4**. **[2 marks]**

11.2 Use evidence from **Figure 6** to explain whether red hair is caused by a dominant or recessive allele. **[3 marks]**

11.3 Identify the genotype of person **1**. Choose **one** answer. **[1 mark]**

homozygous dominant   homozygous recessive   heterozygous

11.4 A heterozygous female and a homozygous recessive male wish to have a child.

Draw a genetic cross diagram to calculate the likelihood of the couple having a child with red hair. Give your answer as a percentage. **[4 marks]**

> **! Exam Tip**
>
> You need to give both the sex of the person and the colour of their hair in **11.1**.

12   Variation exists within all species.

12.1   Define the term variation.   **[1 mark]**

12.2   You have two sunflower plants, **A** and **B**. You collect 20 seeds from sunflower **A** and 20 seeds from sunflower **B**. Using the seeds from the plants, suggest how you could carry out an investigation to determine the effect of genes and the environment on the growth of sunflower plants.   **[6 marks]**

> **! Exam Tip**
>
> Plan this out step-by-step, clearly showing what you would do with the seeds and the results.

13   A group of students set up an experiment to investigate osmosis in cells. They used two sections of Visking tubing to represent two different cells. The students filled each piece of Visking tubing with a different solution:

- cell **1** contained 20% sucrose solution
- cell **2** contained distilled water

The students then placed both pieces of Visking tubing in a beaker containing 5% sucrose solution and left them for one hour.

The experimental setup is shown in **Figure 7**.

> **! Exam Tip**
>
> Visking tubing has microscopic holes in it.

Figure 7

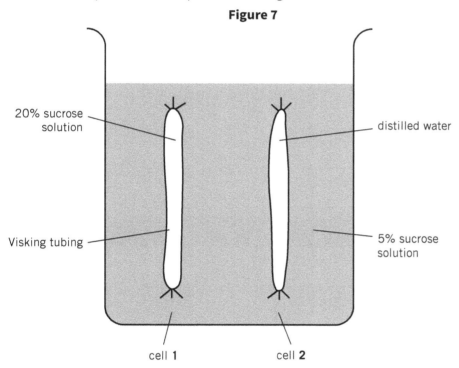

13.1   Identify which part of the cell the Visking tubing represents.
                                                                 [1 mark]

13.2   Give **one** variable the students should have controlled.   **[1 mark]**

13.3   Explain the results observed by the students after one hour.
                                                                 [4 marks]

Knowledge

Cloning

A **clone** is an individual that has been produced **asexually** and is genetically identical to its parent. There are several different methods for producing both plant and animal clones, but there are benefits and risks associated with cloning.

Methods of cloning

Tissue culture

Small groups of cells from part of a plant are added to a mixture of plant hormones and used to grow identical new plants. It is expensive but it allows thousands of new plants to be made from one tiny piece of plant tissue. This is important for preserving rare plant species and growing plants commercially in nurseries.

Cutting

An older, simple method used by gardeners to produce many identical plants from a parent plant. A branch is normally taken from the parent plant, its lower leaves removed and the stem placed in compost. Sometimes the stem is dipped in hormone powder to encourage root growth.

Embryo transplant

Cells are split apart from a developing animal embryo before they become specialised, then the identical embryos are transplanted into host mothers.

Benefits	Risks
• large number of identical offspring produced • quick and economical • desired characteristics guaranteed	• limits variation and causes reduction in gene pool • clones may be vulnerable to diseases/changes in the environment • ethical considerations around cloning living organisms

Adult cell cloning

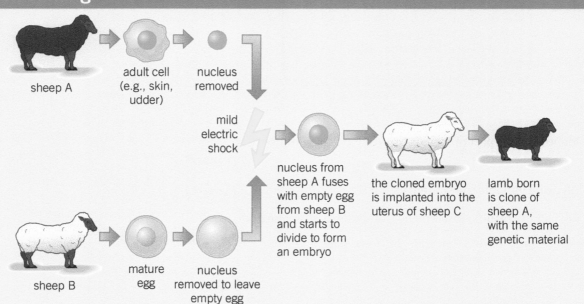

Genetic engineering

Genetic engineering is a process that involves changing the genome of an organism by introducing a gene from another organism, to produce a desired characteristic.

For example:

- Bacterial cells have been genetically engineered to produce useful substances, such as human insulin to treat diabetes.
- Plant crops have been genetically engineered to be resistant to diseases, insects, or herbicides, or to produce bigger and better fruits and higher yields. Crops that have undergone genetic engineering are called **genetically modified** (GM).

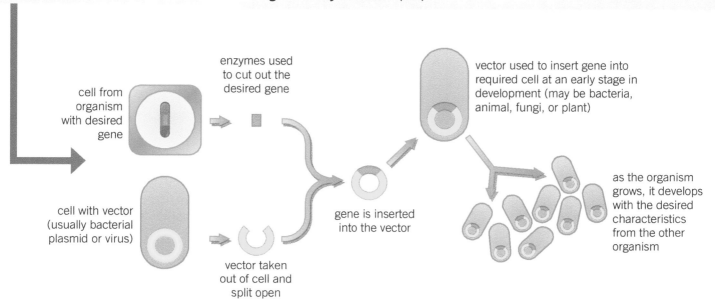

There are many benefits to genetic engineering in agriculture and medicine, but also some risks.

Benefits	Risks
<ul><li>potential to overcome some inherited human diseases</li><li>can lead to higher value of crops as GM crops have bigger yields than normal</li><li>crops can be engineered to be resistant to herbicides, make their own pesticides, or be more resistant to environmental conditions</li></ul>	<ul><li>genes from GM plants and animals may spread to other wildlife, which could have devastating effects on ecosystems</li><li>potential negative impacts on populations of wild flowers and insects</li><li>ethical concerns, for example, in the future people could manipulate the genes of children to ensure certain characteristics</li><li>some believe the long-term effects on health of eating GM crops have not been fully explored</li></ul>

 **Key Terms**   Make sure you can write a definition for these key terms.

asexual   clone   cutting   embryo transplant
genetic engineering   genetically modified   tissue culture

Retrieval

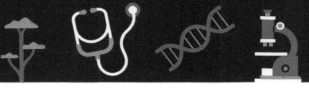

Learn the answers to the questions below then cover the answers column with a piece of paper and write as many as you can. Check and repeat.

	B18 questions	Answers
1	What is variation?	differences in the characteristics of individuals in a population
2	What can cause variation?	genetic causes, environmental causes, and a combination of genes and the environment
3	How do new phenotype variants occur?	mutations
4	What are some examples of modern cloning techniques?	tissue culture, cuttings, embryo transplants and adult cell cloning
5	What are some benefits of cloning?	large number of identical offspring produced, quick and economical, desired characteristics guaranteed
6	What are some risks of cloning?	limits variation and reduces gene pool, clones may be vulnerable to diseases/environmental change, ethical considerations around cloning
7	What is genetic engineering?	modifying the genome of an organism by introducing a gene from another organism to give a desired characteristic
8	How have plant crops been genetically engineered?	to be resistant to diseases/herbicides/pesticides, to produce bigger fruits, to give higher yields
9	How have bacteria been genetically engineered?	to produce useful substances, such as human insulin to treat diabetes
10	What are enzymes used for in genetic engineering?	cut out the required gene
11	What is used to transfer the required gene into the new cell in genetic engineering?	vector (e.g., bacterial plasmid or virus)
12	Describe the steps involved in adult cell cloning.	**1** nucleus removed from unfertilised egg cell **2** nucleus from adult body cell inserted into egg cell **3** electric shock stimulates egg cell to divide to form an embryo **4** embryo develops and is inserted into the womb of an adult female
13	What is tissue culture cloning?	using small groups of cells from plants to grow identical new plants
14	Why is tissue culture cloning of plants important?	preserve rare species and for growing plants commercially in nurseries
15	What is cutting as a cloning method?	simple method used by gardeners to produce many identical plants from a parent plant
16	Describe cloning through using embryo transplants.	cells split apart from a developing animal embryo before they are specialised, then the identical embryos are transplanted into host mothers

Put paper here

Put paper here

Put paper here

Put paper here

Put paper here

Put paper here

Put paper here

Now use the questions below to check your knowledge from previous chapters.

B18

Previous questions

Answers

1	What is the cause of Type 1 diabetes?		pancreas produces insufficient insulin
2	What is variation?		differences in the characteristics of individuals in a population
3	Give three things all control systems include.		receptors, coordination centres, and effectors
4	What do organisms need energy for?		• chemical reactions to build larger molecules • muscle contraction for movement • keeping warm
5	Give four internal conditions controlled in homeostasis.		• body temperature • blood glucose concentration • water levels • ion levels
6	What are the male and female sex chromosomes in humans?		XX – female, XY – male

Put paper here (×2)

Working Scientifically

Practise answering questions about working scientifically using the example below. You need to be able to apply your skills and knowledge to other working scientifically skills too.

Evaluating an investigation – improvements

Improvements to experiments should focus on improving the confidence in a conclusion. All experiments can be improved by:

- Using a wider range of the independent variable. This allows you to check that the identified pattern holds true for a wider range of data.

- Repeating the experiment more times. This minimises the effect of smaller random errors on the calculation of the mean value.

In addition, many experiments can be improved by using different measuring equipment. For example, you could choose:

- more precise measuring equipment, to allow you to read closer to the true value

- data logging equipment, to monitor changes over time

- recording equipment, e.g. a video camera, to accurately monitor rapid changes.

Practice

Look again at the equipment and method used in a Required Practical. What improvements could you make if you had to perform the investigation again?

Practice

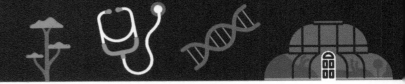

Exam-style questions

01   Some plant crops have been genetically modified to improve their characteristics.

01.1   Explain what is meant by the term genetically modified.   **[2 marks]**

_____

_____

_____

01.2   Reorder sentences **A–E** to describe how crops can be modified through genetic engineering. The first and last steps have been completed for you.   **[4 marks]**

Step 1: The desired gene is removed from the nucleus of a donor cell.

A   The bacteria are allowed to infect plant cells.

B   The foreign gene is integrated into the plant cells' DNA.

C   This 'foreign' gene is inserted into a plasmid (a circular piece of DNA).

D   Bacteria reproduce quickly, producing many copies of the desired gene.

E   The plasmid, now containing the desired gene, is inserted into a bacterial cell.

Step 7: Plant cells grow into plants displaying the desired characteristic.

_____

> **!** **Exam Tip**
>
> Tick off each sentence as you use it, but don't cross it out completely in case you change your mind.

01.3   Give **one** advantage of the genetic modification of plant crops compared to cross breeding plants to gain a desired characteristic.
   [1 mark]

_____

_____

02   Insulin is a hormone secreted by the pancreas.

02.1   Explain the role of insulin in the body.   **[2 marks]**

_____

_____

_____

02.2 People with Type 1 diabetes have to inject themselves regularly with insulin. It is possible to genetically engineer bacteria so that they contain the gene for human insulin. This insulin can then be used to treat diabetes. Describe the main steps in the procedure of genetically engineering bacteria in this way. **[6 marks]**

! **Exam Tip**

'Describe' questions are asking for *what* happened, so go through the steps one at a time. Use key words and technical terms in the appropriate places.

_____

_____

_____

_____

_____

_____

_____

_____

02.3 Insulin originally used in the treatment of diabetes was extracted from pigs. Suggest **two** advantages of using insulin from genetically engineered bacteria rather than from pigs. **[2 marks]**

_____

_____

_____

03 A scientific magazine published the following article.

> MioneTech, a US-based biotech company, reported today that it had successfully started the first human trials of a gene replacement therapy to cure Hunter syndrome, a previously incurable disorder. This inherited disorder prevents cells breaking down some sugars, leading to developmental delays, brain damage, and even death.
>
> The trial uses a form of DNA scissors called zinc finger nucleases (ZFNs), which cut both strands of the DNA double helix at a precise point. A virus is then used as the vector to transfer a 'healthy' replacement gene into the patient's DNA.
>
> The company claims that the revolutionary new treatment will change patients' lives for the better. People with Hunter syndrome require weekly infusions of a missing enzyme; the gene replacement therapy involves a single 3-hour operation.

! **Exam Tip**

Go through the text with a set of highlighters.

For example, highlight the type of protein in blue, the social issues in pink, and the ethical issues in green.

Colour coding large blocks of text makes them easier to read and find the information you need.

03.1 People with Hunter syndrome are missing a protein from their cells. Using the information from the article, name the type of protein molecule that the replacement gene will code for. **[1 mark]**

03.2 Evaluate the ethical and social issues of using gene replacement therapy to treat Hunter syndrome. **[6 marks]**

04 Some species of tomato have been genetically engineered to be frost-resistant.

04.1 Suggest **two** advantages to a farmer of growing frost-resistant tomatoes. **[2 marks]**

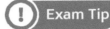

> **! Exam Tip**
>
> This answer is going to be specific to the climate and the area where the tomatoes are grown.

04.2 To make frost-resistant tomatoes, genetic material is taken from a flounder fish. These flat fish are adapted to live in very cold water by producing an antifreeze chemical. Describe how frost-resistant tomatoes are created using genetic modification. **[6 marks]**

05.1 Define what is meant by a clone. **[1 mark]**

05.2 Identify which of the following techniques would **not** produce clones. Choose **one** answer. **[1 mark]**

tissue culture   selectively breeding animals

plant cuttings   bacterial reproduction

> **! Exam Tip**
>
> Read the question carefully.

05.3 Describe the main steps involved in producing new plants through tissue culture. **[4 marks]**

05.4 Give **one** advantage and **one** disadvantage of producing new plants through tissue culture. **[2 marks]**

06 Adult cell cloning is a relatively new technique.

06.1 Define what is meant by adult cell cloning. **[2 marks]**

06.2 Describe **one** possible use of adult cell cloning. **[1 mark]**

> **! Exam Tip**
>
> Whilst there are many possible uses, pick one that is likely to be on the mark scheme.

06.3 In 1997, Dolly the sheep was the first large mammal to be cloned. Describe the main steps involved in adult cell cloning used to produce Dolly. **[5 marks]**

07 Some crops are genetically modified.

07.1 Describe the main steps in genetically modifying a crop. **[4 marks]**

07.2 Name **one** characteristic crops are genetically modified to possess. **[1 mark]**

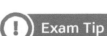

> **! Exam Tip**
>
> Make sure your argument is balanced.

07.3 Discuss the arguments for and against using genetic engineering to modify food crops. **[4 marks]**

08 A group of students were asked to investigate the effect of temperature on the enzyme lipase. They chose to add lipase to full-fat milk and use an indicator to demonstrate when digestion had taken place. The students first mixed equal volumes of milk and sodium carbonate solution in a beaker. This caused the milk to become an alkaline solution. The students then used the following method:

1 Take 10 cm³ of the milk solution and add to a test tube. Place in an ice bath at 0 °C.

2 Leave the solution for 15 minutes to acclimatise.

3 Add a few drops of phenolphthalein indicator. Phenolphthalein is pink or purple in strongly alkaline solutions but becomes colourless when the pH drops below pH 8.

4 Start the stopwatch.

5 Shake the test tube to mix the contents thoroughly.

6 Stop the stopwatch when the solution becomes colourless.

7 Repeat steps 1–6, using water baths heated to 20 °C, 30 °C, 40 °C, 50 °C, and 60 °C.

> **! Exam Tip**
>
> Go through the method and pick out the variables.
> This will give you a good understanding of what the student actually did.

08.1 Explain why the action of lipase on full-fat milk causes the phenolphthalein indicator to change colour from pink to colourless. **[3 marks]**

08.2 The students recorded their results in **Table 1**.

Table 1

Temperature in °C	Time in s	Reaction rate in s⁻¹
0	800	0.0013
20	170	
30	110	0.0091
40	110	
50	360	0.0028
60	–	–

> **! Exam Tip**
>
> s⁻¹ means 1/s
> If you're not sure what to do, see if you can work out the reaction rates given.

Complete **Table 1** by filling in the missing values for the reaction rates at 20 °C and 40 °C. **[3 marks]**

08.3 Explain why the students were unable to obtain a result at 60 °C. **[3 marks]**

08.4 Plot a graph of temperature versus rate of reaction on **Figure 1** to determine the optimum temperature for lipase action. **[3 marks]**

Figure 1

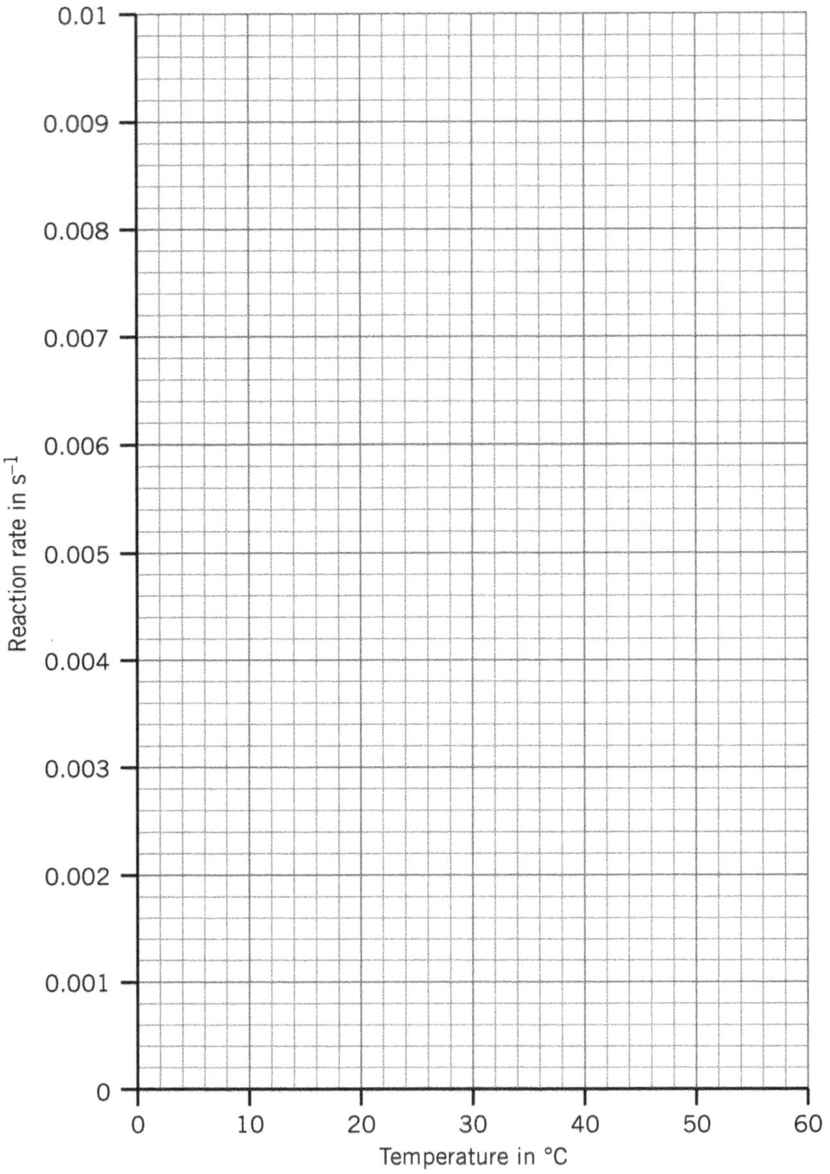

A graph with y-axis labelled "Reaction rate in s⁻¹" ranging from 0 to 0.01 in increments of 0.001, and x-axis labelled "Temperature in °C" ranging from 0 to 60 in increments of 10.

> **! Exam Tip**
>
> Always draw a line of best fit. This can be straight or curved depending on the data.

08.5 Explain why the rate of reaction increased between 0 °C and 30 °C. **[3 marks]**

08.6 Suggest and explain **two** improvements the students could have made to their investigation. **[4 marks]**

09 Animal and plant cells both contain a number of sub-cellular structures. These include mitochondria and the nucleus.

09.1 Describe **two** other sub-cellular structures both types of cell contain. **[4 marks]**

09.2 The number of mitochondria varies between different cell types, as shown in **Table 2**.

Table 2

Human cell type	Mean number of mitochondria per cell (to the nearest 100)
small intestine	1600
skin	200
muscle	1700

Write down the range in the number of mitochondria in human cells. **[1 mark]**

09.3 Explain the data shown in **Table 2**. **[3 marks]**

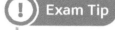

> **! Exam Tip**
>
> Think about the functions of the different cell types and what they need energy for.

10 Two students were asked to investigate whether plant leaf surface area is affected by light intensity. They decided to study the leaves on laurel bushes found in two locations: one area was in direct sunlight and the other was partially shaded by a building. They studied eight leaves in each section. The students recorded their results in **Table 3**.

Table 3

Section of laurel bush	Leaf surface area in cm²								Average
	1	2	3	4	5	6	7	8	
direct sunlight	72	72	68	72	68	68	70	70	70
shaded	72	76	70	64	82	72	84	72	

10.1 Complete **Table 3** by calculating the average leaf surface area for the laurel bushes found in the shade. **[1 mark]**

10.2 Calculate the uncertainty in leaf surface area for the shaded leaves. **[2 marks]**

> **! Exam Tip**
>
> Always look out for anomalous results when you're asked to calculate an average.

10.3 One student concluded that leaves found in the shade have a larger surface area than leaves found in well-lit areas. The second student argued that it is not possible to form a conclusion from this data. Give **two** reasons why the second student was correct. Give reasons for your answers. **[4 marks]**

10.4 Laurel leaves have a complex shape. The students estimated the surface area of a leaf by drawing around the leaf on squared paper and adding up the number of squares contained within the shape. Suggest **one** alternative approach the students could have taken to estimate the leaf surface area. **[1 mark]**

Knowledge

B19 Evolution

Theory of evolution

Evolution is the gradual change in the inherited characteristics of a population over time.

Evolution occurs through the process of **natural selection** and may result in the formation of new **species**.

Darwin's work

Charles Darwin proposed the theory of evolution by natural selection after gathering evidence from a round-the-world expedition, experimentation, and discussion.

This theory states that all living species evolved from a common ancestor that first developed more than three billion years ago.

Darwin published this theory in *On the Origin of Species* (1859). His ideas were considered controversial and only gradually accepted because:

- they challenged the idea that God made all of the Earth's animals and plants
- there was insufficient evidence at the time the theory was published, although much more evidence has been gathered since
- mechanisms of inheritance and variation were not known at the time.

Other theories of evolution

Other theories, such as that of Jean-Baptiste Lamarck, were based on the idea that the changes that occur in an organism over its lifetime could be passed on to its offspring – inheritance of acquired characteristics. Lamarck's theory proposed that all animals evolved from primitive worms. We now know that in the majority of cases this type of inheritance cannot occur.

Process of natural selection

The theory of evolution by natural selection states that:

- organisms within species show a wide range of variation in phenotype due to differences in their genes
- individuals with characteristics most suited to the environment are more likely to survive and breed successfully – 'survival of the fittest'
- the alleles (versions of a gene) that cause these characteristics are then passed on to their offspring.

Mutation

There is usually a lot of genetic variation within a population of a species – this variation arises from **mutations**.

A mutation is a change in a DNA sequence:

- Mutations occur continuously.
- Very rarely a mutation will lead to a new phenotype, but some may change an existing phenotype and most have no effect.
- If a new phenotype is suited to an environmental change, it can lead to a relatively rapid change in the species.

Evolution timescales

In some cases, such as the evolution of antibiotic–resistant bacteria, natural selection can bring about change very quickly.

It took around 40 years for dark peppered moths to become dominant in the population, to match the darkened trees that occurred as a result of the industrial revolution.

However, to produce an entire new species rather than just a different population usually takes much longer. It has taken millions of years for the organisms present on Earth in the 21st century to evolve.

Lamarck's model

In Lamarck's model of evolution, giraffes have long necks because each generation stretched up to reach the highest leaves. So each new generation had a slightly longer neck.

Speciation

Alfred Russel Wallace independently proposed the theory of evolution by natural selection.

He published joint writings with Darwin in 1858 on the subject, prompting Darwin to publish his book the next year.

Wallace is best known for his work on warning colours in animals and for his pioneering work on the theory of **speciation**.

Speciation is the gradual formation of a new species as a result of evolution.

Process of speciation

A species is a group of organisms with many features in common that can breed successfully, producing fertile offspring.

More evidence and work from scientists over time have led to our current understanding of the theory of speciation.

1 **isolation** – two populations of one species become separated

2 **genetic variation** – the populations have an increasing number of genetic mutations as they adapt to their different environments

3 **natural selection** – natural selection occurs so that the better-adapted individuals reproduce and pass on the alleles that code for these characteristics

4 **speciation** – eventually the two populations are so genetically different they cannot breed to produce fertile offspring

Isolation of populations

The most common way that populations become separated is by geographical isolation. Populations become physically isolated, for example, by a new mountain range, a new river, or an area of land becoming an island. This is often a result of earthquakes or volcanic eruptions.

Sometimes organisms are separated by environmental isolation. This is when the climate changes in one area where an organism lives, but not in other areas.

Fossils and extinction

Fossils are the remains of organisms that are found preserved in rocks, ice, and other places. The fossil record shows that many different species have appeared and then died out over millions of years.

Evolution is happening all the time. There is a natural cycle of new species appearing whilst others become **extinct**.

 **Key Terms** **Make sure you can write a definition for these key terms.**

| evolution | extinction | fossil | genetic variation | isolation |
| mutation | natural selection | speciation | species |

Retrieval

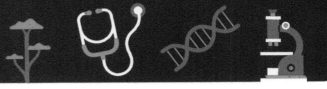

Learn the answers to the questions below, then cover the answers column with a piece of paper and write as many as you can. Check and repeat.

B19 questions

Answers

1	What is evolution?	change in the inherited characteristics of a population over time through natural selection, which may result in a new species
2	Who first proposed the theory of evolution by natural selection?	Charles Darwin
3	What is the theory of evolution by natural selection?	all species of living things evolved from a common ancestor that developed billions of years ago
4	What are the main steps in natural selection?	• individual organisms within a species show variation • individuals with characteristics most suited to the environment survive and reproduce • the alleles that code for these characteristics are passed on to the next generation
5	Describe Lamarck's idea of inheritance.	organisms change over their lifetimes and these characteristics can be inherited
6	Why was the theory of evolution by natural selection controversial?	• challenged the idea that God made all of Earth's animals and plants • insufficient evidence at the time • genes, inheritance, and variation were not understood
7	What is a mutation?	a change in a DNA sequence
8	How do new alleles arise?	through mutations
9	How long does evolution take?	in rapidly reproducing species like bacteria it can occur very quickly, but in most species it takes many years, in some case millions
10	Why can bacteria evolve rapidly?	they reproduce at a fast rate
11	What is speciation?	gradual formation of a new species as a result of evolution
12	What is a species?	a group of organisms with many features in common that can breed successfully producing fertile offspring
13	What are the main steps in speciation?	isolation of two populations, genetic variation results in beneficial characteristics, these are passed on by natural selection, eventually populations can no longer breed to produce fertile offspring
14	What are two ways species become isolated?	geographical isolation and environmental isolation
15	What are some examples of geographical isolation?	new mountain range, new river, new island formed from a volcanic eruption
16	What are fossils?	remains of organisms from millions of years ago, found in rocks

Put paper here

Now use the questions below to check your knowledge from previous chapters.

Previous questions

Answers

	Previous questions	Answers
1	Define the term heterozygous.	two different alleles present in an organism
2	Where in the cell are proteins made?	on the ribosomes
3	Describe the steps involved in adult cell cloning.	**1** nucleus removed from unfertilised egg cell **2** nucleus from adult body cell inserted into egg cell **3** electric shock stimulates egg cell to divide to form an embryo **4** embryo develops and is inserted into the womb of an adult female
4	Name the four main components of blood.	red blood cells, white blood cells, plasma, platelets
5	What are artificial hearts used for?	keep patients alive whilst waiting for a transplant, or allow the heart to rest for recovery
6	What is a genome?	the entire genetic material of an organism
7	What are the male and female sex chromosomes in humans?	XX – female, XY – male
8	How many chromosomes do normal human body cells have?	23 pairs

Put paper here

Maths Skills

Practise your maths skills using the worked example and practice questions below.

Significant figures	Worked example	Practice
Scientists often give numbers that are expressed to two or three significant figures (s.f.). This is to avoid giving irrelevant or unnecessary figures in a very small or large number, or to avoid introducing error in a result. Significant figures can also be used to make large or complicated calculations easier. A key point to remember is that leading zeroes (before a decimal point) are *never* significant.	Zeros within a number count as significant figures. For example, 3.28034 has 6 significant figures. Leading zeros are never significant, so 0.00760 has 3 significant figures. **Example 1:** Round 2.837076 to 3 s.f. First count the significant figures from left to right, giving 2.83 to 3 s.f. As the 4th digit is a 7, the answer is rounded up, giving 2.84. **Example 2:** Round 0.03601 to 3 s.f. Number the significant figures, remembering that leading zeros are never significant. As the 4th digit is a 1, the answer is not rounded up, giving 0.0360.	**1** Round 0.009909 to 3 s.f. **2** Round 53879 to 2 s.f. **3** Round 0.005089 to 1 s.f. **4** Round 98347 to 2 s.f. **5** Round 3.5175 to 3 s.f.

 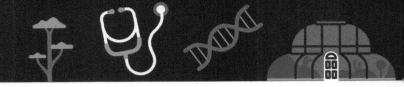

Practice

Exam-style questions

01 New species develop as a result of natural selection.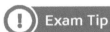

01.1 Define the term species. **[1 mark]**

_____

_____

01.2 In 1858, Darwin proposed his theory of evolution by natural selection. Use the words from the box to complete the passage that describes how organisms evolve by natural selection. **[4 marks]**

characteristics	die	DNA	genotype
phenotype	similarities	survive	variation

 Exam Tip

Not all the words will be used. Don't let this worry you.

Individual organisms within a species show _____

as a result of differences in their DNA. Individuals who have

characteristics that are most suited to their environment are more

likely to _____ and reproduce. The individuals

pass on these favourable _____ to their offspring.

This results in more individuals displaying these favourable

characteristics in their _____ .

01.3 Describe how Lamarck's theory of evolution differed from Darwin's. **[2 marks]**

_____

_____

_____

02 Peppered moths have two naturally occurring colourations:
- pale colouration – provides camouflage against clean tree trunks
- dark colouration – provides camouflage against a black background

During the industrial revolution of the late 1800s, factories produced pollution in the form of soot.

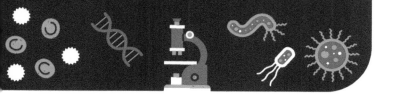

Figure 1 shows the results of a study of moths carried out during this time.

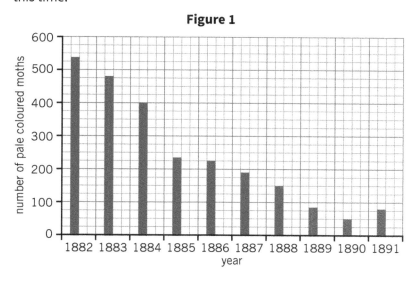

Figure 1

02.1 The data for the number of dark coloured moths over the same time period is shown in **Table 1**. Add this data to the graph.

[3 marks]

Table 1

Year	1882	1883	1884	1885	1886	1887	1888	1889	1890	1891
Number of dark coloured moths	110	180	220	270	335	410	490	540	600	570

02.2 Describe the patterns shown in the graph between 1882 and 1891. **[3 marks]**

_____

_____

_____

_____

02.3 Use your graph to state the year in which the dark coloured moths became dominant in the population. **[1 mark]**

_____

02.4 Explain the pattern shown. **[6 marks]**

_____

_____

_____

_____

_____

_____

03 Water birds have long, webbed feet. One theory of evolution suggests that over the years, due to straining their toes to paddle through the water, these birds developed elongated, webbed toes that help them swim more efficiently.

03.1 Name the scientist that proposed this theory of evolution. **[1 mark]**

03.2 A different scientist suggested that webbed feet evolved as a result of natural selection. Describe how webbed feet would evolve by natural selection. **[4 marks]**

03.3 Give **one** reason why people did not believe Darwin's theory when he first proposed it. **[1 mark]**

03.4 Darwin's theory of evolution by natural selection is now widely accepted. Give **one** piece of evidence for evolution by natural selection. **[1 mark]**

> **(!)** **Exam Tip**
>
> Remember to relate your answer to change over years. This was referred to in the main part of the question.

04 A group of scientists develop a drug called 'Drug 2030' to treat bacterial infections. In trials, the drug proves highly successful at treating many bacterial infections. However, some bacteria have a natural resistance to the active agent in Drug 2030.

04.1 Explain how resistance to Drug 2030 could lead to changes in the population of bacteria. **[6 marks]**

04.2 Describe the features of a successful antibiotic drug. **[2 marks]**

04.3 An increasing number of strains of bacteria are becoming resistant to antibiotics. Suggest and explain **two** steps that people should follow to help reduce the number of resistant strains of bacteria. **[4 marks]**

> **(!)** **Exam Tip**
>
> This is a hypothetical drug to see if you can apply what you know about other drugs and developing antibiotic resistance to a new situation. Do not spend any time worrying about what this drug does, or panicking that you haven't heard of it before.

05 The flow diagram in **Figure 2** shows the main steps in speciation.

Figure 2

Two populations of a species become isolated.

↓

There is a wide range of variation within each population.

↓

↓

The populations are now so different they cannot interbreed to produce fertile offspring.

05.1 Complete the missing stage in **Figure 2**. **[1 mark]**

05.2 State the cause of variation within the population. **[1 mark]**

05.3 Populations can become separated as a result of geographical isolation. Describe **one** example of how this can occur. **[2 marks]**

06 Speciation is the formation of new species in the course of evolution.

06.1 Which of the following statements is true about speciation? Choose **one** answer. **[1 mark]**

A new species has formed when the new organism cannot produce fertile offspring when breeding with the ancestor species.

A new species has formed when the new organism can produce fertile offspring when breeding with the ancestor species.

A new species has formed when the new organisms can produce fertile offspring with each other.

A new species has formed when the new organisms have different behaviours to the ancestor species.

① Exam Tip

Put a cross next to the ones you know are incorrect and a question mark by the ones you are not sure of.

06.2 Which scientist developed the theory of speciation by studying warning colouration in animals? Choose **one** answer. **[1 mark]**

Darwin   Wallace   Lamarck   Mendel

06.3 Explain **one** way in which speciation can occur. **[3 marks]**

07 Life on Earth began 4 billion years ago. It is estimated that 5 billion different species have lived on Earth. Of these, it is estimated that 14 million species are alive today, and 1.2 million species alive today have been identified and classified.

07.1 Calculate the proportion of species estimated to be alive that have not yet been identified. **[3 marks]**

① Exam Tip

Be careful with which numbers you select for the calculation in **07.1**.

07.2 Suggest **two** reasons why the proportion of species identified is only a small fraction of the total estimated number of species. **[2 marks]**

07.3 It is estimated that 1250 species per year become extinct. Compare the current rate of extinction with the mean extinction rate since life began on Earth. **[4 marks]**

07.4 Suggest **three** reasons for the difference in extinction rates calculated in **07.3**. **[3 marks]**

08 Overfishing in the North Sea between the 1960s and 1990s significantly depleted fish stocks. To try to support fish populations the Government brought in a number of new rules for deep sea fishing. One of these rules requires the use of large-mesh fishing nets that contain large holes.

08.1 Suggest and explain why fishing vessels were required to use nets with large holes. **[3 marks]**

08.2 Following the period of heavy fishing in the North Sea, scientists discovered that fish species had started to breed even when they were still small. Explain how changes to the minimum fish breeding size occurred. **[6 marks]**

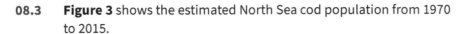

Exam Tip

The *y*-axis is in thousands of tonnes. Be sure to use this unit in your answer. Just using tonnes would be incorrect.

08.3 **Figure 3** shows the estimated North Sea cod population from 1970 to 2015.

Figure 3

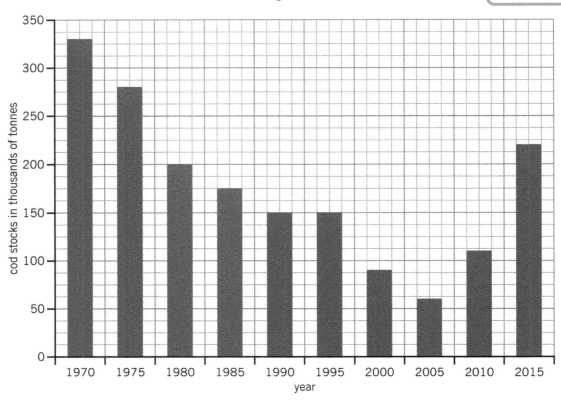

Evaluate the success of the Government's strategy to support North Sea fish stocks. **[3 marks]**

08.4 Estimate the North Sea cod stocks for the year 2020. Justify your answer. **[4 marks]**

09 People with anaemia often have a low red blood cell count.

09.1 Suggest **one** symptom of anaemia. **[1 mark]**

09.2 Explain how a red blood cell is adapted to its function. **[3 marks]**

09.3 Erythropoietin (EPO) is a drug that can be used to treat people with severe anaemia. It increases the number of red blood cells in the bloodstream. Athletes are banned from using this drug. Suggest and explain why athletes are banned from using EPO. **[4 marks]**

10 Some students set up an experiment to investigate osmosis. They set up the equipment shown in **Figure 4** and left it for 15 minutes.

Figure 4

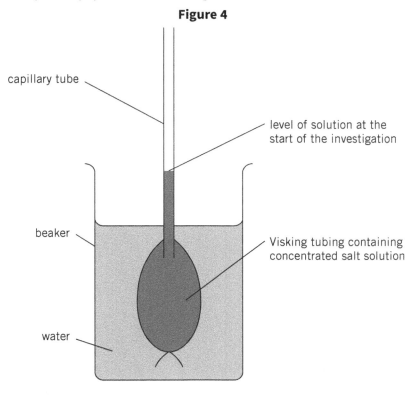

capillary tube

level of solution at the start of the investigation

beaker

Visking tubing containing concentrated salt solution

water

10.1 Complete the sentence with the correct bold word. **[1 mark]**

The salt solution is **isotonic** / **hypertonic** / **hypotonic** to the water.

10.2 Predict and explain the results you would expect the students to find. **[3 marks]**

10.3 Explain what would happen if a cell taken from a leaf was placed into the solution inside the Visking tubing. **[4 marks]**

11 Different processes, including deforestation, affect the carbon cycle.

11.1 Describe the processes that add carbon dioxide to the atmosphere. **[3 marks]**

11.2 **Table 2** shows the area of forest cut down in one country in 1994 and in 2004.

Table 2

Year	Area of forest cut down in km²
1994	15 450
2004	27 772

Explain the reasons for the trend seen in **Table 2**. **[3 marks]**

11.3 Explain the consequences to the atmosphere of the trend seen in **Table 2**. **[3 marks]**

OXFORD
UNIVERSITY PRESS

Great Clarendon Street, Oxford, OX2 6DP, United Kingdom

Oxford University Press is a department of the University of Oxford.
It furthers the University's objective of excellence in research, scholar-
ship, and education by publishing worldwide. Oxford is a registered trade
mark of Oxford University Press in the UK and in
certain other countries.

British Library Cataloguing in Publication Data

Data available

978-1-38-203382-4

10 9 8 7 6 5

Paper used in the production of this book is a natural, recyclable product
made from wood grown in sustainable forests.

The manufacturing process conforms to the environmental regulations
of the country of origin.

Printed in Great Britain by Ashford Colour Press Ltd.

Acknowledgements

The publisher and authors would like to thank the following for permis-
sion to use photographs and other copyright material:

Cover: sciencepics/Shutterstock

Photos: p7: Jack Bostrack, Visuals Unlimited/Science Photo Library; p8:
Rattiya Thongdumhyu/Shutterstock; p35: Jose Luis Calvo/Shutterstock;
p57: Power and Syred/Science Photo Library; p97(t): Iakov Filimonov/
Shutterstock; p97(m): Wolfgang Zwanzger/Shutterstock; p97(b): Anibal
Trejo/Shutterstock; p102: TravelMediaProductions/Shutterstock;
p105(l): Cat Downie/Shutterstock; p105(r): outdoorsman/Shutterstock;
p155: Frans Lanting Studio/Alamy Stock Photo; p156: Hintau Aliaksei/
Shutterstock; p174: Rattiya Thongdumhyu/Shutterstock; p178: Jose Luis
Calvo/Shutterstock; p202: Michael W. Tweedie / Science Photo Library.

Artwork by Q2A Media, Barking Dog Art, GreenGate Publishing, and
Oxford University Press.

Every effort has been made to contact copyright holders of material
reproduced in this book. Any omissions will be rectified in subsequent
printings if notice is given to the publisher.